PRAISE FOR *REST IN POWER*

"[Sybrina Fulton and Tracy Martin] have published a beautiful, searing account of their experience. *Rest in Power* is an intimate portrait of their slain son and a detail-rich chronicle of the year from his death to his killer's acquittal."

—*The Washington Post*

"*Rest in Power* is a devastating and agonisingly detailed account of Trayvon's life and death, and of the Black Lives Matter movement that followed. With Fulton and Martin taking consecutive chapters to tell the story, it unfolds like a true-crime serial: labyrinthine, episodic and appallingly real."

—*The Guardian*

"*Rest in Power* is a heart-wrenching account and an important history that should be required reading."

—*Jezebel*

"In *Rest in Power,* Trayvon's parents, Sybrina Fulton and Tracy Martin, gather the pieces and attempt to present the whole of who their son was when he was just a boy—before he became a martyr. . . . But as much as the book is about Trayvon's life, it's also a meditation on the criminal justice system. . . . Fulton and Martin also offer a glint of hope—in the rallies for justice, the support which extended from Hollywood to the White House, and the birth of the Black Lives Matter movement, which brought together people who understood that, no, Trayvon wasn't an angel *because* he was a human being. *Rest in Power* stands as a reminder—not only of Trayvon's life and death but of the vulnerability of black lives in a country that still needs to be reminded they matter. It also offers a prayer that someday, as Fulton writes, 'the killing will stop' and 'the healing will begin.'"

—*USA Today* (3½ out of 4 stars)

"[*Rest in Power*] is filled with the heartache and anguish only parents who have lost a child can fully understand. . . . [Fulton and Martin] share family stories and anecdotes about Trayvon, giving readers a rounded, more complete picture of the teenager who was gunned down. . . . [They] are not heavy-handed on the dramatics; they speak honestly and boldly and win empathy and understanding through their expression of their bleak reality. The authors also provide answers not readily found in the avalanche of news covering this story, and the book should foster further discussions on the issues of race and violence in America. A brave, heart-rending narrative from the parents who lost their son far too soon."

—*Kirkus Reviews* (starred review)

"Fulton and Martin share a remarkably candid and deeply affecting in-the-moment chronicle of the explosive aftermath of the murder. Writing in alternate chapters, they share every detail of their shock, grief, and grueling quest for justice. . . . Given the unconscionable shooting deaths of young black men, many by police, that followed Trayvon's, this galvanizing testimony from parents who channeled their sorrow into action offers a deeply humanizing perspective on the crisis propelling a national movement."

—*Booklist* (starred review)

"Not since Emmitt Till has a parent's love for a murdered child moved the nation to search its soul about racial injustice and inequality. Sybrina Fulton and Tracy Martin's extraordinary witness, indomitable spirit, and unwavering demand for change has altered the dynamics of racial justice discourse in this country. This powerful book illuminates the grief and commitment to reform that Trayvon Martin's death has mobilized; it is a story fueled by a demand for justice but rooted in love."

—Bryan Stevenson, author of *Just Mercy*

Rest in Power

REST IN

The Enduring Life of Trayvon Martin

POWER

Sybrina Fulton and Tracy Martin

Spiegel & Grau

NEW YORK

*To the memory and legacy of our
fallen son, Trayvon Martin*

CONTENTS

❧

INTRODUCTION

Sybrina Fulton

⁓

For all that is secret will eventually be brought into the open, and everything that is concealed will be brought to light and made known to all.

—Luke 8:17

How can I show you the hole in my heart?

How do I write about the death of my son?

Words can be weak instruments. It's almost impossible to convey the devastation and pain, the bottomless loss, heartbreak, and helplessness—the feeling of being broken into pieces that will never come back together again, not all the way. One piece of me has gone missing and it will stay missing, forever. There is nothing in its place.

The child I lost was a son, a boy who hadn't yet crossed the final threshold to becoming a man. He had been seventeen for only three brief weeks, still in the beautiful and turbulent passage through childhood's last stages, still on his way to *becoming*. Instead, he will be remembered for the things he left behind.

The bullet that pierced his heart.

The blood that stained the ground.

The crime-scene photographs of his corpse.

And the famous hoodie picture.

The fight to find an answer to the question of why he died, in a place where nobody seemed to care and where even the people whose *job* it was to care were eager to move on, to forget.

I can never forget. Nobody ever "gets over" the death of a child. All I can do is remember, and in remembering I pay homage to my son in the hope that the truths I tell can help others and that maybe, someday, through God's grace, what happened to my son will never happen to another mother's child.

His is the story of a life cut tragically short, but it's also the story of a boy who in death became a symbol, a beacon, and a mirror in which a whole nation came to see its reflection. It's the story of a young life that at its seeming end was transfigured into something else. The truth is that my son took his last breath and that will never change. The hole in my heart will never heal. They say when an adult dies you bury the past; when a child dies you bury the future. But though his physical life ended, he isn't yet finished leaving his mark on the world. And so I will never stop saying his name and telling others the story of his life and his death, and all that followed. His spirit lives on, and even his death may yet be redeemed.

This is the story of my son, Trayvon Benjamin Martin.

❧

The call comes at the start of a workday. I have just left my desk at the offices of Miami-Dade County's housing agency, a cluster of cubicles in a downtown office building, and retreat to my car where I am now sitting, Miami sunshine flooding in through the windows. But I don't notice the sunlight and haven't even turned the car on. On the other end of the phone is my ex-husband, Tracy Martin. It's the second time he's called me today. He says something about our son I don't quite understand, which will soon become clear: the previous night, on Sunday, February 26, 2012, at approximately 7:17 P.M., our son, Trayvon Martin, was shot to death in Sanford, Florida, sprawled out on the wet grass of a Florida townhouse complex, a single bullet hole in his seventeen-year-old heart. The call shuts out the sunlight and the sounds around me. I feel myself falling down a long, dark shaft, in silence, alone.

My name is Sybrina Fulton, and in that moment one life for me ended and another began. Before that day—before Trayvon's death— chances are I would've lived and died without you ever hearing my name. I am one of the mass of Americans living an anonymous life of infinite complexities in the struggling suburb of an American city— one of the unheralded people whose weeks go by in a predictable rhythm of work and school, church and picnics, week after week, from cradle to grave. Happily. Before that phone call, there had been very few dark days. I've suffered through deaths of older relatives, like most people, and persevered through the tragedy of my brother Ronnie's car accident, which left him a quadriplegic. But I felt that God had always protected me, watched over me. Sundays found me in church in Opa-Locka near our home: Sunday school at 9:30 A.M., church services at 11:00. We believed in the Lord and believed we were blessed. We also saw enough chaos and pain around us to know that life is fragile and happiness isn't guaranteed. But nothing—no blessing or fear—prepared me for this.

Trayvon's funeral was on March 3, 2012, less than a week after I'd received that shattering call from Tracy. I thought that call was the worst moment of my life. I was wrong. The news over the phone, as devastating as it was, was just words, an abstraction. Burying my son's one and only body—a grotesque reversal of the usual order of life and death—was many times worse. I couldn't fully grasp then, and can only barely remember now, the details of the terrible day when Trayvon's body was put to rest. I walked through the day in a daze. We had celebrated his birthday only twenty-eight days before, on February 5. Just a week earlier, I had been thinking about Trayvon getting his driver's license. I had been thinking about his junior prom. I was thinking about what he was going to do with the rest of his life. Now, instead, we were preparing our son for his eternal rest.

We buried him in white: white suit, powder blue accents, and white shoes. And we sent him off in a baby-blue casket, with his name engraved on the side. With his fresh haircut and smooth, unblemished skin, he looked like he was going to his high school prom. The body was placed in a mausoleum drawer in a Miami cemetery. Yet I never believed that he was there. From the minute I learned that he had died, I always felt his presence. We buried his shell, but his spirit—who Trayvon was and who he always will be—remains. I believe this with all of my heart. That was the one thought on my mind from the moment I heard the news of his death. It's what I wanted, wished, and prayed over, and it came true. Trayvon Martin was soon *everywhere*: in demonstrations, marches, and rallies; from Miami, the city where he lived, to Sanford, Florida, the small town near Orlando where he was killed, to the Million Hoodie March in New York City, to hundreds of newspaper and magazine articles and millions of tweets and Facebook posts, to endless prayers from untold supporters, and, soon, all the way to the White House. Whenever a child walks in darkness, danger, and fear, and wherever people honor my son's life and protest his death, his presence lives.

It is now four years since my son's death. In the midst of indescribable devastation, my favorite Bible passage, Proverbs 3:5 and 3:6, always comes to guide me, and it reads:

> *Trust in the Lord with all your heart. Lean not unto your own understanding. In all your ways, acknowledge Him and He shall direct your path.*

After the funeral, in the midst of the trial of the man who shot Trayvon and the tribulations that followed, none of which I would ever fully comprehend, I put my faith in God, and a path was laid before me. We brought the tragedy of Trayvon Martin to the world, using his death as a call for change. We tell Trayvon's story in this book, along with our own story of how two ordinary parents from Miami, Florida, became activists in bringing their son's case to the world, in the hope that there won't be any more heartbreaking cases like his anywhere else.

Not in Sanford, Florida, where my son was shot dead on February 26, 2012.

Or Jacksonville, Florida, where Jordan Davis, seventeen, was shot dead by a forty-five-year-old man who objected to the music Jordan and his friends were playing in their car.

Or Ferguson, Missouri, where Michael Brown, eighteen, was fatally shot by a police officer.

Or Cleveland, Ohio, where Tamir Rice, twelve, was shot by a police officer as he played with a toy pistol in a park.

Or Staten Island, New York, where Eric Garner, forty-three, died after being put in a choke hold by an officer during an arrest for selling single cigarettes from a package without a tax stamp.

The list goes on and on, one tragic case after another, for too many years, and with too many victims to count or properly remember. Our case is far from the first incident of senseless gun violence; it was definitely not America's first racially motivated killing. But it was the first in a wave that reignited people's passion for the cause of injustice. I never imagined that my voice would be not only heard but heard by so many, and that it would become one of a chorus of voices shouting "I am Trayvon Martin!" in support and solidarity of our fight to make his death matter and not be forgotten. I could never have imagined that my son would become, in death, a symbol for injustice.

We tell this story in the hope that it will continue the calling that Trayvon left for us to answer and that it might shine a path for others who have lost, or will lose, children to senseless violence. We tell it in the hope for healing, for bridging the divide that separates America, between races and classes, between citizens and the police. Most of all, we tell it for Trayvon, whose young soul and lively spirit guide us every day in everything we do.

Rest in Power

CHAPTER 1

Sybrina

Our Lives Before

∽

Who was Trayvon Martin? I've been asked that question a million times since his death. In death, Trayvon Martin became a martyr and a symbol of racial injustice, a name and a face on T-shirts, posters, and protest signs.

When he was alive, of course, he was none of those things. He was simply a boy, growing into a young man, with all of the wonder and promise and struggle that that journey entails.

What else was he? He was loved. Trayvon had struggles—academically, even behaviorally at times—but he loved his friends and family, sports, music, and his dreams of flight. And he saw that love returned and those dreams coming within his reach. In other words, he was a boy, and because he was mine, he was (along with his brother) one of the most important and cherished boys in the world.

His story begins with my own.

My mother named me Sybrina with a *y*. When I was born, Sabrina with an *a* was a very common name. "I wanted her name to be different," my mother said. And so it was Sybrina, and if our given birth name is an indication of our destinies, then from the beginning I was blessed and cursed to stand out.

I was born in Miami, but we soon moved to Opa-Locka, which was a working-class Miami suburb. My mother worked at the post office as a clerk. My birth father was a longshoreman, who died young from heart failure. In 1978, when I was eleven, my mom got remarried to a police officer who worked on the streets of Miami. I was a flower girl at my mother's wedding, dressed in a flowing ivory gown, hair styled up in a bun, and happy. My stepdad was a powerful, strict, and taciturn presence in our house. We lovingly called him Dad.

I was the baby, the youngest of six children, with two brothers who always looked out for me; an older sister; and two stepsisters. We weren't rich, but my parents made sure we were all well provided for. We never had to worry about our electricity being turned off or not having a place to stay or a car to drive. We had big Christmases, went on summer vacations, and always attended church on Sunday. We were taught the importance of work. My parents had good jobs and high expectations, and they expected me to get a good job, too. Nobody gave anything to me. I had to earn and work for everything I wanted.

We lived in a predominantly black neighborhood, although within the neighborhood there was a blend of different nationalities: Cuban, Jamaican, Bahamian, and Haitian. Back then, in the 1970s, Opa-Locka was a paradise. Children played everywhere: in the street, at the school, in the park. There was a house where a lady sold candy and a corner store where we would get soda and chips. Early on, my mom and dad taught me and my two older brothers the proper way of doing things. As soon as I came home from school, I had to change into my play clothes, and before I was allowed to go out and play I had to clean up and do my homework. Then and only then would I be allowed to go outside. We'd play tag and run up and down the street. Even then my dad, the disciplinarian policeman, gave us our perimeters: we had to stay within the two stop signs on our street.

Opa-Locka was changing during the 1970s, like a lot of America at the time, suffering from an influx of drugs and an escalation of street violence. Despite that, my mom and dad created a loving and safe environment for us: what went on outside our doors was different, separate, foreign. There were problems raging out there, but we didn't see or feel them. We were protected. I never saw the violence; I never saw drugs.

By the time I was in my teens, my dad had become a detective, but he didn't bring the energy of his job home. He was always polite with us, but still very strict. I had a curfew. People couldn't just walk through our home. Sometimes I'd go to other people's homes and their parents would allow the children's friends to just walk all over the place. My friends had to be in the same room where I was: if I was in the den, they had to be in the den.

And, of course, I wasn't allowed to start dating until I was sixteen.

I felt comfortable in the easy flow and ordinary rhythm of our humble community, but the truth is I didn't want to be like everybody around me. From a young age, I craved something different, and for me education was the path to a less ordinary life. In middle school, I pursued a series of passions, always backed by my parents. I took classes for acting, etiquette, and modeling, and even learned how to play the piano and clarinet, and I also ran track. When I graduated from high school, there was no question that I would attend college.

My dream was to go to school in Tallahassee, where I had friends—until my older cousin told my mother that everybody went there. So she decided that I needed something different.

"I'm not sending my money—or my daughter—there," my mother said. "Sybrina, pick another school."

I flipped through a book of colleges and, almost at random, settled on Grambling State University in Grambling, Louisiana, a place I had never visited, where I knew no one, and that, honestly, I knew nothing about. I just picked it because I wanted to get away from Miami, do my own thing, be my own person, and follow my impulse to do something different. I had never been away from home before, without my parents, other than to attend summer camp.

My mother, impressed with my determination, approved.

My mom, my Auntie Leona, and my brother Mark drove me to Grambling. When we arrived, I checked in to the freshman dorm and got my room key. My family and I went upstairs to my standard dorm room: two beds, two desks, four walls, small space. *Okay, it's just like summer camp,* I thought. My mom, my aunt, and my brother helped me move in. We cleaned up everything, made up my bed, plugged in the clock, unpacked my clothes, and hung them in the closet.

It was time to say goodbye.

We all hugged, and Mama kept up a patter of encouraging talk as she slowly moved toward the door: "Sybrina, you will be fine"; "You're going to do great"; "You've always liked to do things on your own"; "You always did like to be adventurous."

"This is awesome and I'm so proud of you," she said at last, as they were leaving.

I walked out after them down to the sidewalk and watched their car start to pull out, when suddenly it all hit me at once like a big wave: this *wasn't* a good thing. In fact, it was the *worst* thing in the world. I started sniffling. Then crying. Then boohooing. Then screaming. Making all this horrible noise in front of the entire freshman dorm. I don't know where it all came from, but soon I was screaming so loud that my family could hear it from their car, and they turned around and drove back to where I stood. My mother popped open the door and came over to me.

"Sybrina, what's wrong with you?" my mother asked.

I felt like a puppy that had been left alone in the woods. I looked at her with pitiful eyes.

"Sybrina, look at all these people staring at you!" my mother said, gesturing to the students and parents now watching at us.

"I don't care, I don't know these people," I said, getting back into the car with them, ready to drive away from Grambling forever, and go back home. Instead, they took me to Captain D's, a fast-food sea-food restaurant, for lunch.

"Oh, my God, I cannot believe you are doing this," my mother said, because I'd always been strong. But in that moment I realized how much family really meant to me—not just the idea, but the physical presence of family, the closeness, the way the people you love can create a kind of soft, gentle barrier around you that makes everything seem easier. When my family left me, alone in that strange place, that lonely place, I felt a chill wind, a sense of isolation I'd never known before. After a while I calmed down and slowly went back into the dorm. A year and a half later I was still homesick, and when I came home for Christmas break, I never went back. I enrolled in the University of Miami for one expensive semester, before transferring to what was then called Florida Memorial College, where I majored in English with a minor in communications.

My ambition was a career in television, either as a reporter or someone who worked behind the scenes, but when I interned at a Miami television and radio station, Channel 10 and 99 Jamz, everyone told me, "You're going to have to leave Miami to go to one of the smaller markets to get more experience."

I thought about it, but worried, *Maybe this is going to be just like Grambling, homesick all over again.*

I decided I wanted to remain close to home. In 1989, I left college to do what I had always done: go to work. My first full-time job was working for Miami-Dade County as a console security specialist.

I sat at a desk that faced a wall of small TV monitors, fifty in all, each connected to a closed-circuit camera around the county. I was also given seven different two-way radios that connected me to various nearby security companies. My job was to monitor the cameras and alert the security companies by radio whenever I saw something suspicious or whenever an alarm went off. So I kept an eye out for anything I thought might be suspicious—never targeting a demographic category. I learned how to size people up rather quickly, without having to resort to simplistic profiling.

It was a job in security, I suppose, except it wasn't dangerous; occasionally there would be a minor break-in or other petty crime to report, but mostly my shift included homeless people sleeping where they shouldn't, vandalism, and cats and dogs triggering false alarms. It was a good, solid job. I was in my twenties. I was dating and had been proposed to twice. I felt like I was at the beginning of something; the start, maybe, to a life that worked, surrounded, still, by the family I loved in my hometown.

∾

It wasn't love at first sight. But Tracy Martin grew on me. I met him at the Miami-Dade County Solid Waste Management Christmas party in 1993. I was still working for the county, but had been promoted to code-enforcement officer, writing tickets for violations, mostly to people dumping trash in front of their homes. It wasn't a glamorous job, but it offered stability. I was still good at quickly sizing people up. But when Tracy's brother Mike, who worked as a truck driver for the county, brought Tracy over to meet me, he wasn't easy to size up or understand.

Tracy was *very* tall, thin, and really lean. When he said, "How you doin', Sybrina?" his baritone voice was inflected with a thick accent from a faraway place—well, not that far away: he told me he was born in Miami but raised in East St. Louis. But it wasn't his voice that drew me in: we seemed to click from the start. He was friendly and funny, and I just felt, somehow, although I still can't figure out why, I just felt we had met before.

He asked me out a few weeks later. Everything about Tracy Martin was different. He was hilarious and gentle, but also bold and self-confident. His already impressive height was topped by a high-top fade. I liked him, and came to love him, enough to say yes when he proposed. We were both twenty-seven.

On June 11, 1994, we were married in a big Miami wedding, filled with friends and family, at a banquet hall. We moved into a small, two-bedroom apartment. In the beginning, it was Tracy, my son Jahvaris, then an active and intelligent four-year-old bundle of joy, and me, beginning a new life of hard work, faith, and family.

~⚬~

Our baby, Trayvon, was born the following year, on February 5, 1995. My mom and Tracy's mom were with Tracy and me in the delivery room. I wasn't asleep, just relaxed from the anesthesia, and in that state I remembered the prediction of a psychic I had visited some years before. I had gone with a friend, thinking I'd only wait for her while the psychic performed her reading. When we got there, the psychic looked at me, and even though I was at the back of a line of people outside, she took me by the hand and said, "I'll read you first."

She was a middle-aged Puerto Rican woman wearing a bright-colored dress covered in gold beads, and she led me into her reading room. She began shuffling tarot cards and then placed them down on the table. She then took my hand in hers and started peering down at my palm.

She told me she could see my future clearly. "You're a strong person, ambitious, very spiritual, and you will live a long time. You care about people, like to help people. As for children, you'll only have boys, never girls."

I wasn't sure if I believed in fortune-tellers, but I sensed that what she was saying was true and felt a quick surge of mixed emotions. I had always been close to little boys; everybody in our community seemed to do so much for little girls—teaching them, keeping them safe—and I felt that boys needed someone on their side, too. But, of course, I also knew that black and brown boys had a harder struggle ahead of them—not only with the temptations of drugs and crime, but just to get the basic things that should have been theirs by right: education and employment. So I was always there for my two brothers and my male cousins and nephews. And now I promised myself that I'd always be there for my son, Jahvaris, and also the baby that was now pushing to escape my womb and come out into the world.

Trayvon came out screaming. After they cleaned him off and wrapped him in a blanket, the nurse laid him on my chest and I thanked God for this miracle, this ultimate blessing. I could feel his heart beating so fast, right alongside mine, so close that it made me cry. Then and there, I made a promise: to do my best for this child, as a mother, an example, a counselor, and a friend.

From the beginning, Trayvon was a playful child. We called him "Crazy Legs" at one point, because his legs were so long, just like his dad's. As soon as he could crawl, those legs were moving, and little Trayvon was trying to escape that two-bedroom Miami apartment. He was always on the go. He would bother everything, and sometimes I'd make him sit down and watch TV, just to keep him still. He loved cartoons, was glued to them: *Ninja Turtles, Batman, Superman, Barney,* and most of all, *Winnie the Pooh,* which he watched so much that we exchanged Crazy Legs for "Pooh" as his nickname, and even dressed him as Winnie the Pooh for Halloween two years in a row.

By 1997, I had returned to Florida Memorial University to complete my degree. Trayvon was two and Jahvaris was six, two little boys I'd dress in identical clothing, always sitting side by side under my chair or on my lap while I was studying in the university library or at home. I took them everywhere with me because Tracy was always working. From early on, I impressed on them the importance of excelling. "I graduated from high school and college, and you have to not only do what I did, you have to exceed what I did," I would tell them. "Because each generation has to do a little bit better than the last generation."

When Trayvon was five, Tracy and I split up, but agreed to share custody. Trayvon and Jahvaris would spend the weekdays with me, and then Tracy had them on the weekends, picking them up at the house on Friday afternoon and bringing them back either Sunday night or Monday morning. It wasn't always easy, but we stayed close.

By the time Trayvon was nine, he had begun calling me "Cupcake" because, he said, "you're so sweet." He wanted to do everything for me. If I was sick, he wanted to be my doctor. When I was tired, he wanted to be the cook. He could already make breakfast and, soon, dinner. He carried grocery bags, moved furniture, cleaned the house, babysat his young cousins, washed my car, *everything*.

Sometimes I would even pretend that I couldn't do things just to give him a chance to do the work he loved. He would tell me, with his big smile, "I've got it, Cupcake."

He was a mama's boy, always with me, always affectionate, kissing and hugging me, sitting beside me, walking alongside me and holding my hand. But as he grew, his world expanded. He would introduce himself to everyone who crossed his path and then dub them a "friend."

I always taught my sons the importance of good manners. Once, when I took Trayvon and Jahvaris to visit my mom and dad, Trayvon rushed in and just started talking like he had been there the entire time. No *Good evening. How are you?* Just talking a blue streak. I marched him right back outside that door.

"You will *not* come into my mother's house without speaking!" I told him.

And I made him make his entrance all over again, this time saying, "Good evening. How are you this evening?"

Whatever he did, he did with all of his heart and soul. He didn't just ride his bike; he had to build a ramp, on which he would ride on his bicycle—*fast*—so the bike would take him high into the air. He played football for two youth teams, basketball, wrestling, and played drums in the school band. When he turned fourteen and his junior league football days were over, he kept going to the park. He worked at the concession stand with his father, who ran it, but he also worked with the younger kids at the park, making sure they had their uniforms, helping them get on the field on time, and doing whatever else he could, until I had to say, "Trayvon, we have to go home now!"

Two summers before his death, Trayvon found his future in Opa-Locka, at the airport near our home. That summer, he joined

Experience Aviation, a summer camp founded by the legendary pilot Barrington Irving. Irving was raised in inner-city Miami and, in 2007 at age twenty-three, became the first black pilot to fly solo around the world. Miami to Miami. The flight took ninety-seven days and twenty-six stops to complete. He designed his summer camp to help kids become more knowledgeable about aviation and, through aviation, build their skills in other areas, including reading, math, and science. One day at the camp, Trayvon sat in the cockpit of Barrington Irving's globe-trotting airplane. When he came home, he still had stars in his eyes. "Mom, I know what I'm going to do," he told me. He had decided on a career in aviation: either as a mechanic (because he could fix *anything*) or as a professional pilot. He couldn't decide which, except that he was determined to *be around planes.*

He was a child of Miami, Florida, the great melting pot of nationalities: whites, African Americans, Puerto Ricans, Cubans, Haitians, Bahamians, South Americans, Chinese, Vietnamese. . . . People from all over the world call Miami home. We taught Trayvon to respect the differences of others, but also to always remember who he was. He was an African American. But that was never *all* he was. We sent Trayvon Martin into the world not as a young black man, but as a young man.

By the time he was seventeen, Trayvon was 140 pounds and almost six feet tall. He was a typical Miami teenager, eager to do everything all at once. He'd already seen a world outside Miami: I'd taken Trayvon and Jahvaris on skiing and snowboarding trips to Colorado so they could have a white Christmas, and we'd recently been to New York, where Trayvon fell in love with the Statue of Liberty, Times Square, and the Empire State Building and saw his first Broadway play. He was *very* particular about his clothes and his appearance, his haircut, his cologne, and, most of all, his shoes. He collected Air Jordans, though I couldn't afford to buy a new pair of $100 to $200 shoes every time a new style was released. "If you can earn the money, I'll take you to get the shoes," I would tell him. He went to work, doing odd jobs for family members and friends—washing cars, cutting grass, trimming hedges, pulling weeds, babysitting—until he had enough for the shoes. Sometimes, if he fell short, I would pay the difference, and Trayvon would stand in line from six A.M. until the store opened at ten—because he always had to be the first to get whatever was new.

When he said he wanted the new $80-a-bottle Issey Miyake cologne, I drew the line, for a simple reason: it was too expensive! Instead, I gave him a bottle as a birthday gift when he turned seventeen, on February 5, 2012. Two weeks after that, we celebrated my birthday by going horseback riding. We were all beginners. But Trayvon, who had only ridden ponies before, led our group as if he'd been riding all of his life.

I can still hear him calling his friends to tell them about the horseback ride on his ever-present cellphone. He kept earbuds in his ears at all times, because he could use them to listen to music or talk on the phone. And he rarely removed his gray or black hoodie, which he wore spring, summer, winter, and fall, even though Miami really only has one season: *hot*.

At first, I didn't like the hoodie, and would tell him to take it off. It was something the teenagers were wearing that I wasn't used to. Hoodies weren't in style when I was growing up. But Trayvon, who felt he was making a fashion statement, would rarely remove it. So once I realized that all the teenagers were wearing them, I was okay with it.

As he got deeper into his teens, his teachers generally found him pleasant and smart. But there were some dark clouds, too. Problems began just before the start of his eleventh-grade school year, when I transferred him from Miami Carol City Senior High, a school he loved, to a good school closer to our house, Dr. Michael M. Krop Senior High.

Away from the teachers and friends who'd been his community for years, he didn't always apply himself. At Carol City, in advanced classes, he had been a B and C student; at Krop, he was making Cs and Ds. By the fall of 2011, school seemed to take a backseat to everything else that was happening in Trayvon's life: his haircut, his clothes, his social activities, going to parties, and, of course, girls. He lost focus. I kept telling myself that these were the typical ups and downs that a lot of teenagers go through, that Trayvon was still the same person I'd known for his whole life. And he was a good kid. Still, Tracy and I started to worry.

He started missing classes, and then entire school days. When he would show up to school, he would frequently be late. The school receptionist would call the house to report his absences.

At first, they would reach my older brother, Ronnie, who, after being left a quadriplegic in an automobile accident many years ago, had come to live with us. Like all of us, Ronnie adored Trayvon, who helped take care of him, frequently cooking meals and feeding him. So when the school called to report tardiness and absences, Ronnie would cover for Trayvon, and word never got back to me.

When I finally caught wind of the calls, I started taking Trayvon to school myself, which, strangely, he liked. It gave us a chance to talk—about small things, but the sort of talks that teenagers need in order to feel a connection to their moms, to be reminded of the gentle, familiar intimacy of family during a time of tough transitions—but our time was always short. "Hurry, Trayvon! Let's go!" I was forever saying, because I needed to get to work on time. Like so many mothers I've met, the shortage was never love or concern or desire. But time was short.

Trayvon was still finding his share of trouble. In February 2012, he was disciplined for being in an unauthorized area of the school and writing "WTF" on a locker in the school hallway. When the security guards searched his backpack, they found a screwdriver, which they called a "burglary tool," and some women's jewelry: rings and earrings. Trayvon admitted the jewelry wasn't his, but because he wouldn't tell the administrator who it belonged to, he received a ten-day suspension from school.

This had gone too far. When he came home, I sat him down. We were in my living room, him on the sofa, me on the love seat, me dressed for work, him in his everyday jeans and polo shirt, me demanding answers, him quiet and very careful with his words, because he knew I was upset and, even worse, disappointed in him.

"Why did you have it?" I asked him about the jewelry. "Where did it come from?" I tried to stay calm, but I'm sure my voice was laced with tension.

He said it belonged to a friend, whose name he wouldn't reveal—and would never reveal—to me or to the school administrators. I had always impressed on Trayvon and his brother the importance of making commonsense decisions—and this didn't make sense. This was much bigger than skipping school; I needed to know *why*.

"Where. Did. You. Get this?" I asked again, my voice rising.

"From my friend," he said.

"What's the friend's name?"

He looked away and said nothing. The silence between us lingered for a few moments.

"You're going to have to be more responsible," I said, finally.

"I know," he said.

"If you keep getting suspended you're not going to graduate on time," I said. "And if you don't graduate, you're going to have to stay in school for an extra year."

"Oh, no, Mom, I want to graduate," he said.

"Well, then you need to work hard and stay out of trouble," I said. "You need to stop doing whatever all of those other kids you are associating with are doing."

"Well, I'll just be by myself," he said.

And I said, "That sounds like a good plan."

For the first few days of his suspension, he was at home, and my mother, brother, and aunt Leona kept him busy doing odd jobs. For the second week of the ten-day suspension, he was set to go on a trip with his father to Sanford, Florida, a city of around fifty thousand people just outside Orlando. Tracy was going to Sanford to attend a convention.

The week before he was to leave for Sanford, Trayvon grew tired of all the odd jobs we were lining up for him. He was ready to get out of Miami. So Tracy, who had to work and couldn't drive up to Sanford until Friday, suggested that Trayvon go a few days earlier than him and spend time with Tracy's girlfriend, Brandy, and her son, Chad.

Tracy thought it might do Trayvon some good to go with him to Sanford, and said he would use the opportunity to talk with Trayvon, father to son, to get him back on the right track before he went back to school the following week.

Trayvon, eager to get out of the house and into a new place with new friends, agreed.

৵৹

On the night of February 21, a Tuesday, my youngest brother, Mark, and I drove Trayvon to the Greyhound bus station so he could catch the five-hour, multiple-stop ride from Miami to Orlando, the nearest stop to Sanford, where Brandy would pick him up and take him to her townhouse in nearby Sanford. Trayvon had his cellphone with the earbuds, as always, in his ears. He was wearing a new pair of basketball shoes, khaki pants, sweatshirt, and his gray hoodie.

"I love you, see you later," I said, kissing him goodbye.

"Love you, too, Mom," he said as he exited the car and disappeared into the bus station.

We were almost back home when my cellphone rang.

"I missed the bus," Trayvon said.

"What?"

He gave me some story about how he walked away from the station for a moment and when he came back the bus to Orlando was gone.

"Do you not want to go?" I asked.

No, no, he said, he wanted to go.

"Can you come back and get me?" he asked.

I was frustrated that he'd missed the bus. What did he have to do other than wait for the bus to come? But I didn't say anything to him about it. I just turned the car around and drove back to get him. Since there wasn't another bus to Orlando that night, we drove him back home. By ten P.M. we were fast asleep, and by seven A.M. we were up and sitting around the breakfast table.

As always, I had to get to work. So after breakfast I drove Trayvon to Tracy's house, and Tracy took him back to the Greyhound station.

That was Wednesday, February 22, 2012. After I said a quick goodbye to Trayvon at his father's house, I rushed off to work, still feeling a low vibration of anxiety about how Trayvon's journey would go, whether he and Tracy would get a chance to talk, whether Trayvon would return to school on Monday with his head on straight, like he'd promised me he would, ready to shake off these setbacks and move forward with his studies and his dreams, all the things we'd talked so much about. I had no idea that would be the last time I would ever see my son alive.

Five days later, I got the call from Tracy.

"Trayvon," he began, his voice breaking, "is gone."

CHAPTER 2

Tracy

∽

February 26, 2012–February 27, 2012

Sometimes, I still see him, running across the public park football field, his shoulder pads too big for his slim frame, but his spirit large enough to make up the difference. The Optimists football club would retire his jersey—number 9—but one team wears it on the back of their helmets, as a reminder of the friend and teammate they lost. I still go to that field all the time—I run the Optimists football program as a volunteer. And while I know it's not my son, I see Trayvon running across that field again in every kid there. I think of them all as my sons, and my responsibility to them goes beyond football. I'm there to help them, guide them, and do my best to make sure that what happened to Trayvon won't happen to them.

I sometimes wonder, *What if?* What if Trayvon hadn't been killed? What would he have become? But those questions are pointless, unanswerable. All I can do now is remember all that he was to me, the son I considered my best friend.

"I love you," I told Trayvon on the day that he died.

He had called me to ask for the phone number for the local pizza delivery service.

"Do you have enough money for pizza?" I asked him, just to make sure that Trayvon and Chad had money left over from what I had given him earlier.

"Yes, we've got enough," he told me.

"I love you, Tray," I remember saying.

I always make it my business to tell my kids or my significant other "Hey, I love you" whenever we're going to be apart.

It gives me some comfort to know that the last words I said to him before he died were "I love you." And that his last words to me were "Dad, I love you, too."

∽◦∾

I was born in Miami but raised in East St. Louis, Illinois. The Mississippi River separates East St. Louis, Illinois, from St. Louis, Missouri, and although the two cities are separated by less than a mile, they are many worlds apart. I grew up in the Roosevelt Homes projects on Forty-fourth Street and Bunkum Road. The first thing that was instilled in me was to be patient, careful, and respectful to everyone I met, not just because it was the right thing to do, but because it could be the difference between life and death. The sound of gunshots was as common as the sound of car horns on those streets, and the neighborhood was a hot spot for gangs. So you had to respect the people, the territory you were in, and the constant potential for violence.

Coming from where I did, the sight of a dead body, or a crime scene, was hardly news—until one day it was my son whose body was surrounded by the yellow police investigation tape. I've known death before—both of my parents are deceased, I've had friends shot and killed, relatives who passed away young from accidents and disease. This was all part of growing up in East St. Louis. But even then, nothing compares to the loss of a child. It's a different level of hurt than anything I've known, a hurt that sears your mind, body, and soul, that never subsides.

· · ·

My father's side of the family lived in Miami, so I often visited when I was young. But my heart was set on staying with my mother and my family in East St. Louis, where I was the youngest of four boys.

East St. Louis is a small city, almost 99 percent black, and surrounded by predominantly white suburbs. So there were certain areas where we knew we couldn't go. I've been called "nigger" by people in passing cars as I walked along the roads of East St. Louis, and I remember seeing handwritten signs saying "No Niggers Allowed." Some people argue that racism goes both ways, that it affects everyone, and maybe that's true. However, African Americans are more often on the receiving end of it, and black boys catch the majority of its hell. When I became a parent, I would tell my sons, "Hey, racism is alive and well, and you have to watch out for it all of the time." While the subject of racism is a conversation that America struggles to have, we as African Americans have to have the conversation all the time.

My mother always advised her kids, "If you see somebody coming at you with any kind of racism, run."

I remembered my mother's advice when I was around fourteen. While I was walking with some friends, a car full of white young men passed by. They threw bottles at us and called us niggers. We kept walking. The next thing you know we saw that same car coming back, and my mother's words came back to me in a hurry.

Run. And that's what we did.

So just like my mother told me, I told my kids, including Trayvon: "If you see yourself about to get into a racial confrontation, eliminate yourself from the equation."

Run, because the confrontation isn't worth it.

Run, because the confrontation may escalate.

Don't stop to discuss it. This is NOT the time to have a conversation about race. If you have to protect yourself, do so. But if you can, just run.

Why run? My mother was from the South, so she knew what racists were capable of—racial terrorism was still going strong when she was growing up in the civil rights era. For her, running from racists—back when the racists you were running from might be law enforcement, civic leaders, or even elected officials—made all the sense in the world. As for me, I was raised in all-black East St. Louis, an island of poverty and violence surrounded by affluent white suburbs. Racial tensions ran high. No matter what progress had been made, there was no changing how some people felt about us.

And while we didn't have to worry about the Klan in East St. Louis, I knew good and well that if there *was* a racial confrontation, no matter the right and wrong of it, the black person involved would be saddled with a presumption of guilt. Running made sense to me, too.

A generation later, I had to give my sons the same instructions my mother gave me. Progress is sometimes hard to find. And it was better for them to be aware, so they could protect themselves and extract themselves from the situation simply by running from it.

I'm a truck driver now, which might not sound like a dream job, but even as a kid I was always fascinated by truck driving, and sports, especially basketball. My friends and I always said that basketball was going to take us out of the ghetto, and I was pretty good at it. I wanted to play in college, but my grades weren't up to par. So I started focusing on work at a very young age, never even considering a college education.

I passed through a variety of jobs, but I really didn't have any goals set at the time. I got into some trouble at a young age, hustling to get some money in a place where money was hard to find, being young and hungry and angry all at once. I wasted years. I knew I had to look for a different way of life.

My oldest brother, Willie "Mike" Williams, was driving a truck for Miami-Dade County Solid Waste Management in Miami and convinced me to leave East St. Louis. It was a hard decision, but in March 1993, I made a permanent move to Miami. The day I arrived in Miami, my brother Stephen Martin took me job hunting. And that's how I landed my first Miami job, working at Glass Carving Enterprises, as a laborer in their glass factory warehouse. Within the year, I was promoted to driving a truck, delivering glass across South Florida. I'd finally found some stability.

In the years that followed, my focus was on work and playing amateur softball, something that I'd grown passionate about while living in sunny Florida. Then one day Mike invited me to come along with him to the annual Miami-Dade County Solid Waste Management Christmas party. It was December 1993.

The party was in a hall. Mike was introducing me to a lot of the people he worked with when we saw Sybrina and some of her friends. The first time I saw her, she was wearing blue jeans and a denim vest with a purple heart embroidered on it. Mike introduced us. We spoke to each other for a while, and then she told me that she had a career with the county and didn't have any interest in a young unemployed man with no goals.

Meaning me.

I assured her that not only was I employed but I had goals and dreams of becoming a family man. Later that night we exchanged phone numbers, and a few weeks later we went on a date.

One day I invited her on a date, and drove her out to Miami Beach. I had an engagement ring in my pocket, and there, on a stretch of sand, I got down on one knee and said, "Will you marry me?"

It wasn't elaborate, but it was sincere.

And she said yes.

We were married on June 11, 1994, and moved into a two-bedroom apartment in what is now known as Miami Gardens, a Miami suburb. We weren't rich, but that was our castle. It was me, Sybrina, and Jahvaris, who was two when we met and who I raised as my own child. Then came my pride and joy, Trayvon.

I cut the umbilical cord and was the first to hold him. We were bound from the start—me, Sybrina, Jahvaris, and baby Trayvon—from the moment he came home from the hospital. He was an active baby, and almost from the time he was born, he was crawling—and bawling—trying to come after me. Every time I opened the door, he wanted to go, he wanted to move. "Outside," he would say as soon as he learned to speak. It may have been his first word. He just *loved* going outside. Playing in the dirt, rocks, whatever he could find. Adventurous. Friendly, and not afraid of anything.

I don't think he ever used the bassinet we bought for him. People gravitated to him. "Oh, he's so cute," they would say, picking him up and loving him. He was my joy.

We were blessed. Everyday people, yes. Not rich, ever, but rich with love. For five years, we lived together as a family, but as time went by Sybrina and I found ourselves on separate paths. Back then, Sybrina was a homebody—she was tightly focused on her education and her job and her kids. Meanwhile, I had started playing softball more seriously, traveling to amateur tournaments across Florida and nearby states with my team. We were playing three or four nights a week in the Miami area and going for tournaments some weekends, all of which put a strain on our marriage. The kids used to call me "Disneyland Dad" because when I was at home it was always a party, an event, a celebration. I didn't care much for sitting still; I had so much love for my kids. They were everything to me.

I gave everything to my kids; I didn't give my all to my marriage, and it eventually came to an end. I moved out, meaning out of the house, not out of the family.

Sybrina was the custodial parent, and the kids primarily lived with her, but Trayvon still spent as much time as he could with me— we let the kids share their time between us however they wanted. Whichever house they were in, they knew they were always welcome and deeply loved.

One day when Trayvon was nine, we headed home after he finished one of his youth football games in the park. "Do you want something to eat?" I asked as we drove home. No, he said, he was too tired. When I got him home, I put some oil in a pan on the stove to fry some wings and French fries. But while the oil was heating up, Trayvon and I lay down in the bedroom and both of us fell asleep. I woke up to the smell of smoke. I ran to the kitchen and threw a towel over the burning pan to try to smother the fire, but grease splattered all over me, leaving third-degree burns on my lower extremities.

I screamed out, "Trayvon!"

Then I blacked out.

Trayvon woke up and came running into the kitchen. He dragged me out of that burning kitchen. If he hadn't awakened, we might have both been dead. My son saved my life. And on the night of February 26, 2012, I wish I could've saved his.

As time went on, I found out from Sybrina that Trayvon was having trouble at school. We sat down and discussed ways of correcting the issues. I have to admit, I was worried, not about losing my child to the streets, but seeing the son we had raised become a young adult and forgetting about the values that we instilled in him. As soon as we found out about his suspension, we confronted Trayvon— something he didn't look forward to because he knew how strict we were about certain things. But the truth is I never thought Trayvon had gone astray. His life wasn't out of control; he wasn't a bad kid. He was a teenager, and teenagers sometimes do unexpected things—that wasn't an excuse, but a reality I tried to keep in mind, to keep from overinterpreting his growing pains as something darker. Still, this was an important moment to intervene, to make sure he stayed focused on his goals and dreams. I knew all too well what could happen when a young life gets derailed.

He was in his junior year, and we encouraged him to focus on getting past the suspension and finishing up strong so he could go into his senior year with high expectations, ready to tackle the challenges ahead. We wanted so much for him to follow the same path as Jahvaris, who was already doing well in college.

"Recognize the mistakes you have made, and let's correct them," I told him. "We know you're not a bad kid. We know you're not going down a bad path. But we're going to cut off the things that are detrimental to your future. We're going to get things right."

. . .

I was planning to drive up to Sanford that weekend to visit my girl-friend, Brandy Green, and I knew from his previous trips that Tray-von liked visiting her in Sanford, so I decided to take him with me. I thought it would be good to get him away from whatever distractions he was experiencing as a teenager.

The plan was for him to go up a couple of days early, on Tuesday, so he could spend some time with Brandy and her son, Chad—he regarded Trayvon as an older brother. I would drive up on Friday to join them when I got off from work.

"Give yourself a little 'me' time," I told Trayvon when I dropped him off at the Greyhound station that Wednesday. "Think about what you are going to do when you go back to school next week."

"Okay, Dad," he said and turned to go into the bus station. I watched him walk away and felt that, even with this struggle, things were going to be okay.

I'd first met Brandy Green two years earlier at a convention we were both attending for a Masonic organization whose mission was "dedicated to a unifying understanding of God and the betterment of humanity." On the weekend of February 24, 2012, two years later, we were returning to the same convention in Orlando.

Brandy worked as a juvenile detention officer in Orlando, supervising kids in trouble between the ages of eleven and eighteen—kids locked up for fighting, drugs, probation violations, prostitution, disobeying court orders, and other infractions. Some of the kids grew up without a mom or dad. They were kids without supervision or guidance, looking for love and acceptance in the wrong places.

Brandy knew troubled kids, and she knew that Trayvon wasn't one of them.

When he arrived in Orlando on the Greyhound bus, Brandy was waiting for him in front of the station.

"You hungry?" she asked, even though she already knew the answer: Trayvon was *always* hungry.

They drove to Flyers Wings & Grill in West Orlando for the jumbo

25-wing special: wings, fries, a soda, the works. After lunch, they drove to Brandy's home at the Retreat at Twin Lakes, a three-bedroom, one-car-garage townhouse. The Retreat would be familiar to anyone who's spent time in southern or central Florida: it was a classic Florida subdivision, right off the interstate that led straight to Orlando. It was a secluded and sunny place to live.

By the time Trayvon hopped on that bus to Sanford, the Retreat had suffered from foreclosures, and along with the foreclosures, burglaries. The community had reportedly been burglarized eight times the year before, enough for the residents to establish a neighborhood watch, with volunteer, unarmed security guards patrolling the area. Their mandate was to call the police if they saw any suspicious activity.

Even though I usually visited Brandy in her Sanford townhouse about twice a month, I didn't know anything about any of that at the time. And neither did Brandy, for that matter. She worked in Orlando from 2:00 to 10:30 P.M., on a different schedule from her neighbors. She and her son kept to themselves and never knew that there had been burglaries in the neighborhood, much less a neighborhood crime watch. Brandy loved living in the Retreat. It was quiet. Gated. Peaceful. Kids playing outside. She never even noticed the foreclosures, never saw a burglar.

"Chad will be home later," Brandy told Trayvon before leaving for work that afternoon. "Make yourself at home. Whatever you want in the refrigerator, it's all yours."

When she returned that evening, Brandy found Trayvon and Chad asleep. Chad was in his room; Trayvon was in the spare bedroom. Friday would be the start of a very big event for Orlando: the NBA All-Star Weekend. Brandy bought Trayvon and Chad tickets for one of the highlights of the weekend, a game featuring the best rookies and second-year players. That day she picked the boys up after the game and drove to meet me at Orlando's DoubleTree hotel, where the Masons' convention would be held.

I knew Trayvon was in great hands with Brandy because they got along from the first time they met. When they arrived at the Double-Tree, and I saw Trayvon's big smile, it made my day.

Throughout the weekend, as we always did, Trayvon and I talked: about his school suspension, about what he would do when he returned to school that following Monday, and about his future.

"What do you want to do with your life?" I asked him at the hotel.

"Well, I want to go to college, but I know I have to work hard to get there," he said.

He said he wanted to go to the University of Miami or Florida A&M University. He wanted to go to aviation school, but was also interested in Florida A&M, one of the largest historically black colleges and universities in the country.

Today, the pieces of those final few days come back to me like the prelude to a nightmare. At the time, though, it seemed so normal. Brandy and I went to the convention on Friday, and Trayvon and Chad ordered room service in the DoubleTree hotel room we booked for them to stay in that day.

We went to the room and checked on them: he was wearing cargo shorts with multiple pockets, flip-flops, a T-shirt, and, as always, his hoodie. I sat with him awhile, and talked more about his problems at school, his slipping grades, and his suspension, how he needed to get down to business when he returned to school if he wanted to go to college.

"Because if you don't get into college, what are you going to do?" I asked him.

He mentioned his cousins who were working at the Port of Miami, loading cargo ships.

"Dad, if I don't get into college, I could get a job at the port," he said. "Some of the guys working there make a hundred and fifty thousand dollars a year."

"Coming out of high school and going straight into the workforce shouldn't be your goal," I told him. "You should aim higher than that. You're only seventeen. You only have a couple of teenage years left. And your expectations should be getting higher as you get older. You don't want to get stuck in Miami all of your life. You need to take whatever chance you have to see the world."

The Port of Miami is a great way to earn a living. But I wanted more for my kid.

"I know, Dad," he said.

On that Friday evening, after the convention was done for the day, the four of us drove back to Sanford. We dropped Chad off at his grandmother's house because his father was taking him to a youth football game the next day, and Brandy, Trayvon, and I went back to her house and went to sleep. The next day, the three of us drove back to Orlando for the convention, and we sent Trayvon back up to the hotel room, where he went back to sleep. Later that afternoon, we went to watch Chad play his football game at a public park thirty minutes outside Sanford.

When Chad's football game ended, Brandy and I headed to a surprise birthday dinner for one of her friends from high school, leaving Trayvon with Chad and my nephew Steve, who everybody calls "Boobie." Boobie had borrowed his sister-in-law's car so that he could drive Trayvon and Chad wherever they wanted to go. We felt the kids were safe with Boobie, who was twenty-one and had a day off from his job, and was happy to take care of the boys. Neither of them were any trouble, and later Boobie would say that he understood why some of his friends called Trayvon "Mouse." Because he wasn't afraid of anything, because he could fit in with any group, and because, most of all, he was just so calm and quiet.

We gave the boys money for food and a movie, but Chad was tired after the game, so Boobie decided they'd skip the movie and just relax at Brandy's townhouse. They went into the garage, where Brandy had set up some furniture and a television so the kids would have a place to hang out. Boobie and Trayvon played the card game tunk for a dollar a round, while watching movies and calling friends on their cellphones. By the time we returned, after midnight, everybody was asleep: Chad in his room, Trayvon in the spare room, and Boobie in the garage.

The next morning, Sunday, February 26, Brandy and I went to visit some of my friends, leaving Trayvon and Chad with Boobie. Around eleven A.M., Boobie wanted something to drink, so he searched his cellphone for nearby stores on Google Maps, and the closest to pop up was a 7-Eleven at 1125 Rinehart Road, no more than a half mile from Brandy's apartment.

"I'm going to the store to get something to drink," Boobie told Trayvon.

"I'll ride with you," Trayvon told Boobie.

Trayvon put on his white Air Jordans, beige jeans, a sweatshirt, and his gray hoodie. The cousins drove to the 7-Eleven, where Boobie went inside and bought a soda while Trayvon stayed in the car. Then Boobie drove Trayvon back to Brandy's house. It was now 11:30 A.M. Boobie gave him a hug inside the car and said, "Okay, Bro, see you next time I'm in Miami.

"Love," said Boobie.

"Love," repeated Trayvon, and he got out of the car and walked back into the townhouse.

Somewhere between five and six P.M., while they were watching the pregame show for the All-Star game, Trayvon asked Chad if he wanted anything from the store.

"I'm going to walk to the 7-Eleven," he told Chad, meaning the 7-Eleven where he and Boobie had driven earlier that day.

Chad said he wanted some Skittles.

Trayvon left the townhouse and walked for about ten minutes to the 7-Eleven. As always, his earbuds were in his ears and he was surely listening to his music or talking to a friend on his phone.

He arrived at the 7-Eleven shortly before 6:23 P.M., according to the store's security camera, which showed him inside the store in his hoodie, buying a can of Arizona Watermelon Fruit Juice and a bag of Skittles. Then he left the store to walk back toward the house, talking to his school friend Rachel until a few seconds before 7:16 P.M., when the call was suddenly disconnected as he walked through the Retreat at Twin Lakes.

Trayvon was outside, which is where he always loved to be.

It was raining.

And someone was watching.

"Hey, we've had some break-ins in my neighborhood," the neighborhood watchman told the Sanford Police Department dispatcher, "and there's a real suspicious guy, uh, it's Retreat View Circle, um, the best address I can give you is one-eleven Retreat View Circle. This guy looks like he's up to no good, or he's on drugs or something. It's raining, and he's just walking around, looking about."

"Okay, and this guy, is he white, black, or Hispanic?" asked the dispatcher.

"He looks black," replied the neighborhood watchman.

∽✧∽

We returned to Brandy's townhouse at ten-thirty that night, and immediately checked on the kids.

Chad was asleep upstairs in his bedroom, but there was no sign of Trayvon.

"He went to the store," Chad said once we awakened him.

"Store?" I said. It was late for a trip on foot to the store. "How long has he been gone?"

Chad had lost track of the time.

"I don't know," he said.

Brandy checked all of the doors. The sliding glass door to the backyard was unlocked. There was no sign of Trayvon, inside or outside. She locked the sliding door. We looked around. Everything seemed secure.

I called Trayvon's cellphone. It went straight to voicemail.

I called my nephew Boobie's cellphone. It went straight to voicemail, too.

Well, maybe they decided to go to the movie and they turned off their phones, I thought. Or, even more likely, their phone batteries were dead.

I kept calling both of their phones and kept getting both of their voicemails.

I had been up since three or four that morning. A seventeen-year-old out past eleven P.M.? Again, normal. Surely, Trayvon would be back soon. And since he had a key to Brandy's house, he could let himself back inside. I took a hot shower. I lay down on the bed and was soon fast asleep.

At seven A.M., Brandy woke up, and immediately went to check on Trayvon. She checked Chad's room. Nothing. Trayvon's room. Still nothing. Downstairs. The kitchen. The garage. Nothing, nothing, nothing.

"Baby," she said, waking me up. "Trayvon's not here."

Now, I *was* worried. Again, I called his cellphone. Again it went straight to voicemail. I called Sybrina in Miami, and told her that Tray hadn't come home, and she told me to call Boobie, who would surely know where Trayvon had gone.

I called Boobie's cell and, finally, he answered.

"Where are you?" I asked.

"Man, I'm at home," he said.

"Where's Tray?"

"He should be home," he said, meaning Brandy's townhouse.

"What time did you see him last?"

"I left him at the house at eleven-thirty in the morning," Boobie said.

I began babbling. "Boobie, he's not here, he hasn't been here, not since early evening."

I called another nephew, Kevin, who lives in nearby Oviedo, Florida, thinking, now praying, that maybe Trayvon had gone up to visit him. He hadn't seen Trayvon, either. We woke up Chad and began grilling him, and he kept telling us the same thing: "He was going to the store to get something to drink, and I asked him to get some Skittles for me."

Brandy began making calls. She called her job at the juvenile detention center in Orlando. Has someone named Trayvon Martin been arrested? "No," she was told. She called the Orange County Sheriff's Office and asked the same question. Again they said nobody arrested.

I called 911 and said, "I need to file a missing person's report."

They asked me all the particulars: name, age, description, last seen, et cetera, et cetera. I told the dispatcher, "He's not from this area, and he has just turned seventeen."

"Okay, sir, we're gonna dispatch somebody out there," the operator said.

I went outside to wait, expecting Trayvon to come walking up at any moment with an explanation of where he'd been and what he'd been doing all night.

Instead, within thirty minutes, several police officers came driving up to Brandy's townhouse.

∼⋙∽

It was still early morning when Detective Chris Serino, an investigator for the Sanford Police Department's general investigative section, introduced himself and the two officers who came with him.

Serino was a stocky guy who looked like a television detective: close-cropped dark hair, sunken eyes that seemed to have seen pretty much everything, and a button-down white shirt with a tie that was loosened at the neck.

I gave him all of the details: that my son, Trayvon, hadn't come home from the store the night before; that he wasn't from this area; that he didn't have a driver's license or other form of identification.

Detective Serino asked me if I had a recent photograph of Trayvon. Of course I did, I told him, and showed him a picture on my digital camera that I had taken of him a week before. The detective looked at it and then went outside to his car and returned with a folder. It had started drizzling by then, so he asked if we could all go into the townhouse.

We sat down at the kitchen table.

"I'm going to show you a photo, and you tell me if this is your son," he said in his deep, gravelly voice.

He pulled out a picture, and laid it on the table in front of me.

"Is this your son?" he asked.

I looked at the picture, and today, four years and an eternity later, I still find it hard to describe how I felt. My mind spun. My chest ached. My eyes spilled over with tears. And I began sobbing and screaming. Later, Brandy, who was upstairs, told me that the scream was like nothing she had ever heard before, a bloodcurdling shriek that shook the house and could probably be heard in all two hundred and sixty-three townhouses at the Retreat at Twin Lakes, and for blocks, miles, worlds, around.

The picture burned a hole in my heart. It showed my seventeen-year-old son, as lifeless as a broken rag doll, on the wet grass, no more than a hundred yards from Brandy's townhouse. One of his legs was folded back on itself, and his eyes were slightly open, staring into a stranger's camera. The sweatshirt he wore beneath his hoodie was stained blackish red with blood from the gunshot wound to his heart.

Trayvon was dead.

By the time I regained my composure, a police department chaplain had arrived. But I couldn't be consoled. Not now. Not over this.

I asked the detective what happened.

All he said was that there had been an altercation, that Trayvon had been shot, and that the person who shot him "has made an assertion of self-defense." He asked for my cooperation, patience, and understanding. No one, it seemed, had been arrested. I knew immediately that the killer wasn't black.

And that is where it all began.

CHAPTER 3

Sybrina

⌐∾

February 27, 2012

Tracy Martin and I were divorced in 1999, but we remain bound forever by our two sons: Jahvaris, now twenty-five, and Trayvon, forever seventeen.

Friends would sometimes say, "Oh, they get along so well for them to be divorced." And I would say, "Listen, I'm still trying to get rid of my ex-husband. Everybody else can get a divorce and their ex-husband is gone and they're done with them. Mine is still always around me, mainly because of Trayvon's tragedy. But we've always respected each other."

The telephone call that came on February 27 would bind us together in ways I would never have imagined.

It was the start of my workday. After twenty-four years in various government positions in Miami-Dade County, I had become a program coordinator for the Miami-Dade Housing Agency, working to bring housing back to residents who had been moved out of their homes in recent years. Dilapidated public-housing projects had been torn down, displacing generations of residents.

By that February some new housing had finally been completed on the acres of empty lots. The former residents, who had to undergo background checks and an additional screening to qualify for the new units, were skeptical and, in some cases, scared to come back because of various qualifications they needed to return. I was assigned to bring the displaced residents back to a new mixed-income housing development called NorthPoint at Scott Carver, built where the projects had once stood. These were new two-, three-, and four-bedroom apartments and townhouses, and I was on a mission to do whatever I could to bring people back and give them a better and nicer place to live. I had a community office in Liberty City, and Trayvon and Jahvaris would frequently come along as I hosted meetings for former residents so we could explain what was going on and hear their feedback. I wanted my sons to see what my work was about, see how communities were built and sustained, and appreciate that they always had a roof over their heads, and a wide extended family of grandparents, uncles, aunts, and cousins who would always care about them.

I was in my cubicle office in downtown Miami when my cellphone rang. "Trayvon didn't come home last night" was all that Tracy, in his deep, East St. Louis baritone, said. Everyone was busy at work in the other cubicles around me. I couldn't talk in the office. So I took my cellphone into a conference room and stared out the window. Another sunny Miami day. *Trayvon didn't come home,* I thought, which in and of itself alarmed me. It wasn't like either of my sons to stay out and not let us know where they were. Even Jahvaris never stayed out without calling—and he was then a grown man at age twenty-one. Tracy said he wasn't sure what was going on. He said his cousin Steve, who we call "Boobie," had been with Trayvon the day before.

"Call Boobie," I said. "He'll know where Tray is."

"I'll call you back," Tracy said.

I don't remember exactly how long it took him to call me back or exactly what I did while I waited. I know I went back to my desk, where I couldn't do anything. I know I called my sister, and told her what Tracy said about Trayvon not coming home.

"Do we need to go up there to Sanford and help him look for him?" she asked.

I said, no, that Tracy was handling it. But I kept thinking, *What's happened?* I started stressing. I knew I wasn't going to be able to concentrate on work until Tracy called me back. It was so unusual for Trayvon to stay out all night without calling. I knew there was no point in being at work with all of this uncertainty. So I got up from my desk and went to my supervisor's desk.

"I have to go," I said. "I have an emergency at home. Something's happened to my son. I don't know what it is, but I need to leave."

I didn't give him any more information than that. Because I didn't have any more information to give.

"Okay, Sybrina," my supervisor said.

I picked up my purse and my things and I left the office. To this day, I've never returned.

I took the elevator down to the lobby, walked out of the building and into the parking lot, where I climbed into my car. I just sat there thinking, *Where could he be?*

He's probably with Boobie, I told myself. *Maybe they were watching a movie or something and he fell asleep and didn't call his dad to let him know where he was.*

He's with Boobie, I just kept thinking. *He just went somewhere with Boobie. They got in late. They fell asleep. They're at Boobie's house. They went to the movies and it was late and he didn't want to go all the way back to the house. So he stayed with Boobie and fell asleep. And he planned to call his dad the next morning.*

I'm not sure how much time had passed. My memories from that day are still gray. All I can remember is that I was still in the parking lot, sitting in my car, when Tracy called me back.

He said the police had come over to the house and shown him a picture.

"What kind of picture?" I asked.

Tracy was talking, but I could barely understand what he was saying.

"Trayvon gone. Trayvon gone," he kept repeating. "Trayvon is gone."

"Gone?" I said. "Gone where?"

"Somebody killed him," said Tracy. "He was shot and he's gone. Dead. Murdered."

"No!"

I couldn't allow myself to believe it.

"Did you see the body?" I asked.

"No, the police showed me a picture," Tracy said. "They're still here now."

He said that the picture showed Trayvon dead on the ground, shot through the heart.

I cut him off. "That's not him," I said. "That's not Trayvon."

"Yes," Tracy repeated. "I saw the picture."

"That's not him," I said. "You go see the body. You go see the body *physically* to make sure that that is him."

My heart couldn't allow my mind to believe what Tracy was telling me. I couldn't accept any of it. Not shot, not murdered, not dead. I couldn't even begin to comprehend it; I was numb with disbelief. I went into denial. It hadn't happened, couldn't have happened, would *never* have happened. Even though Tracy kept telling me that it was true.

"What did they say happened?" I remember asking at some point, though I was still far from accepting any of what Tracy was telling me.

"Trayvon hid behind this building and this guy was following him," he said.

"Did they arrest this man?" I asked him.

"No, not yet."

And we hung up.

I immediately made two calls, one to my mom and one to my sister. I wasn't crying. It hadn't really hit me yet. I was lost in a swirl of confusion, not allowing myself to believe what Tracy had just told me, but feeling like I needed to tell my family what he said. I called my mom first. I seemed to be on autopilot. I remember dialing her number and repeating to her what Tracy had told me.

"Tracy called and said Trayvon was . . ." I stammered. Then let it out. "He said somebody shot and killed Trayvon."

"What?!" my mom screamed.

"Tracy said somebody shot and killed Trayvon!"

"Are you sure?" she said.

"That's what Tracy told me," I said.

Next, I called my sister and told her the same thing.

"Tracy called and said Trayvon has been shot and killed!"

And she said exactly the same thing as my mother.

"No!" she said. "Are you sure?"

"That's what Tracy told me," I said again, although I still didn't allow myself to believe it.

"I'll meet you at your house," my sister said.

I started the car. I drove out of the parking lot. I pulled onto the I-95 expressway, going over everything I'd been told. I still wasn't crying, because I still didn't believe it. *It's not Trayvon, it's not Trayvon, it's not Trayvon,* I kept repeating as a prayer, in the hope that it might come true. I was driving north on the expressway, heading toward home. Still not a tear. I passed the exit for Miami Beach. I kept going over what Tracy had said.

Okay, he didn't come home, I thought. *Maybe something* did *happen.* Now the reality was starting to sink in. I kept replaying Tracy's words over and over again. *Oh, my God. Did he say that Trayvon had been shot? Did he say Trayvon had been killed? Did he say Trayvon had been murdered? Was he talking about my son? My baby?*

And then, in the middle of traffic on I-95, it hit me like a punch to the stomach.

It was true.

I put on my right turn signal and pulled over onto the shoulder, right before the exit for NW Sixty-second Street/Dr. Martin Luther King Boulevard. I stopped the car and put on my hazard lights.

And there, on the side of the highway, with hundreds of cars whizzing by, with the roar of the traffic all around me, with my baby dead on the ground from God-knows-what, I broke down. I cried. I wailed. And, finally, I screamed out to God.

NO!

"Why?" I screamed out. "Why, why did this happen to him! Why did you let this happen to him! Why, why, why, why, *WHY?!"*

The truth had taken the breath and the life out of me. A darkness descended and everything ached: my head, my chest, my heart. Especially my heart. Everything hurt. I had never experienced the piercing pain I felt in that moment, a hurt so deep it made me think my heart was going to come flying out of my body and explode in midair. It was true. Trayvon was gone. And I was in a very dark place.

Finally, my questions to God about *why* turned into asking God for help in getting through it. I don't recall how long I stayed on the side of that expressway. It might have been thirty minutes; it could have been an hour or two. I lost all sense of time. Cars were flying by. I couldn't see them, hear them, care about them. Because of my tears. I cried some more and I prayed some more and I cried some more and I screamed some more and pleaded with God for help some more.

Please give me strength, God. Please help me, God. Please, please, please, please, please . . .

Finally, I pulled myself together. I still had sense enough to know that I couldn't stay on the shoulder of that expressway forever. I wiped the tears off my face, and I waited. I waited and waited and waited until I felt like I'd gotten myself together, at least enough to continue the drive home. I started the car and resumed my drive home. All I remember of that moment was that it was hot and my whole body was wet with sweat and tears.

When I pulled into the driveway at home, my mom and sister

were outside waiting for me. I remember Tracy calling again to make sure I got home okay. Then more calls from friends and family. Calls and calls and calls and calls.

I couldn't focus on any of that. With that one call, my whole life had been destroyed. My peaceful existence was over. I desperately wanted to see my baby and couldn't let myself believe that he might really be gone. So I went into my bedroom and lay down on the bed, and I didn't come out for the rest of the day, hoping, praying that when I awoke it would have all been a bad dream and that Trayvon would be safe and smiling in our home again.

CHAPTER 4

Tracy

⤳

February 27, 2012–March 8, 2012

The police took off and left me with the photo of Trayvon lying dead on the ground. I was distraught but also desperate for answers. *How could this have happened? And* what *happened?* I walked outside of the townhouse and went around the back, about eighty yards, to the spot where the police said my son had died. It was a typical suburban setting: a communal grassy backyard to dozens of townhouses, with a paved walkway running through it.

The detective told me that he and the two officers with him would return later to do what they called a "walk-through," reenacting the "altercation," at this very spot where it happened. He asked me not to come outside while they were doing the walk-through because the person who had shot my son would be there. For some reason, I agreed. Instead of letting emotions run high, I decided that I would leave the house and get away from the scene when the police came with the gunman, thinking at the time, *Let the police investigate. Let justice take its course.*

But there was nothing stopping me from visiting the crime scene before they arrived. So I walked outside, my face still streaked with tears, and I saw . . . nothing. Not one sign that anything had ever happened. The crime-scene tape, if there had ever been any, had been taken up. The evidence had supposedly been gathered, along with Trayvon's body. The sidewalk was clean. There wasn't a single sign that anything had happened at that place a few hours earlier. It was like the shooting had never happened.

As I was standing there bewildered by how quickly they had erased any sign of my son's death, a television reporter walked up with a small crew.

"Have you heard about the shooting last night?" he asked.

"Yes," I said. "That was my son." And I began to cry again.

We had a brief conversation, and then I began knocking on doors.

"I'm the father of the kid who was shot last night," I said. "Can you tell me what happened?"

Most said they didn't see anything, only heard the gunshot. And then they quickly shut the door.

My sense of hopelessness and despair deepened. Already I could tell: no one seemed to care about a seventeen-year-old kid shot dead in Sanford, Florida.

On Wednesday, February 29, two days later, the shooting of Trayvon Martin had received forty-one seconds of television coverage on Fox affiliate Channel 35 in Orlando, and the local newspapers gave it brief mention, buried deep in the paper.

BOY, 17, SHOT TO DEATH IN SANFORD DURING "ALTERCATION," POLICE SAY, read the headline of the *Orlando Sentinel,* the first and only paper to report the shooting that Wednesday.

At the medical examiner's office, Trayvon's body was listed as a John Doe.

Young black male.

Identity unknown.

The body was off-limits to me. It was stored at the Volusia County medical examiner's office, thirty-three miles away from Sanford. Sanford is in Seminole County, and the county has its own medical examiner's office, right in Sanford. I wondered why they would send Trayvon's body to another county. No one would explain it to me. When I called the medical examiner's office in Volusia County, I was told they didn't allow visitation, even for next of kin.

So I wasn't able to see my son's body.

Why?

Why wasn't I able to see my son? What had they done to my baby? It was now forty-eight hours since my son's death. Sybrina had insisted that I see the body to be one hundred percent certain that it was Trayvon who had been shot and killed. But I was turned away from seeing the body, much less collecting it. I was determined not to leave Sanford until his body was released and my son was headed home, to Miami, for his final rest.

His clothes and belongings—everything from twenty-two dollars in his pants pocket to the bag of candy in his hoodie to his earbuds and his cellphone—were bagged as evidence and held by the Sanford Police Department. But his body was stuck in Volusia County and would be until the Sanford Police Department sent a letter, along with the crime-scene photo, positively identifying the body as Trayvon Martin.

For two days, the body, along with questions over *why* my son was shot, lay in limbo.

On the morning of Tuesday, February 28, not knowing what to do or who else to contact, I decided to go to the Sanford Police Department.

I was still in shock. I couldn't drive. I couldn't speak. Brandy drove me to the police station. It was morning. I don't remember the exact time. No one took notice of me, a six-foot-three, 200-pound black man walking into a police station in sweatpants, a long-sleeved T-shirt, and a baseball cap, with Brandy at my side.

"Good morning, I'm Tracy Martin," I told the receptionist, asking to see Detective Chris Serino.

She called someone upstairs and soon Detective Serino arrived, again wearing a white button-down shirt and loosened tie, and guided us to a conference room.

All I knew at this point was that there had been an altercation and that Trayvon had been shot and killed. Now, in the conference room, the detective elaborated on what had happened on the night of February 26, 2012.

He told me that Trayvon was walking back from the 7-Eleven when the altercation occurred.

I asked the detective who killed Trayvon.

He said the man's name, George Zimmerman, but I will refer to him from this point forward as who he is: the killer. He was a twenty-eight-year-old volunteer neighborhood watch coordinator at the Retreat at Twin Lakes. He was also a student at Seminole State College working on a degree in criminal justice, the detective told me, adding that the killer had never been arrested for anything in his life. "This guy is squeaky-clean," the detective told me.

Detective Serino then told me the killer's version of the altercation: He was sitting in his vehicle, behind tinted windows. Trayvon was walking along the sidewalk, coming back from the 7-Eleven. The killer began tailing Trayvon in his car. Trayvon turned and walked up to the killer's car and asked, "Why are you following me?" The killer rolled down his window and said, "I'm not following you." Trayvon then supposedly asked him, "Do you have a problem?" And the killer replied, "I don't have a problem."

Trayvon began running. The killer got out of his truck, and came around one of the buildings. Trayvon walked up to him again and said, according to the detective, "What's your problem, homes?"

"I don't have a problem," said the killer.

"You've got a problem now," Trayvon allegedly said. At which point, the killer put his hand in his pocket to retrieve his cellphone, and, the detective said, Trayvon sucker-punched the twenty-eight-year-old, knocking him to the ground. And here the detective said my seventeen-year-old son began beating the neighborhood watch coordinator, covering his mouth with his hand and telling him, "Shut the fuck up," while pounding his head onto the sidewalk pavement.

While they were struggling on the ground, the killer grabbed his pistol and shot Trayvon once through the chest.

According to the detective, after Trayvon was shot he put his hands out and said, "You got me, homes."

It sounded like something out of a bad movie. And it didn't sound anything at all like my son. I told the detective that Trayvon wouldn't just walk up to a stranger's car out of the blue and ask, "Do you have a problem?" That was the first thing I questioned. Knowing my son, he wouldn't just go up and confront, much less attack, a stranger.

"Have you arrested this man?" I asked.

"No," he said. "We're interviewing him."

He added that the killer had a license to carry a gun.

"Did you do a background check on my son?" I asked, remembering what the detective had told me about the killer having a "squeaky-clean" record.

"Yes," he replied, and Trayvon's juvenile record was, of course, clean.

"Just because this guy has a squeaky-clean background and a license to carry a gun, does that give him the right to kill my son?" I asked.

"Sir, it certainly does not give him that right," said Detective Serino. He added that he was a father, too, and he told me that he didn't believe the killer's story. "I want to interview him again and catch him in a lie," he said.

The story didn't make sense, but at that point I was focused on getting my son's body released so we could get him back to Miami for the funeral.

I asked Detective Serino if he would contact the Volusia County medical examiner's office so I could arrange to transport Trayvon back to Miami.

He said he would do his best to help get the body released. Then the detective led Brandy and me into a cubicle. "I have something I want you to listen to," he said, and he began setting up some audio files on his computer. I had no idea what he was about to play for me, which turned out to be parts—short snippets—of the 911 tapes of several neighbors who called the police to report that two men were involved in a fight at the Retreat at Twin Lakes on the evening of February 26.

"Brace yourself," the detective told Brandy and me. "You'll hear screams. You'll hear the shot."

Then he hit PLAY.

The calls were to report the altercation, and you could hear it still going on in the background on the tapes.

The sound was, at times, fuzzy. Still, listening to those tapes was horrifying. I was actually listening to my son being shot and killed.

The detective played a few seconds of one tape, a few seconds of another tape.

"This one has some screams on it," he said. We leaned in closer. Again, there was a lot of commotion on the tape, but you could clearly hear what I knew were death screams, the last moments of Trayvon's life. These screams still haunt me and are impossible for me to describe. I heard a shriek, a howl. I thought it sounded like the word "Help!" It was followed by the sound of a gunshot, the single, fatal shot that took the life out of my son.

"Was this your son screaming?" the detective asked me when the tape went silent.

I was shaken up, in a daze, as anyone would be after hearing the screams and the shot that led to the death of their child. I shook my head like, *Man, I don't know.* Later, the detective would say I shook my head and said, "No," meaning it *wasn't* my son screaming, meaning the screams came from the killer. At that moment, however, I couldn't tell for sure who was screaming, and, hearing those screams for the first time, I didn't want to know.

I didn't ask him to play the tapes over again so I could identify which screams were Trayvon's and which belonged to the man who shot him.

"I don't want to hear it anymore," I said.

Detective Serino assured me that he would do everything that he could to arrest the man who killed my son, and said that he wanted to "interview him again and catch him in a lie."

More bad news followed. Not only would there not be an arrest of the man who shot my son, I would soon learn that the Sanford Police Department allowed Trayvon's killer to walk out of the police station and go home to his bed while Trayvon's body remained at the Volusia County medical examiner's office.

I felt helpless, powerless, facing a situation I just couldn't understand. My son was dead. The man who shot him walked free. And no one seemed to be doing anything about it.

I didn't know where to turn. Three days after the shooting, I was still in Sanford. Still trying to get my son's body released. I was expressing my frustration to my brother Steve, and he said, "Give Patricia a call." He was referring to Patricia Jones. She's a lawyer, now a legal adviser for the Miami-Dade Department of Corrections and Rehabilitation, but back then she was an assistant public defender, working with people who couldn't afford to hire private attorneys. She'd once worked as a criminal defense attorney.

Patricia was also a family member. She had known Trayvon since the day he was born.

"Tracy, what's going on?" Patricia asked me over the phone.

I tried to explain—the shooting, the aftermath, the confusion, the lack of an arrest. I could barely talk about it. The shock was still too fresh. Patricia shook me from my stupor.

"Something's not right, Tracy," she said after I told her the story the best I could. "We have to apply some pressure."

"Okay," I managed to say. "But how?"

"I need you to call Ben Crump," she said.

Then she told me a little about Benjamin Crump. Crump, at the age of forty-two, had already become one of the most prominent African American attorneys in the country. He was born in Lumberton, North Carolina, the oldest of nine kids. He had first noticed racial inequality in fifth grade the same way a lot of us first notice it. He looked around. He asked his mom, "Why do people on that side of the tracks have it so much better than people on our side of the tracks?" Since 1997, he had fought—and won—some of the most important recent civil rights cases, along with Daryl Parks, his partner at their Tallahassee law firm, Parks and Crump. Crump had taken on a wrongful-death case against the state of Florida for the parents of Martin Lee Anderson, a fourteen-year-old who died in early 2006 after being kicked and beaten by guards at the Bay County Sheriff's Office Juvenile Boot Camp in Panama City, Florida, and won more than $10 million in settlements. After the guards who beat Anderson were tried and acquitted, Crump told the media, "You kill a dog, you go to jail. You kill a little black boy and nothing happens."

Crump's law firm's motto is "We help David fight Goliath and win."

Patricia told me she would contact Benjamin Crump on my behalf.

In early March 2012, Crump was busy in court as usual, working on another civil rights case. But Patricia kept calling him, leaving messages, sending texts and email. She became a thorn in his side. Finally, Crump called back.

"What is it?" he asked Patricia, during a lunch break. "Why do you keep calling me?"

"Well, you're the only person for this case," said Patricia.

"But what's the case?" Crump asked.

She gave him the background about Trayvon's shooting and then asked Crump if he would talk to me, so I could give him the story from my point of view.

Shortly after that, I was on the phone with Attorney Crump. I was still in shock, and my manner was meek and mild. I was still barely able to speak about what had happened to my son.

"Trayvon was seventeen years old," I told him. "He was walking from the 7-Eleven, and a neighborhood watch volunteer pulled a nine-millimeter pistol and shot and killed him. The police said Trayvon was unarmed, and the police also said they aren't going to arrest the man who shot him. All my son had was a bag of Skittles and a can of iced tea."

"Hold on," said Crump. "Let me make sure I understand this. Your son was walking home. He was unarmed. The neighborhood watch volunteer had a nine-millimeter pistol?"

"Yes, sir," I said. "And he shot my son in the heart."

There was a long silence. "You don't need me on this case," Crump finally said. "I'm an officer of the court and we see people all the time, people with no evidence against them at all, get arrested on an innuendo, on a suspicion, on a 'somebody said you look like somebody. . . .' But here, you've got a person who has the proverbial smoking gun in his hand, with an unarmed teenager dead on the ground."

He took a breath. "*Of course,* they're going to arrest him," he said. Then he repeated, "You don't need me on this case, Mr. Martin. Give it a couple of days. They are going to arrest him."

Crump went back to his case. I went back to trying to get my son's body released for his funeral in Miami, believing justice would prevail and the killer of my son would soon be arrested.

I have a close and longtime friend at Roy Mizell & Kurtz Funeral Home in Fort Lauderdale, Cameron Mizell. I called him from Sanford asking for a favor.

"Trayvon was killed and we need to get the body back home," I told him. "Could you pick him up in Volusia County, drive him home, and get him ready for a funeral on Saturday?" I asked, meaning Saturday, March 3, which was only a few days away.

"Yes, of course," he said.

Before I drove back to Miami, I made one last call to the Sanford Police Department, letting Detective Serino know that I wasn't satisfied with the answers I had received about Trayvon's death, and that I would be back after I laid my baby to rest.

The funeral home sent what's called a "First Call Car," a van without windows, specially fitted with a stretcher on the inside to hold a body that's being transported to a funeral home for embalming. They picked up the body at the morgue in Volusia County, and transferred it to the van, and took my son on his last ride back home. The funeral home's representatives called me once they were on the road. Only after I knew for certain the body had been picked up did I start driving back home. On the way, I asked the funeral home director if it would be okay for me to see Tray as soon as they got him back home.

He warned me that it wouldn't be a good idea, because the body had been in the cooler and it would not be a pretty sight. "You wouldn't want to see a loved one in that state," he said. "That's not how you would want to remember your child."

The idea of my son's body sitting in a cooler for days—"in that state"—hit me like a punch. But I took his advice and waited until they prepared him.

As soon as I pulled into town, I drove over to Sybrina's house, carrying the picture that the police detective had given me of Trayvon lying dead on the ground. Even though Trayvon's body was now back in Miami, Sybrina and her family still couldn't—or wouldn't—believe that he was dead.

"Tracy, are you absolutely sure?" Sybrina's sister asked me.

I asked her if she wanted to see the picture that the police had shown me.

She said she did, and one of Sybrina's brothers did, too, so I showed them the picture. But Sybrina couldn't look at it. She wasn't in a state to do anything. I gave two friends a shopping list, and they went out to buy Trayvon's last outfit, the clothes he would wear in his casket. I wanted him to wear white with powder-blue accents because those are the colors Trayvon told me he wanted to wear to his high school prom. My friends found him a white suit and a powder-blue necktie and vest at the mall in Fort Lauderdale. I met them at the mall, then Sybrina and I went to the funeral home, where we picked out a baby-blue casket lined in white, with his name engraved on it.

Now I had to choose his grave site. I went to the Dade Memorial Park in North Miami, where my mom, dad, and grandmother and other family members were laid to rest. A member of the cemetery staff drove me around on a golf cart, looking for what he called "a decent plot."

We rode around for a while and eventually pulled over. We got off the golf cart and walked toward an empty plot, a path forcing us to walk over other people's graves.

I stopped. "No. I don't want Trayvon buried in the ground." I didn't want to imagine anyone walking across his grave.

A member of the cemetery staff told me about their mausoleum, where, by coincidence, Trayvon's great-grandmother Nettie Spotford and his cousin Cory Johnson were buried. Cory's fiancée had purchased a space in the mausoleum right next to Cory's. Once she'd heard about Trayvon's shooting, she'd offered to help us however she could. While we were still at the cemetery she called me up and said, "Tracy, I heard you are looking for a plot?"

I offered to purchase the plot in the mausoleum next to Cory from her. We would lay Trayvon to rest there.

Our fight to find the truth about what happened to our son continued throughout the preparations for his funeral. Attorney Crump still hadn't agreed to work on our case, but he did send his associate, a young civil rights attorney named Jasmine Rand, down from Tallahassee to meet with us. On the day she came, the house was filled with family and food, and a feeling of almost unbearable grief. Being a young attorney she was nervous about meeting us: not just because it was such an emotional time, but also because Jasmine is white. She later told me that before she opened the door, she was anxious about how she would be perceived, and wondered if we'd be resentful toward her because, as far as she knew, a white person had just killed our son.

But the last thing on our minds was the color of her skin. We were still shell-shocked, still numb, but already some of our strength was returning—we were focused on getting answers, and if Jasmine was going to help, we welcomed her.

Jasmine Rand called my cellphone from her car on her way to meet us. She was headed to Sybrina's house, and I had to apologize: we were running late because I was in the mall picking out the suit in which to bury Trayvon. For a moment no one spoke: I think the pain of that surreal moment radiated from one end of the phone to the other. Jasmine asked me to please not apologize and said that she would be ready to meet whenever it would be convenient for us.

We met later that same day. Sybrina, Jahvaris, and I took the attorney to Jahvaris's room, where we told her what details we knew about what had happened to our son—and then she told us what she thought she and Parks and Crump could do for us.

"If they decide to accept the case, I can promise that Benjamin Crump, Daryl Parks, and I will fight harder than anybody to have the killer arrested," she said, adding that even with those efforts, no specific outcome could be guaranteed. "But if it is going to happen," she said, "it will happen with Ben Crump."

We signed the papers for the Parks and Crump law firm to take our case.

The viewing, at Richardson Funeral Home in Miami, was on Friday, March 2. So many people came to view the body: Trayvon's family, friends, and classmates, as well as friends of the family. Our family arrived last. I walked through the crowd of mourners and began the longest walk of my life: down the funeral home aisle toward my son's open casket. I approached the casket and saw Trayvon lying there, his face placid, his body uncharacteristically still, in his white suit. Showing no sign of the violence that had prematurely snuffed out his young life, he actually looked at peace.

I leaned over and kissed him on his lips.

They were cold.

I rubbed his hands.

Cold.

I broke down. Sobbing. I stood there, holding on to the casket, feeling that something deep and essential, something irreplaceable, had been stolen from me that I could never get back. I fell hard into a dark, dark place. As much as I wanted to speak to all the people gathered there to join us in mourning and comfort, I couldn't speak. I felt that no one could fully understand the pain of what I was going through, and I didn't have the words to make it clear. I was being eaten alive—I was so close to his body, but would never see my son again in this life. My best friend, Tommie Liddell, stood by my side, and as close as we were, he couldn't even find a way to comfort me. I was trying to be strong for my family, and they were all right there for me: Brandy and her family, my brothers and sisters, Sybrina and Jahvaris, all of my family and friends. But nothing and nobody could save me from my sorrow now.

The next day, our family arrived at the Antioch Missionary Baptist Church in Miami Gardens for the funeral in two limousines provided by the funeral home—I rode with Sybrina, Jahvaris, and two of my other children, Takira and Demetrius. As other family members walked out of the first limo and into the sanctuary, we gathered our thoughts and tried to calm our emotions. The church could hold more than a thousand people, we were told, but it had apparently swelled past its capacity and people were lined up outside. A lot of them were there for us, and to see Trayvon, who many knew as "Slimm," for the last time. But there were strangers, too. As of yet, nobody really knew the story of what brought us to this point, only the stray details that were being passed along by word of mouth and in a handful of sketchy news stories that had come out: a young man had been shot and killed. But they had all come to bear witness. I was dazed, but moved that so many people had come to remember our son. I looked over at Sybrina, who seemed closed inside herself, her face lined with the suffering of the previous days. I looked down at the flower on my suit to make sure it was on straight. Sybrina and I—and our whole family—all wore white; my suit was in the same style as the one Trayvon wore. I took off my suit after the funeral and placed it in a plastic bag with the flower still pinned to the lapel. I would never wear it again.

Finally, our limo door was opened and we got out and walked up the front steps of the church. We were all crying. The doors to the church opened and the choir was singing, but I couldn't hear or see anything but the casket resting at the altar at the front of the church. I was led to my seat, too hurt to even know what I was doing. I only vaguely remember the funeral service, led by Pastor Ludence Robinson.

He recited Psalms 89, 90, and 91, psalms about strength, trust in God, and the power we have to rise, even above death. Although he didn't know Trayvon or the circumstances of his death, the pastor read from Job 36:15, which deals with unexpected tragedy and loss: "But those who suffer he delivers in their suffering; he speaks to them in their affliction."

The congregation rose and one by one passed by Trayvon's casket, taking a last moment to pay their respects to our son, who was also a son of our community, a son of our city. Many of the mourners stopped by the first row, where we sat, to give us a hug or a kiss and offer words of comfort. I accepted it all in a daze. As we prepared to leave the church for the cemetery, I broke down again, knowing that when that casket closed, I would never see Trayvon again. Not in this life.

We left the church and climbed back into the limousine. Sybrina, Jahvaris, Takira, Demetrius, and I were driven to Dade Memorial Park, passed through an alley of glorious old trees and up to the sturdy mausoleum, a pink granite wall of graves.

The pallbearers, which included two of my nephews, Sybrina's nephews, and a few of Trayvon's friends, lifted his casket from the hearse and walked it to the wall, as the pastor began reciting verses and prayers.

"As much as it pleases God Almighty to take upon himself the soul of our dear brother Trayvon Martin, we now commit his body to the ground," said the pastor.

"Earth to earth.

"Ashes to ashes.

"Dust to dust.

"In the sure and certain hope of the resurrection of the dead," he continued. "For the Lord Himself will descend from Heaven with a shout, with the voice of the archangel, and with the trumpet of God, and the dead in Christ will rise."

At that, Trayvon's casket was slid into the mausoleum drawer and sealed up. We all stood there for a moment and felt something missing from among us. An absence. An aching.

And then there it was again, the silence.

No trumpet calls. No shouts of outrage. No arrest.

Nothing. Only silence.

After the funeral, my sense of hopelessness and despair deepened, and I called Benjamin Crump again.

"Attorney Crump, it's Tracy Martin," I said. "When we talked before you said that if they didn't do anything, to call you back and you would help me."

"They didn't arrest him?" Crump asked. I could hear shock and surprise in his voice.

"No, sir," I said, reporting back to him what I'd heard from the Sanford police. "They told me that because of this thing called the Stand Your Ground law, they're not going to arrest him."

Crump said that was odd. Stand Your Ground, I'd come to find out, is a law in Florida and more than two dozen other states that allows the use of force when someone is faced with the "fear of death or great bodily harm."

"Mr. Martin, I'm going to help you," he immediately said.

Crump would later tell his associates that he was going to try to help us, the family of Trayvon Martin, a seventeen-year-old killed by a neighborhood watchman in Sanford, Florida. Apparently, that news didn't exactly bring cheers of support. It was another "non-high-producing" case, in lawyer terms, in which the attorneys would spend their time, money, and resources on a case in which probably no arrest would ever be made or settlement won.

"You're probably right," Crump told his associates. "But we've got to do something about this."

He instructed Jasmine Rand to "try to put some pressure on the Sanford police to do the right thing."

Crump still hadn't officially taken on the case, but he called me back for more information, and I told him everything I knew, which at that point was still very little. "I went down to the Sanford Police Department," I said. "And they let me hear a 911 tape to identify the voices."

He cut me off. "There are 911 tapes?" he asked.

"Yes, there are 911 tapes where you can hear screaming and a gunshot."

Shortly after that, Chief of Police Bill Lee held a press conference to announce that there were no immediate plans to arrest the killer for the shooting of our son. That's the moment Crump fully committed to taking on our case, I would later discover. I was on the phone with him at the time and heard him yelling down the hall of the law office to Jasmine Rand.

"Draft the lawsuit!" he said.

"What lawsuit?" Jasmine asked.

"The chief of police just announced he's not arresting George Zimmerman for killing Trayvon; he held a press conference," Crump told Jasmine. "Can you believe it? A press conference to remind the people of Sanford that our people's lives don't matter. Now it's time for us to remind him that we do matter."

Crump told Jasmine to write the public-records lawsuit to sue the Sanford Police Department for a copy of the 911 tapes.

"That's impossible. We haven't even sent a public-records request yet, so the suit is not ripe [meaning ready to be filed]," Jasmine said.

To which Crump responded, "Well, write a public-records request for the 911 tapes, fax it, and then write the lawsuit."

"But don't we need to give them time to respond before I file the lawsuit?" Jasmine asked.

Crump's answer was simple. "No." The message from Bill Lee earlier that day was all he needed to hear in order to know what he now needed to do.

Two days later Crump received a call from the Sanford Police Department's attorney. They wouldn't release the tapes, they said, because the case was still an active investigation. Jasmine already had the lawsuit ready to file, demanding that we, as Trayvon's parents, had the right to view any photographs of him and listen to any audio recordings of his last moments, including visual or audio depictions. "I want them to know I mean business," Crump told me and Sybrina. "They're not going to sweep Trayvon Martin's death under the rug."

I met Benjamin Crump for the first time in person in Sanford a few days later. He was an interesting character. He was clearly well educated and wore a sharp business suit, but he also had the sort of deep Southern accent that some people associate with uneducated individuals. But the words would just flow—not like honey, but in a sharp rhythm like the beat of a drum. He wasn't aggressive or edgy or slick—he was polite but efficient, clearly a dogged, hard worker. He apologized several times for telling me in our first encounter that they were going to arrest the man who killed my son. "Hey, man, I apologize," he said. "I figured a kid with a bag of Skittles and a can of iced tea, getting shot and killed by a neighborhood watch volunteer? I thought it was a no-brainer that they would arrest the man who shot your son."

It was less than two weeks after Trayvon's death and Crump, as we came to call him, had already come up with a strategy on how to bring attention to Trayvon's death, apply pressure on the police to arrest the man who had killed him, and expose the truth of what happened that night in Sanford.

His plan was to take the case to the media.

Attorney Crump put me on the phone with Ryan Julison, a media specialist who had previously worked with an attorney named Natalie Jackson—a lawyer who worked with Crump on cases from her office in Orlando. Julison ran a one-man public relations consultancy in Orlando. Even over the phone, I immediately had confidence in Ryan Julison, who seemed like a smart and savvy media wizard ready to bring his time and experience to our case. Julison had been in the public relations business for more than twenty years, but the economic crisis of 2008 wiped out his job as the head of communications for an Orlando real estate company. He decided to start his own media consulting firm, and along with his normal clients he found a sector that desperately needed a person of his expertise working with attorneys who represented regular people in need of assistance. He had worked with a variety of families—not in civil rights cases but what he called "regular people in trouble." When Julison heard our story, he wanted to help and he began volunteering his time, connections, and knowledge.

On the phone with Ryan, I was still emotional, feeling helpless and still having trouble expressing myself. I managed to tell Ryan that I was frustrated that the media didn't seem interested in the death of my son. Ryan told me that he and Ben Crump might be able to change that and shine a national spotlight on my son's death. Both of these men felt so strongly about this that they would donate their time to our cause for free.

But in exchange, we would have to be willing to go in front of the media and tell our story.

As I said before, I'm a truck driver.

I had never spoken into a media microphone, never done a newspaper interview. Not local, or regional, much less national. But I was prepared to do whatever it took to get answers and, hopefully, find justice.

"It's not going to be easy; you're going to have to relive your grief every day, answering the same question over and over again," Ryan

Julison told me right there at the beginning. "Every one of these media interviews can be invasive, but this is the only way for you to find justice. You are going to have to express your emotions and your inner grief. You're going to have to be incredibly strong to go out and bare your soul in your quest for justice."

"I understand," I said. "I'm ready."

I'm not sure I was. At that point, Trayvon was an unknown teenager killed with a can of fruit tea and a bag of Skittles. We had to put a face to that story and give it an emotional life. We had to make people care.

The media was interested in photos of Trayvon. We gave Ryan Julison what we had that was easily accessible: the photos we used in his funeral program. He sent those photos to various members of the media. The one that would turn out to be published the most was the picture of him in his red Hollister T-shirt. Some would later accuse us of trying to confuse people by using a photo of him when he was much younger, to pretend that he was smaller and less developed than he really was. But that's not the case. We simply provided the media with photographs we had access to, and they chose what they wanted to run.

That was the first move.

But we couldn't stop with a photo or a press release. Now that people had a face to attach to the name, we needed to tell the story of the human being behind that picture. It wasn't an easy story to tell, initially. Some editors, reporters, and producers weren't interested. Others were reluctant to be the first to make a story out of the case of a young black man shot by a white neighborhood watch volunteer. We heard that one editor called it a simple, everyday story of a "fight gone bad." The media didn't go looking for the story, so we had to go looking for the media.

The fuse began burning on March 7, ten days after Trayvon's death, when the first national media coverage about the case appeared on the Reuters news service, followed the next morning by a report that aired on *CBS This Morning*.

Family of Florida Boy Killed by Neighborhood Watch Seeks Arrest

BY BARBARA LISTON | ORLANDO, FLORIDA

The family of a 17-year-old African-American boy shot to death last month in his gated Florida community by a white Neighborhood Watch captain wants to see the captain arrested, the family's lawyer said on Wednesday.

Trayvon Martin was shot dead after he took a break from watching NBA All-Star game television coverage to walk 10 minutes to a convenience store to buy snacks including Skittles candy . . . the family's lawyer Ben Crump said.

"He was a good kid," Crump said in an interview, adding that the family would issue a call for the Watch captain's arrest at a news conference on Thursday. "On his way home, a Neighborhood Watch loose cannon shot and killed him."

Trayvon, who lived in Miami with his mother, had been visiting his father . . . in a gated townhome community called The Retreat at Twin Lakes in Sanford, 20 miles north of Orlando.

As Trayvon returned to the townhome, Sanford police received a 911 call reporting a suspicious person.

Although names are blacked out on the police report, Crump and media reports at the time of the shooting identified the caller as George Zimmerman, who is listed in the community's newsletter as the Neighborhood Watch captain.

Without waiting for police to arrive, Crump said, Zimmerman confronted Trayvon, who was on the sidewalk near his home. By the time police got there, Trayvon was dead of a single gunshot to the chest.

"What do the police find in his pocket? Skittles," Crump said. "A can of Arizona ice tea in his jacket pocket and Skittles in his front pocket for . . . Chad."

Zimmerman could not be reached for comment on

Wednesday evening at a phone number listed for him on the community's newsletter.

Crump said the family was concerned that police might decide to consider the shooting as self-defense, and that police have ignored the family's request for a copy of the original 911 call, which they think will shed light on the incidents.

"If the 911 protocol across the country held to form here, they told him not to get involved. He disobeyed that order," said Ryan Julison, a spokesman for the family.

"He [Zimmerman] didn't have to get out of his car," said Crump, who has prepared a public records lawsuit to file on Thursday if the family doesn't get the 911 tape. "If he never gets out of his car, there is no reason for self-defense. Trayvon only has Skittles. He has the gun."

Since Trayvon, a high school junior who wanted to be a pilot, was black and Zimmerman is white, Crump said, race is "the 600-pound elephant in the room."

"Why is this kid suspicious in the first place? I think a stereotype must have been placed on the kid," Crump said.

That article got our story out of Florida. In one stroke, it was a national story. Reuters gave us credibility and national distribution for our message: this was a story of justice denied an innocent child, shot to death in the night with no one arrested, no one held accountable. On the same day the Reuters story was published, Ryan Julison had arranged for me to be interviewed about the case on *CBS This Morning*. Unbelievably, the next morning, March 8, Charlie Rose, at his desk in the New York City studio of the nationally televised show, was talking about Trayvon.

"The parents of a teenager who was shot and killed near Orlando last month will hold a news conference today," he said. "They are outraged that no one has been arrested in a case that has serious racial overtones. Mark Strassmann is in Sanford, Florida. Mark, good morning."

I was standing with the reporter at the Retreat at Twin Lakes. This was my debut on television, but I wasn't yet out of the fog of grief—just a few weeks ago, I never would've conceived of any of this, of my son's death or the official stonewalling that followed it. Or me standing by the patch of grass where my son was killed, speaking to the entire nation on television.

"He was lying right here, wasn't he?" the reporter asked me, adding, "It must be a little . . . still kind of odd to be here?" he asked me.

"Yeah, it is," I said. I didn't know what else to say.

The reporter then told the national television audience the facts of the story: "Seventeen-year-old Trayvon Martin, Tray to his family, lived in Miami. He loved horses and dreamed of becoming a pilot. This high school junior was visiting relatives last month when he was shot and killed inside this gated subdivision of townhomes."

"He meant the world to me; he meant the world to his mother," I said. "And it's just sad that he's been taken away from us. He was just up here, just to relax. He wasn't up here to return home in a body bag, and that's just the part that really tears me up."

I was starting to find my voice, even though I knew it wasn't coming out exactly right. The reporter went on.

"When Tray was only nine he pulled his father from a burning kitchen," said the reporter.

I hadn't expected this—but the camera was on me and I knew I had to say something. I just didn't know what was going to come out of my mouth. Or if I could even hold it together to talk. We had been told by Crump and Julison that there might be tough questions, but I hadn't had time to prepare. I looked at the reporter and felt something uncontrollable welling inside me.

I broke down and cried on national television. "He was my hero; you know what I am saying?" I said. "My son saved my life, and for me not to be able to save his life is just . . . it's hard.

"My kid went to the morgue, and this guy went home and went to sleep in his bed," I said. "There is no justice in that."

The reporter finished by telling the television audience, "Sanford police hope to finish up their case and get it to local prosecutors by this weekend. They are not releasing the half-dozen 911 calls until that investigation is complete. And, Charlie, we're told on one of those calls you can hear the sound of the gunshot."

The fuse was now burning faster. After the *CBS This Morning* taping we received calls from many more media outlets. At this point I had no idea what was ahead of me. I knew that it would take more than me to get the world to hear me out, or care about my son's story. I knew that Sybrina would have to gather herself and accompany me to tell our side of the story. And that would take some convincing.

The day after the *CBS This Morning* segment aired, we held a press conference, with attorneys Ben Crump and Natalie Jackson; my nephew Boobie, who held Trayvon's framed football jersey; Brandy Green; and me in front of Natalie Jackson's office in Orlando. I told the cluster of mostly local newspaper and television reporters about Trayvon, what had happened to him, and how it seemed that nothing was being done about it. My emotions were raw and my words passionate, and I hoped that the reporters could feel my love and grief for my fallen son.

"It's senseless," I said at the press conference. "We feel justice hasn't been served."

Crump called the killer "a loose cannon." And then he said, "Why?": Why did he follow Trayvon? Why did he confront him? Why was a neighborhood watch volunteer patrolling his neighborhood with a gun? And if Trayvon did fight back after being confronted, what was wrong with that? As the attorney Natalie Jackson said at the press conference: "Trayvon didn't know the neighborhood watch captain had a gun."

Shortly after our first press conference in Orlando, Crump called Reverend Al Sharpton. Crump and Sharpton knew each other from the case of Martin Lee Anderson, the fourteen-year-old black boy killed at the boot camp–style detention center in Panama City, Florida, but Reverend Sharpton had never been to Sanford before Crump called him asking for his help in our case. And he certainly had never heard of us or Trayvon.

But he recognized injustice when he heard it, and he listened as

Crump spoke his usual blue streak the first time they discussed the death of our son.

"I want you to talk with the father," Crump had told Reverend Sharpton, and I got on the phone and told the famous reverend what happened, and how there was no recourse with those in authority. I began crying on the phone, and Reverend Sharpton was moved to action. He booked us on his MSNBC television show *Politics Nation,* and Crump and I taped a segment from Sanford. "The family is calling for justice," I said on the show. "We don't want our son's death to be in vain. We're looking for answers. I don't have an understanding as to why my son is dead to this day."

Not long after that show, Reverend Sharpton told Sybrina and me he didn't believe in "drive-by activism." "If we're gonna be in it, we're gonna be in it until we win," he said. "And we're gonna win because we have no other choice. We cannot allow a legal precedent to be established in a city [meaning Sanford] that tells us it is legal for a man to kill us, tell any story he wants, and walk out with the murder weapon."

The reverend's words were true—and we didn't have to fight just against a legal precedent, but a cultural one, too. One thing this case revealed to us was that a kid could be killed in this country and people would step up and *defend the killer.* Not only some twisted members of the public, online bloggers and racists, but even some police officers. What is it about this country that allows that to happen? But we also discovered that we weren't alone in thinking this was crazy. So many people at this rally drove two hours, eight hours, to make a statement that, no, this won't stand. And people like Reverend Sharpton have stood behind us the whole way.

Soon, the Sanford Police Department would claim that the killer hadn't been arrested due to the Stand Your Ground law. I came to understand that the law meant that if you feel your life is being threatened, you can defend yourself by shooting your assailant.

The problem that I had with this was: If this was a Stand Your Ground case, if the killer was in true and immediate fear for his life, why did he follow my son? Why did he trail and confront the person who caused such fear?

"Outrageous," Sharpton said of the Stand Your Ground defense. "I can't for the life of me understand how they can justify not making an arrest! Arrest does not mean conviction, but there is probable cause here even with this [Stand Your Ground] law that we would question. This is a national outrage to many of us."

Then the show was over, and, once again, the silence began. No arrest. No justice. Nothing.

I did hear from some of my friends, who had seen me—and attorney Crump—on television. "Who is this dude?" one of them asked, mentioning Crump's accent and manner of speaking.

They didn't understand the brilliance of this man. The police, despite their initial assurances, had given up on the idea of arresting the killer, claiming that Florida law prevented it. The recommendation of the Sanford Police Department investigator Chris Serino had been to at least charge the killer with manslaughter—but even that recommendation was not addressed. When the lead investigator is essentially telling you, "I have enough information and evidence to at least arrest this individual for manslaughter," but then his superiors seemed to be saying to you, "No; we're not going to do anything," it left us with nothing in hand at all, least of all any trust in the judicial system to bring light to the crime committed against our child. We didn't have faith in that process at all.

We were being told, both in words and in actions: *It's already happened. There's nothing to do or see here. Go back home to Miami. Don't worry about this.*

But Crump said no, we're not going away. We're going to make the world pay attention. And it was working.

After the show with Reverend Sharpton, Crump told me that I did fine on television. Still, I was only half the story. The other half, Trayvon's mother, Sybrina, was still in her house in Miami, still unable to fully understand, much less speak publicly about, the terrible events that had left her son dead.

"We have to get Sybrina involved," Crump told me. "She's the mother, and people need to hear from her. They need to hear from both of you."

CHAPTER 5

Sybrina

⌒

February 27, 2012–March 8, 2012

Losing my child ripped my heart in half; it is indescribable pain. I could not get out of my bedroom.

My bedroom had always been my haven, filled with my favorite things, all in my favorite color: purple. Purple is my birthstone, the purple of amethyst, the ancient stone that, it's written, Moses said was filled with the spirit of God, bestowing power and strength. Almost everything in my room was purple: walls, carpets, sheets, pillows, flowers, accents, decorations, and more. After Trayvon's death, even the purple seemed dead, and the brightest color, the color that had always comforted me, lost its radiance. Everything was gray.

My mind spun around and around on this one thought: every child needs their mother, and when my son needed me most I was not there for him. I could not get this thought out of my mind. It took the life out of me and put me in a strange paralysis. I couldn't eat, couldn't sleep, couldn't do anything but lie in bed and cry. Within a few days I'd developed a new routine to cut off my exposure to the world: brush teeth, shower, change clothes, and fall back into bed, where I'd lie for hours and, then, days. People would come to visit, but I wouldn't come out of my room. I didn't want to see anybody, speak to anybody, or hear another word about the events that left my son dead.

One day, while I was in the shower, just letting the water run over me, lost in my grief, a song suddenly came to me.

My world was upside down, but the song, from some faraway corner of my memory, was like a life raft, something that I could grab on to in my endless gulf of grief. I couldn't sing the song, couldn't even speak it. Who could sing at a time like this? But the lyrics were stuck in my head, repeating themselves:

> *I'm living this moment because of You*
> *I want to thank You and praise You, too*

I knew the song from church. It was the gospel standard "Your Grace and Mercy" by the Mississippi Mass Choir from Jackson, Mississippi. It was a song about salvation, about overcoming seemingly impossible obstacles, about somehow continuing to live in the shadow of death and the depths of despair. The song gave me strength, or at least enough to get through the next minute, the next hour, and, soon, the next day. I would sing to my boys all the time and would ask them if I sounded like what they heard on the radio. They always said yes.

Still, I didn't want to see anyone or hear any news about the events in Sanford, Florida. Most of all, I *never* wanted to go to Sanford, and my feelings about the town were so strong that I made a vow, a promise to myself: *I'm never going to Sanford,* I told myself over and over again. *Never, never, never going to Sanford.*

Alone at home I prayed and cried, prayed and cried. I just wanted Trayvon's body to be returned home so we could give him a proper homegoing service and burial.

Tracy would call to update me on the latest problems and road-blocks. He couldn't identify the body, couldn't visit the body, couldn't get the body released in order to bring the body home. And, of course, there had been no arrest of the man who had killed our son, the neighborhood watch captain whose identity, at that point, I didn't know and didn't want to know.

"They're not giving me any information," Tracy kept telling me, except that the police had told him they were probably never going to arrest this neighborhood watch captain, even though he'd admitted shooting Trayvon and they had the gun he'd used to shoot him.

I would listen to what Tracy had to tell me. But he seemed worlds away.

"Anyway, I'm never going to Sanford," I would reply. "You need to straighten everything out, and find out what happened. Because I'm never going there, *never* going to Sanford."

I managed to pull myself out of bed and out of my room for my son's funeral.

The sun was shining, but it was a dark day. For me, the darkest. The day was just a blur. I don't remember most of it, except for one image, which kept returning to me again and again over the days that followed: my son lying dead in his casket, in his white suit with his light blue tie, almost with a smirk on his face, as if to tell me, "I'm gone from Earth, Mom, but I'm okay." As if he were trying to comfort me like he always did. As if he were saying, "I've got it, Cupcake."

After the funeral, I managed to get out of the house to visit my pastor, Arthur Jackson III at Antioch Missionary Baptist Church. Pastor Jackson knew Trayvon. Trayvon was a member of the church and the youth ministry, and he was learning to run the video cameras that record the Sunday services that we would attend. Trayvon got involved and started attending more because of the youth minister, Reverend Dwayne Fudge, Sr. So now I found myself going there for strength and comfort. My faith and trust in God were unbreakable. They were the only things unbroken in me. But I believed I was in a spiritual crisis.

I was ushered into his office, and he immediately hugged me in greeting. I'm sure I looked like a nervous wreck. Later, Pastor Jackson would tell me that he'd been expecting someone weeping out of control, mad, shouting profanity or expletives, but I wasn't there to blame God—I never blame God—I was just desperately seeking help, somehow to make sense of this.

For some reason, I had started visualizing my own mind like a puzzle that had been put together and once formed a clear picture, not perfect, but one that made sense. Now that puzzle was broken and in disarray, and I could not find a way to put the pieces together.

"I know the pieces are there, but I can't see the image," I told Pastor Jackson as I sat across from him at his desk. Now I started crying and trembling, and my hands were shaking and my voice cracking, and I could barely speak.

"I have one son about to graduate from college," I said, referring to Jahvaris. "And another son who was about to graduate from high school," I said, referring to Trayvon.

I was having trouble keeping the thread. "I just feel like I'm just not myself, like I'm not me," I continued. "It just doesn't feel like this should be happening . . ." I tried to say more but kept having to stop when I would break down crying. "I don't want to lose my mind.

"I keep thinking about my oldest son, Jahvaris," I told my pastor. "I don't want him to someday say, 'I lost my brother to gun violence and then my mother lost her mind.'"

He put his hand on my forearm.

"These trials and tribulations that you're going through won't make you who you are; it will reveal who you are," he told me. "It's not going to make you strong; it's going to reveal the strength you have. It's not going to make your character; it's going to reveal it. The strength you have is already inside of you, and this tragic event is going to reveal it."

He came around from behind his desk and sat beside me, and we talked some more. I found myself feeling calm, even feeling some flicker of strength returning to me, just from the conversation. I come from a long line of strong women, I remembered, and I knew I was strong, had been strong all of my life. Even when I didn't feel strong,

I told myself, *I am strong*. And so I became strong. But you never know how strong you are until you are tested. And now I faced the ultimate test for any mother.

When I was done he prayed for me. Then we embraced each other and I just cried on his shoulder.

I walked out feeling better, still broken, but better, still far from whole, but stronger. I left knowing that I was going to someday get up out of my purple bedroom. Just not yet. I still didn't know how to get back to the person that I was. I knew that my life would forever change because of what happened to Trayvon. I just didn't know how to get back into life and find whatever my new "normal" life might be. I felt I would never know anything even close to happiness again.

Finally my sister, my cousin, and one of my nephews got me out of the house with a trick: they told me they just wanted to take me for a drive. So I pulled myself together, came out of my room, and climbed into my sister's Camry, expecting a quick loop through the streets around our house and then back to bed. Before I knew it, we passed one of my favorite restaurants: Red Lobster.

"I'm hungry; let's stop here," my sister said.

Before I could object, we were pulling into the parking lot and, soon, sitting at a table. Just when the waitress brought the menus, my cellphone rang.

It was Tracy and the attorney Benjamin Crump.

"You need to come to Sanford," Tracy began.

"Never, never, never," I replied, just as I'd already told him a million times: *I am never going to Sanford, Florida, where my son was shot and killed.*

"If we're going to get the nation to listen to us, if we're going to try to open people's eyes to Trayvon's death, then both of us have to do it," said Tracy. "Both of us have to speak to the media. Both of us have to do television and newspaper interviews together."

"I'm *never* going to Sanford!" I repeated.

He passed the phone to Crump, and he started saying something about the 911 tapes from the night Trayvon was killed. Tracy heard the tapes, Crump said, and they had "evidence unlocking what happened that night in Sanford," a blow-by-blow of the shooting. However, the police wouldn't release the tapes, even though Crump and his associates had filed official papers demanding the 911 tapes be released.

I got up from the table with my cellphone and went outside into the Red Lobster parking lot.

Tracy got back on the phone, repeating that it was important that I come to Sanford, to speak to the media with him, to demand the release of the 911 tapes and shine a light on what happened to our son. I didn't understand why he needed me to speak to the media. That was not me. It was my sister, not me, who sang in the church choir; my sister who'd come up to testify before the congregation. Not me. Not Sybrina. Sybrina was a mother and not someone who had anything to say into a microphone. And, anyway, I had been pretty clear, *I'm never going to Sanford*.

"You handle it," I said.

Then he said something that immediately lifted me out of Stage 1 of the grieving process—Denial and Isolation—and immediately propelled me into Stage 2:

Anger.

"They're not going to arrest him," Tracy said, meaning the police weren't going to arrest the man who shot our son. "And we have to get the word out to the media about that—"

I cut him off. "What do you mean they're not going to arrest him?!" I asked. "They have the person who killed Trayvon. They have the weapon. Why aren't they going to arrest him?"

"They have this Stand Your Ground law," Tracy said, explaining the law. I didn't understand it then, but surely do now. *How could that law apply to this case?* I thought. *With a seventeen-year-old armed with only a bag of candy and a can of iced tea?*

I felt my strength returning, felt the old Sybrina rising up within me.

"Okay," I said. "I'm coming."

I hung up the phone and marched back into the restaurant and told everyone what happened. And we left. Immediately. Drove home. Packed some clothes. And just like that we were all on the road—my sister, my cousin, my mother, and me—within a couple of hours after the call.

I was leaving Denial and Isolation behind. I was going to stand up for my son. I was going to fight to get answers as to why he was killed. I was going to do whatever was necessary to make sure that his death would not be in vain.

I was angry.

And I was going to Sanford.

CHAPTER 6

Tracy

⤙∽⤚

February 29, 2012–March 9, 2012

"You ever hear of Murphy's Law?" Sanford Police Department detective Chris Serino asked the killer during a police interview on Wednesday, February 29, 2012.

I didn't hear it till much later, but when I did, it gave me chills. Not because the killer was monstrous and violent, but because he was so composed, casual. So sure of his own victimhood, so indifferent to the life he'd taken.

"You ever hear of Murphy's Law?"

"Yes sir," the killer replied.

"Okay, that's what happened. This person was not doing anything bad. . . . You know the name of the person that night?"

"Tayvon."

"Trayvon," Detective Serino corrected him.

"Trayvon? Martin?" the killer asked.

"Trayvon Benjamin Martin. He was born in 1995, February the fifth. He was seventeen years old. An athlete probably. Somebody who was going to be in aeronautics. A kid with a future. A kid with folks that care. In his possession we found a can of iced tea and a bag of Skittles. And [twenty-two] dollars in cash. Not the goon."

"Goons" were what they called the gang members based in and around Sanford and Orlando, Florida. The detective continued his questioning.

"Um, you have any prior training in law enforcement at all?"

"Just the legal side of it," he said.

"Constitution of law," said Serino. "Okay, but as far as identifying people and stuff like that, as far as what to look for . . ."

The killer told him that there had been a PowerPoint presentation at a neighborhood watch event.

"Okay, I wasn't privy to that," said Serino. "But if you guys continue neighborhood watch, typically speaking at nighttime the [criminal] garb is black on black on black with a black hoodie. Now, this guy had a dark gray hoodie. It was dark but his pants were beige. Not quite your, you know, prime suspect type." After a discussion of previous burglary in the community, and what the shooter said Trayvon was doing on the night he was killed, Serino said, "You know you are going to come under a lot of scrutiny over this, correct? Okay, the profiling aspect of the whole thing. Had this person been white, would you have felt the same way?"

"Yes," he said.

~✴~

I was waiting for Sybrina in Sanford, Florida, but it wasn't the Sanford I knew before Trayvon's death, the Sanford of weekend visits with my girlfriend, Brandy, and her young son, Chad. That Sanford was gone for me, forever. Now Sanford was a battleground.

We never wanted Trayvon's death to become a racial issue. Soon, people of all different races would come to support us. And people of all races would be against us. That's just the nature of life. Not everybody's going to agree with you, and not everybody's going to disagree with you. Benjamin Crump did his job in making the case in the media that there might be racism behind the shooting and the lack of an arrest. But for us, from day one we wanted our message to be: It's not about race. It's about the senseless killing of an unarmed kid and the injustice of the Sanford Police Department, as I would later say in a hearing, which we felt was trying to sweep it under the rug.

I knew, as Crump himself said, race was the elephant in the room: a white man—or at least a white-identified man—killed a black kid. So it wasn't surprising to me that so much of the coverage approached it from that angle. It worried me, though. Because we knew that once it became a racial issue, once it was more than the plain and simple act of a kid walking home shot dead—people were going to be divided. Once you throw race into the equation, mothers in the white community that could identify with Sybrina's pain of losing a child are left to choose: am I loyal to my motherhood or am I loyal to my race? They would likely never put it in those terms themselves, but I'd lived through enough events where at some point people stop caring about the truth or the complications; all they care about is whether you're on team Black or team White.

That's why we didn't want Trayvon's death to have racial implications. We were after justice and wanted to build a groundswell of support, not have Trayvon's death become another point of division. Aside from losing racist supporters, who we probably wouldn't get or want anyway, we were worried about people of goodwill getting turned off because they were tired of the endless battles around race, just at the moment when we wanted them to get engaged. But we may have been naïve to think that it was ever under our control.

And personally, I *knew* racism was part of the story from the day I heard what happened to my son and how lax the police and prosecutors were about the killing. We would soon discover that the killer had called the police forty-six times since 2004.

The truth is, we were battling a system that allowed young African American boys to be killed without any consequences. So race *would* become an issue. Another reason race became an issue was because of where the shooting happened: Sanford, Florida.

Natalie Jackson, the Orlando-based attorney, was a gift. She not only knew Sanford; she was born and raised there and had all of the local knowledge of the town. What Natalie Jackson didn't know about Sanford, her mother did, because she is the town's unofficial historian, especially when it comes to its African American history.

Her name is Francis Oliver. Now seventy-three, Ms. Oliver is a longtime Sanford resident, teacher, activist, and historian who has lived in the city since she was four. One night, I joined our team of attorneys at Ms. Oliver's house for the first of many dinners. She lived in a beautiful, large family home in the Goldsboro community of Sanford, and that night Ms. Oliver, in her long, white dreadlocks and the Christmas apron she wears year-round, cooked us all some soul food: fried chicken, collard greens, and homemade pound cake for dessert. When we sat down, she told me, as she would later tell Sybrina, all about Sanford and its history.

I already knew about Jackie Robinson, the black baseball great who was refused a hotel room in Sanford in 1946, and escorted out of the dugout before his game started after he came to the city for spring training.

"A whole lot of stuff had happened before that," said Ms. Oliver, before launching into the story of Sanford. Originally Sanford was divided into three towns, Sanford, Sanford Heights, and an all-black township called Goldsboro, which in 1891 became the second incorporated African American town in the state of Florida. "Goldsboro had its own identity," said Ms. Oliver. "Its own post office, its own jail, and its own city council. But the city of Sanford, which was mostly white, felt like it was boxed in. It couldn't grow north because of Lake Monroe, and it couldn't grow south because of another town called Sanford Heights, and it couldn't go east because east was nothing but marshland. And it couldn't go west because that's where Goldsboro was, sitting high and dry."

She showed us a clipping from the *Orlando Sentinel* dated September 1, 1991—"Political Sham—The Rise and Fall of Goldsboro." The newspaper article talked about a man named Forrest Lake, Seminole County's "sharpest politician of the early 1900s. . . . But Forrest Lake might also have been one of the worst characters in the shadowy, back-room politics of his day," the Opinion page article read.

"Forrest Lake went to the state capitol in Tallahassee and got the legislature to dismantle the Goldsboro charter and the Sanford charter and the Sanford Heights charters," said Ms. Oliver. "And then three days later he came back with one charter called Sanford."

On April 26, 1911, the legislature passed a bill essentially allowing Sanford to annex Goldsboro and Sanford Heights, and black Goldsboro disappeared. At least as a city unto itself. The black citizens remained, only now they had no town of their own. Their businesses, their city jobs, their post office, their school, their jail, even their streets, or at least their street names, which were changed from honoring Goldsboro's African American founders to numbers, would all eventually disappear. Now the citizens of Goldsboro were on the wrong side of the railroad tracks, which divided the white side of Sanford from the black side. "That's where the hundred-year feud started," said Ms. Oliver. "From that point on there was a wall between the black community of Sanford and the white community. The black citizens of Goldsboro refused to be part of Sanford, and for more than forty years, from 1911 to 1953, Goldsboro and Sanford were in litigation over the money that Sanford owed Goldsboro at the demise of Goldsboro."

A lawsuit was filed by the leaders of the now-defunct Goldsboro in the Florida Supreme Court. "And for forty years they battled Sanford and they never got restitution for what Sanford owed Goldsboro and its citizens," said Ms. Oliver. "They lost the lawsuit and it can never be reopened.

"Goldsboro had room to expand land-wise, but the city of Sanford couldn't expand because of geographical boundaries. There was just no room to grow. In the 1950s Sanford gerrymandered Goldsboro, redrew the boundaries," she said, explaining how most of the black citizens were even now unable to vote on local matters because, through redistricting, they were living in Seminole County and not the city of Sanford. "So white people controlled Sanford, even though they weren't the majority," Ms. Oliver said. "To this day, I can't vote in the city of Sanford because I live in Goldsboro. But the people who live on the next street, just one street away from mine, can vote in the city of Sanford.

"I came to Sanford in 1946, when I was four years old," she said. "We came on the overground railroad, the name for the segregated railroad cars the blacks took to flee Alabama and Mississippi Jim Crow, government-sanctioned racial segregation. My daddy came in search of an all-black city, and landed in Goldsboro, which was still all black, but it wasn't its own city anymore.

"Well, everything was going fine in the 1950s," she continued. Fine at least for segregated Sanford, she said, where blacks and whites stayed separate: in their neighborhoods, businesses, churches, and schools. "Everything was separate. We were divided by a railroad track, and what happened on one side of the railroad track didn't have anything to do with the other side of the railroad track.

"But then, in the early sixties, came the Civic Center," she continued. "The city built this big, beautiful Civic Center and everyone was looking forward to it—until the city manager said that blacks would never be able to use the Civic Center.

"Well, that totally divided Sanford," she said. "After it was built, the white kids were having dances there and things like that. And the black kids decided one night that they were going to integrate the Civic Center.

"I was with that group that night," she said. "I was about seventeen years old in the eleventh grade. It was February 14, Valentine's Day night, 1960, and since it was February, it was cold, at least cold for Florida. There were about five carloads of us. We parked on the side where the river is, and we were walking across the street to the Civic Center. Through the Civic Center's windows, we could see the white kids dancing and having a great time. And we heard a man say, 'Here they come,' and then they turned the fire hydrant hoses on us. As soon as we saw the water hoses we ran back to our cars. I don't know if they were firemen or not. We outran the water. It was too cold to get wet that night. But some of the kids that went there that night were arrested the next day. I've got that article, too, to prove what I'm saying."

Sure enough, she did. "City Won't Tolerate Violence, Demonstrating, Negroes Told," read *The Sanford Herald* headline of March 8, 1960. The story detailed the arrests of six students, who "massed downtown and demanded use of the Civic Center or improved facilities of their own."

"They arrested the boys who they thought had created the idea of integrating the Civic Center," she said.

Despite the US Supreme Court's 1954 *Brown v. Board of Education* decision, Florida didn't integrate its schools until 1971, when the Court upheld the use of busing to achieve integration. "The decree came down from the state of Florida that all schools had to be integrated that year," said Ms. Oliver. Her daughter, attorney Natalie Jackson, was bused twenty miles to a newly built white high school in Lake Mary, even though the school she had been attending was walking distance from her house. "Sanford's only black high school was Crooms Academy high school on Goldsboro Avenue. A lot of the whites didn't want their children to go to that school. So they did all they could to close the school down, including burning the school, setting it on fire."

She showed us a front-page *Sanford Herald* newspaper article from 1970: "Crooms High Is Partially Burned" read the headline.

"They burned down the main building," Ms. Oliver said, "which had all of the school records, but they were able to save the side classrooms. But after they couldn't burn it down, two or three years later the school board shut it down," which sparked a lawsuit, which kept the school open. "Crooms Academy is open to this day. It's a magnet school of technology, and rated number one in the state of Florida."

She took a breath because she was now ready to discuss the present-day Sanford, which, she said, was like any other Florida city, or many Southern cities, in the 2000s when it came to race relations—

at least before February 26, 2012. It was a place that seemed to live up to its slogan, "The Friendly City," and would soon even have its first African American city manager, Norton Bonaparte, Jr., and an African American city commissioner, Dr. Velma Williams.

"Now, after about fifty years, I would say in about 2000, three consecutive new mayors reached out to the black community," said Ms. Oliver. Especially, she added, Sanford's current mayor, Jeff Triplett, a good man who, with the shooting of my son, would become caught in an extremely volatile situation. "Like a character out of a John Grisham novel" is how our attorney Natalie Jackson described him. Triplett is a full-time banker and a part-time mayor. His wife went to the historically black Florida A&M University law school in Orlando. Ms. Oliver is a close friend of Jeff Triplett's mother, and Jeff is known around town as "a nice guy," said Jackson. He became mayor to do his part for his city, only to become caught up in a crisis the likes of which Sanford had never seen.

"Once they started reaching out to the black community, there was the response that, you know, we might get together, we might finally sit down to the table and talk," Ms. Oliver told us. She paused. "And then your son was killed.

"So when Trayvon happened and the neighborhood watch volunteer admitted that he shot him and he went in the front door of the police station and out the back door, well, the black citizens of Sanford and Goldsboro and Seminole County said, 'Enough is enough.' That was the straw that broke the camel's back. But a majority of the white citizens of Sanford didn't come with us. They believed George Zimmerman killed Trayvon in self-defense. So we're separated again."

For me, in the two years I visited before Trayvon's death, the Retreat at Twin Lakes was a sunny place, a gated community like thousands of others across America, where residents spend their hard-earned money for a home that feels safe, protected. Kids played in the streets. Neighbors waved hello. Cars drove down sunny streets with names like Twin Trees Lane and Retreat View Circle.

But the Retreat had a seamy underside that was mostly invisible to me. The media would report that townhouses that once sold for $250,000 were selling for $100,000 or less, if at all. Some people bought at the height of the market and when the bubble burst went into foreclosure. Investors took over, buying and renting out the townhouses to newcomers. Some of the original residents who stuck it out believed that the newcomers, the ones who came after the bust, didn't come alone—they brought something with them: crime.

I never once in my two years of visits saw one thing that alarmed me there, even though burglaries and break-ins were by then a reality of life for some residents.

There was something else I never saw and most residents didn't know about: on the streets and in the shadows, there was a man with a gun.

He carried a Kel-Tec PF-9 9mm pistol in a hidden holster behind his back in the waistband of his pants. And while the homeowners' association at the Retreat had appointed this man the head of the community's neighborhood watch, responsible for alerting police to suspicious activity but prohibited from confronting suspects himself, nobody seemed to know about his gun.

The media would call him a vigilante, but for Sybrina, our family, our attorneys, and me, the killer's gun told us everything we needed to know about him. Because no matter what else is said about this case, one thing is certain: if he hadn't been carrying a gun on the night of February 26, 2012, our son would still be alive.

Just like Ms. Oliver told us, the black community of Sanford had our back, but things started slowly.

At nine A.M. on Saturday, March 3, six days after the killing of my son, two dozen African American residents from Goldsboro, the African American community of Sanford, crossed the railroad tracks and gathered in front of the Sanford police station. Francis Oliver herself was in Alabama, participating in the memorial Martin Luther King, Jr., civil rights march from Selma to Montgomery, and she didn't know about the first rally protesting the shooting of a seventeen-year-old young man at the Retreat at Twin Lakes. Even we didn't know about the protest, and only heard about it later.

No media was present to record the event, just a small group of protesters with a few homemade signs to show their outrage over the shooting of a seventeen-year-old kid in their city, and the lack of an arrest of the man who shot him dead.

"Where is everybody?" Francis Oliver's sister, Debra Detraville, asked her by phone.

"What do you mean?" Ms. Oliver asked.

"We're at the police station," said Debra Detraville.

"For what?" asked Ms. Oliver.

"We came up here because of that boy who got killed with the Skittles," she was told.

Ms. Oliver sprang into action, as she knew someone had to lead the protest in case the police came outside the station. Eventually, she was told that Oscar Redden, founder and vice president of Brothers Keepers, which helps people recover from addictions, was present, sitting in his truck.

"I said, 'Take Oscar the phone and let me talk to him,' and I said, 'Oscar, will you take charge and serve as the spokesperson in case the police come out and try and arrest somebody?'" Ms. Oliver told us she said that day.

Oscar Redden said he would serve as spokesperson. But no police arrived, no attention was given. The protest, witnessed by only the protesters, broke up after not too long, but the protesters would be back in even greater numbers, and this time they wouldn't be turned away: not by the Sanford police, not by the legislature, a water hose, gerrymandering, or fire. This time, the black citizens of Goldsboro, Sanford, America, and the world would stand up, and this time they couldn't be stopped.

And not only would Sybrina and I be with them, but, almost unbelievably, we would be leading them.

But in the beginning, though, I was just like that first little group of protesters: upset, angry, and not getting any answers. For many days I remained in Sanford, still reminded day in and day out of the crime scene right outside the windows. I would often walk out the back door and into the communal backyard to stand at the spot on the grass next to the sidewalk where my son fell dead, trying to visualize what actually happened to him out there. Back and forth I would walk, trying to trace Trayvon's steps, until I finally gave up. The trail had gone cold.

Sybrina came to Sanford for the first time late at night on Thursday, March 8, driving in with her family.

I could see the pain in her face, but I could also see the strength. And when I told her, "We have to try to figure out how to get justice for Trayvon, and get an arrest of the guy who killed him," I could also see determination to do exactly that.

We were both very nervous. But we told each other, "Let's tell the truth. Let's tell what we know. Let's tell who Trayvon was. Let's let America know who Trayvon was." We were both still torn up, leveled, on the brink of a breakdown, and every interview Sybrina would do—at least in the beginning—she would do with a box of tissues.

But we also knew that we had to hold it together, and be strong, for Trayvon.

The next morning, we met the media in our hotel, then went to the Seminole County Clerk of Courts, where Ben Crump filed a public-records lawsuit on our behalf against the Sanford Police Department, demanding the release of the 911 tapes.

At the courthouse, a reporter showed us a photo of a dark-haired man at the Orange County jail.

"This is his mugshot," the reporter told us. "He's been arrested before."

What? I had been told by the Sanford police that the killer not only had no arrest record but was "squeaky-clean." The picture the reporter was showing us, along with the arrest record that she had unearthed, showed that the killer had been detained by police in

2005 for battery of a law enforcement officer and resisting arrest with violence. It was the first time we had seen a picture of the man who had shot Trayvon, and now not only did we have his picture—and a mugshot, no less—we would also soon have his police record, which Crump easily obtained through the county clerk's office, all of which showed that he was not "squeaky-clean."

Later that same day, we met the media outside the Sanford Police Department: me, our attorneys Ben Crump and Natalie Jackson, and, for the first time in public, Sybrina and our son Jahvaris.

Crump spoke first, angrily demanding the 911 tapes. He held up a copy of the killer's arrest record. "We confirmed that George Michael Zimmerman had a police record and the police lied to this family," Crump continued. "They lied to them when they said George Michael Zimmerman was squeaky-clean. . . . And Mr. [Tracy] Martin will tell you in just a second they said that was one of the reasons why they weren't arresting him. . . . He was arrested in 2005 for resisting arrest with violence and battery on a law enforcement officer. These are violent crimes. He had a propensity to be violent.

"Trayvon Martin *was* squeaky-clean. He had *never* been arrested. He was a kid with a baby face who everybody said always was smiling and was always a happy-go-lucky kid. But yet they are trying to cover up for this adult and sweep this under the rug. So this family just can't understand why the police is lying to protect this home-owners' association loose cannon, why they're trying to cover this up, why they are trying to protect him and not to get to the truth of the matter as to why their son was [shot and killed] while he was coming home with a bag of Skittles and George Michael Zimmerman had a gun.

"The 911 tape will show," Crump said at last. "It's gonna be riveting."

One of the reporters asked Crump why we just didn't wait for the process to unfold, since the police were saying that their investigation was ongoing and information would be forthcoming.

"If your child had been shot down, and all you wanted was answers, how long do you wait?" Crump shot back. "How long do you wait when there's this mound of evidence, saying this guy just killed your child, and all your child had was a bag of Skittles? He had a gun. He had a history of violence. . . . This was their child. This is their hope for the future. And he's gone!"

Crump was right about the media, and he and our media relations expert Ryan Julison's strategy of keeping our case alive by taking it to the media would pay off in ways that we couldn't imagine. The announcement of the killer's arrest record became news around the world. We started paying attention to certain journalists who picked up on the story with particular care and ferocity. One of them was Jonathan Capehart at the *Washington Post*. We hadn't met him at this point, but we felt like we knew him. He said things with a directness and eloquence that we didn't have, but that echoed in me and expressed the still-unsorted feelings in my own soul. "As an African American, this case was personal," Jonathan Capehart wrote in one column. "The killer of an unarmed black teenager doing nothing more than returning to where he was staying on a rainy evening had to be held accountable in some way. Any life should not be taken so easily or cheaply. I wrote more than 60 pieces seeking justice for Trayvon as if my life depended on it—because one day it might." Another African American journalist, the *New York Times*'s Charles M. Blow, who had two sons just like Sybrina and I had before Trayvon's death, wrote: "This is the fear that seizes me whenever my boys are out in the world: that a man with a gun and an itchy finger will find them 'suspicious.' That passions may run hot and blood run cold. That it might all end with a hole in their chest and hole in my heart. That the law might prove insufficient to salve my loss.

"That is the burden of black boys in America and the people that love them: running the risk of being descended upon in the dark and caught in the crosshairs of someone who crosses the line."

At our March 9 press conference, Natalie Jackson said, "What's so important about us finding out the criminal history of George Michael Zimmerman? It is important because it gives you the indication of, one, you have a person with a propensity toward violence. Or at least the appearance of a propensity toward violence." She said that the police had investigated Trayvon within twenty-four hours of his being shot. But even though the Sanford police had sophisticated computers and databases "linked to the FBI record searches," they didn't seem to have investigated the man who killed our son. "In this case, one of two things happened," she said. "Either an investigation of [the shooter] was never done, or, two, an investigation was done and there was a decision made to withhold this information from the family and the public. Now, why? That's the question. That's the big elephant in the room."

Crump once again showed the media the killer's arrest record and said, "We just simply went to the Orange County clerk of court public records." He stated the killer's name and birthday and said, "Charged with a third-degree felony in 2005. Resisting officer with violence. Charged with battery on a law enforcement officer. Third-degree felony. . . . *And, so the police had this!* So they knew about his propensity of violence. But yet just chose to not even consider that when they lied to this family saying he was squeaky-clean."

Later, at a press conference, Sanford police chief Bill Lee responded. According to a local television news report, "Lee admitted on Monday that his investigators took Zimmerman's word that he had a clean record and didn't find out about the arrest until days after the shooting." Lee had insisted that they were doing a thorough investigation, but we wondered why it had taken so long for them to mention this huge piece of information.

Although the charges against the killer were eventually dropped, Crump told the media his propensity toward violence remained.

"They should have arrested George Zimmerman," he said.

A reporter interrupted. "Miss Sybrina," she said. "We haven't heard much from you. This is your son. What is your reaction to the fact that your son is no longer here and was shot and killed by a man with at least a history of violence?"

And with that, Sybrina Fulton, standing beside me in her dark business suit and purple blouse—always purple, for strength and positive energy—began to shake, began to cry, and, finally, for the first time in public in this case, began to speak.

When I pressed the police, begging to know why they hadn't made an arrest, they claimed that the person they brought in that night was clean—"squeaky-clean," as they had called him—and that he had taken criminal justice classes, which seemed to give him some kind of credibility.

But the streets were offering different information. The news reports were multiplying—and intensifying. Reuters reported, "A rumor that superiors had quashed an investigator's intent to charge Zimmerman had already made the rounds in the black community, said Velma Williams, the only black member of the five-person Sanford City Commission. 'People were getting suspicious, saying we knew that was going to happen based on history,' Williams said in an interview."

After our first press conference with Sybrina on March 9, Ms. Williams went to the police chief's office with a community activist. "We said, 'Look, chief. Last time I was here I told you a train was coming down the tracks and it was going 50 miles an hour,'" she told Reuters. "I said, 'It's going 150 miles an hour now. And it doesn't have any brakes.'"

It was a train, all right, a very fast train, gathering steam, and we were on the back of it, and we would soon be stoking the engine with our media appearances. One show after another. Until you could feel the momentum gathering beneath our feet as we moved forward with our attorneys, our media expert, and the growing number of people who came to our side in support—particularly when it came to the 911 tapes from the night Trayvon was shot.

We knew there were 911 tapes. I had already heard parts of them at the police station the day after my son was shot. But rumors were now going around Sanford about the parts of the tapes that I hadn't heard. Sanford is a small city and everyone knows one another. Some of the rumors traced back to people who supposedly worked at the 911 call center—or so the attorney Natalie Jackson and her mother, Ms. Oliver, had heard. There were also tapes of nonemergency calls that had been made that night, which included calls between the killer and the police, which some people in Sanford were now talking about. Those tapes apparently revealed that the neighborhood watch volunteer was told not to follow Trayvon and to wait for the police to arrive before doing anything—while the neighborhood watch captain told the police that he was following the suspect. He supposedly emphasized two facts: the suspect seemed suspicious and he looked like he was black.

These rumors seemed to be turning the story of our son's shooting from a mystery into a conspiracy. People were saying that the tapes might show that the killer racially profiled our son, that our son was followed and shot because he was black. This is what the attorney Natalie Jackson told Ben Crump and what Crump told me.

Now more than ever we realized we needed to hear those 911 tapes in full, for ourselves. We had to take our fight for the tapes to the next level.

We continued our strategy of using the media to bring as much light and heat to the case as we could. In and out of airplanes and cars. One television studio after another. The strategy was starting to pay off. As the news spread about Trayvon's shooting, more people began to come to our aide. These were people we didn't know, and some of whom we would never know. But they kept offering support.

Among the first was a law student named Kevin Cunningham. He was a thirty-one-year-old redheaded Irish American studying law at historically black Howard University. "The only race I believe in is the human race," Kevin Cunningham would say when people expressed surprise that a white man played such a key role in the case. He didn't know Trayvon and he didn't know us personally, but he had been drawn to the story through media accounts. Cunningham first heard about our case on a Howard University fraternity website that ran a short piece that began, "A young black kid with a bag of Skittles was gunned down by a neighborhood watch volunteer on a wet Central Florida night." He read the piece and felt himself becoming increasingly outraged by the details. He left the Howard site and logged on to Change.org, a website where people can start petitions for whatever causes they choose.

Cunningham started a Change.org petition: PROSECUTE THE KILLER OF 17-YEAR-OLD TRAYVON MARTIN.

Florida Attorney General Pam Bondi
Sanford Police Chief Bill Lee
US Attorney General Eric Holder
Florida's 4th District State's Attorney Angela Corey

I'm writing you today to call for justice for Trayvon Martin and his family.

Trayvon Martin was only 17 years old when he was gunned down by the Neighborhood Watch captain George Zimmerman. All Trayvon did was go to the store to get his brother some Skittles.

According to police, George Zimmerman admitted to the shooting and killing of Trayvon Martin. Why has he not been charged and his case been handed over to prosecutors?

Trayvon Martin was unarmed when he was shot by Zimmerman. All he had in his hands was some candy when he was followed and approached by Zimmerman—who ignored instructions from police not to confront the young man.

Please uphold justice.

Sincerely,

It was a long shot that an online petition would actually move the case forward, but it sparked a huge buzz online, and the signatures started adding up. On the first day, a hundred people signed the petition, but the numbers kept climbing: two hundred, then three hundred, then a thousand, then two thousand and more. Some of the signatures were friends of Trayvon's and others were friends of ours. But most, like Kevin Cunningham, didn't know us, only knew the story. Within a few days, the number of people who had signed Kevin Cunningham's petition demanding justice and an arrest had grown to ten thousand, and Change.org and Kevin Cunningham transferred the petition to my name and Sybrina's so that we could take the lead on the campaign.

Within two weeks, a thousand signatures would be added to the petition every few minutes, making it the most successful petition in Change.org history at that time. It would soon have two million signatures. It didn't suddenly lead to an arrest, but it kept growing the sense of outrage over the lack of one. The train that Velma Williams had said was going 150 miles an hour was now speeding even faster.

Anger was also building. Every day more and more. A rally in Sanford's Fort Mellon Park was planned for March 22. People from Sanford and around the country were calling the mayor's office, insisting on an immediate arrest. The NAACP was demanding that Sanford Police Department chief Bill Lee, who said that there was not sufficient probable cause to make an arrest, be immediately fired. And US representative Corrine Brown, an African American woman whose district included the city of Sanford, was telling the media, "We want him arrested as we speak *now!*"

CHAPTER 7

Sybrina

∽

March 9, 2012–March 16, 2012

We left Miami for Sanford at around eight P.M., riding in a Toyota Camry belonging to my cousin Penny, whom I call "Sugg" because she's so sweet. I sat in the backseat with my mother and my sister while Jahvaris sat in front, listening to music through his headphones.

Along the way, my cellphone exploded: call after call—friends, family, and media.

"We're on our way," I would tell the friends and family. "I'm okay. Just pray for us."

After driving four hours from Miami, we pulled up to our hotel in Lake Mary, a small Orlando suburb ten minutes from Sanford. The feelings I'd held off during the car trip returned now that we were so close to Sanford, and I was dropped again into a deep gloom. Tracy came to meet me in the lobby of the hotel. I was quiet; he was pushing me to join him in action, which meant taking our tragedy—and our grief—to the media.

"C'mon, we gotta do this," Tracy kept telling me.

And I kept saying, "I'm going home. I can't do this."

But I stayed, and soon we were a team for Trayvon. People thought we were still together as a couple because they never saw the disconnect that most divorced couples have. We were now drawn together in our love for our sons and our fight for justice for the one who had died. Just as we had always done, we had to put everything that separated us as a married couple aside, to do the best we could for our kids.

There was one more thing I had to put aside: blame. I could have blamed Tracy for even taking him to Sanford, where he was shot and killed. I could have been angry at him for what happened, just as I was the time when Jahvaris came home with a broken toe after a few weeks with Tracy one summer. I yelled at Tracy then, "I can't believe this! I send him off with you and now his toe is hanging off to the side!"

But I knew how much he loved his sons, knew how he loves all children, how he acted around them, so I never felt that Tracy didn't do his best—or that he didn't care. I let thoughts of blame go.

It was after midnight by the time we finished talking, and I went up to my room. I said my prayers—*I plead the blood of Jesus to cover me and my family*. The alarm rang just after dawn the next morning, and we were up and driving, following Tracy's directions to the Retreat at Twin Lakes, to Brandy's townhouse, to the place I'd imagined a thousand times in my mind since that first phone call from Tracy two weeks ago. Tracy and the attorneys Benjamin Crump and Natalie Jackson were waiting for us there.

We turned a corner, and, for the first time, I could see the community where my son was killed. The Retreat was a nice, clean development, but beside the big black entrance gate I saw something that shook me: a memorial. I had to look twice to see that it was a memorial for my son. There were footballs, teddy bears, signs, cards, and letters with the name "Trayvon" on them. Everything in tribute to my angel. That memorial—that outpouring from strangers—touched me deeply in a way the place did not. The Retreat was the crime scene, but the memorial was a gift. Strangers telling us through these cards and small tokens of childhood that they knew that the body on the ground was a boy, a human, a life. And that his killing wouldn't be forgotten.

Soon, the memorial would be gone. The city of Sanford, or the people who ran the Retreat, didn't want it at the gate as a reminder of what happened.

Once we were inside the townhouse, I didn't look outside—and I wasn't about to go into that backyard to see where Trayvon was shot and killed. I was doing my best to keep my focus, and my composure.

In the living room, I met Ben Crump and Natalie Jackson. Crump—which is what we called him from the day we met him— was compassionate, professional, and always dressed in a suit and tie. But I could tell he was country. Not country in a bad way. More like Southern-gentleman country. He and Natalie were down-to-earth people who made us feel comfortable, and I immediately had confidence in them. That night, and every day I saw him, he kept saying over and over again that we needed to do media, to get our message out.

"Sybrina, this case is going to be swept under the rug," he would say. "They're not going to arrest George Zimmerman. People want to hear from the parents. People need to hear from you! About how you felt about him, the man who murdered your son, not being arrested. We have to get the story out. You have to tell the story of what happened to Trayvon."

A thing that kept rising up in our tragedy was the issue of race. People were already comparing Trayvon's death to Emmett Till, the fourteen-year-old from Chicago visiting family in Money, Mississippi, where he was lynched on August 28, 1955, after being accused of flirting with a white woman. But at first I felt that our case had little to do with race, at least as far as whether people would find the story sympathetic or not. When I hear a child has drowned, I don't care what race or nationality that kid was. I don't say, "Oh! Was it a black kid?" It doesn't matter. A child has lost a life. When I hear about the death of a child, I think about the parents, the family, the siblings, the friends who are grieving the loss. Who cares about race in the face of that kind of tragedy and injustice? But the more I found out about my son's killer, the more I started to wonder: if it wasn't race, what else could it be?

Those thoughts were racing through my head the first time I went to the government offices in Sanford. Crump said he wanted us to go with him to file the paperwork demanding the release of the 911 tapes. So my sister, my mother, Jahvaris, and I piled into one car, with Tracy and the attorneys in another, a two-car caravan. We exited the Florida Turnpike and took a smaller road toward downtown, where we were greeted with a sign by the side of the road—"Welcome to Sanford"—whose bland cheerfulness chilled me.

We drove into Sanford's little downtown and went into the clerk's office where Crump filed the papers demanding the release of the tapes. Tracy and I didn't actually have to be there, but we wanted to be there to show our support. When we came outside the courthouse, the media was waiting for us. I was still raw, numb, and unsure of what to say. I was strong enough to get out of bed, get out of my house, get out of Miami, and travel to Sanford, but I still wasn't strong enough to speak to the media, and the public, about what had happened to my son.

But there I was, standing in front of the clerk of courts building on Friday, March 9, 2012, just twelve days after my son's death. The media gathered around us in a semicircle. Blinding camera lights. Stares from a dozen strangers. Everyone waiting for us to speak.

"My son left Sanford, Florida, in a body bag, while George Zimmerman went home to sleep in his own bed," said Tracy.

It was my turn to speak, but my voice was deep inside me, and it was hard to get it out. I was visibly trembling, and when I finally spoke, my voice came out high-pitched and at times unclear. My mother, my sister, and Jahvaris stood behind me for support. But I was adrift. I was on the verge of tears and a breakdown right there in Sanford's courthouse square.

"Um . . ." I started. "It was very difficult and it is very difficult for me to deal with."

I gasped for breath, but few words followed.

"I don't understand why we haven't gotten the answers from the police department," I said. "I don't understand, and I don't understand why my baby . . ." At this point, I lost my train of thought. Then began again. "Why this guy was not arrested." Now I was crying. "I don't understand. As a mother, my heart is broken."

Sobbing now, big tears rolling down my face. Gasping for breath. *Flailing*.

"My heart . . . hurts," I said. "I don't understand. He was just a kid. He was just a baby."

I shook my head back and forth, and Jahvaris leaned in and kissed the back of my shoulder for support.

A reporter asked, "What's the hardest part for you when you wake up every morning knowing your son is not around?"

I wiped my eyes and tried to regain my composure. "Just having to deal with him not being with me," I said. "Just having to deal with him not smiling. Just having to deal with him not trying to help me and take care of me. It's just very . . ."

I tried to wipe the tears away. A reporter interrupted. "Ma'am, knowing the circumstances of this, was the man who pulled the trigger a vigilante that night?"

Tracy answered for me.

"I honestly think he was," Tracy said. "He approached him for no apparent reason. It was cold outside. My son had on a hoodie. Does that give you the right to approach an individual just because he has a hoodie on and it was raining?

"He was seventy to one hundred yards away from the back door trying to get home," Tracy said.

Crump added, "Bob, we can't call this guy a vigilante. Because a vigilante would say that something had been done to him," he said.

"Trayvon did absolutely nothing to this guy! He was just walking home. He was seventy yards from his home with a bag of Skittles and a can of iced tea when this guy confronted him, disregarding the police.

"This guy did not have the requisite training to try to approach and detain this young man," Crump continued. "If somebody came up to you in plain clothes as night falls and tells you, 'I'm going to detain you. You wait here.' Why would Trayvon not say, 'Who are you?'"

On the way into the courthouse, a reporter had shown us the killer's mugshot from his previous arrest. Now, during our press conference, the same reporter showed me the mugshot again on her phone. "I'm going to show you his picture, and I want you to look at the picture because I want you to determine something," she said. "He's your son, so you know him best. If he saw this man approach him, do you think your son would be afraid and kind of get a little agitated by the whole thing?"

"He's much heavier than him. He's older than him," I said of the man in the picture. "He would have been afraid. He would have tried to protect himself."

Why hadn't the police shown Tracy or Crump this picture already? I wondered. Then Crump returned to the matter of the tapes. "Why won't they release the tape to the public? Why won't they tell this family the truth? We deserve answers."

We left the courthouse and went to a restaurant and then returned to a hotel to wait for the judge's decision on the tapes. The decision came later that day: the tapes would not be released at this time, but a hearing on the matter was scheduled for more than a week away.

We ended up going home, driving back to Miami, still with more questions than answers.

Back home, we went to Antioch, where on the evening of Sunday, March 11, we had a candlelight vigil for Trayvon. It was a small but emotional group of us: family, friends, and members of the church community, all of us gathered outside the church.

I was sleepwalking through everything, but I could see the church, its outdoor stairs filled with people. Everyone out on the stairs in the drizzle, holding candles. My brother Mark passed some candles to us and we lit them. Watching those candles flickering and sputtering from the rain, I could feel myself falling apart all over again. But I was there, and so were they, this band of supporters, and I had to see them, to greet them, embrace them, and thank them for caring. The crowd began singing the church songs that I loved. But now they all sounded sad, and were painful to hear.

Just get through this, I told myself.

Along with our friends and family came the media. A small podium was set up. One of my aunts said an opening prayer, someone else recited a poem to Trayvon. And we began to pray. Just then, as the darkness descended, it began to rain a little more. The wind became gusty and we huddled under the big church's eaves, to say a few words in memory of Trayvon.

"Not only did I lose a son; I lost my best friend," said Tracy.

I was still too distraught to speak at length. But we were among family and friends in our hometown, so I said a few words. "I think it's just profiling," I said. "I think it has something to do with the fact that he was a young black African American kid."

"We need answers and we need justice," said Tracy. "Not only are we looking for an arrest, we're looking for a conviction."

The rain came down harder, and some of the candles flickered and went out. More prayers were said, along with more demands for justice, and then we all went home to prepare for what we knew would be a very busy week ahead.

Monday, March 12, began with a press conference by Sanford police chief Bill Lee outside the Sanford City Hall. He had been chief for only eleven months. This would be the first time the public and the media would come face-to-face with the police in this case, and it was tense.

We couldn't be there, but Ms. Oliver attended and told us all about it. She was among a group of citizens, mostly from the nearby black Goldsboro community, who came to the city hall to hear the chief speak—and to hear if he was going to at last arrest the man who shot my son. "Norton Bonaparte, the black city manager, was with Chief Lee," Ms. Oliver told us. "And the chief had his whole department, almost, behind him. His sergeants. His lieutenants. His officers."

"We don't have anything to dispute his claim of self-defense at this point with the evidence," the chief said as to why they hadn't arrested the killer, adding that the police had told him not to confront Trayvon or take any action and to wait for the police to arrive. He later elaborated in a memo posted on the city's website: "By Florida Statute, law enforcement was PROHIBITED from making an arrest based on the facts and circumstances they had at the time. Additionally, when any police officer makes an arrest for any reason, the officer MUST swear and affirm that he/she is making the arrest in good faith and with probable cause. If the arrest is done maliciously and in bad faith, the officer and the City may be held liable."

He said that the police were turning over the case to prosecutors in the state attorney's office, which meant that their investigation was coming to a close, apparently without an arrest.

The reporter spoke up. "When someone shoots and kills someone they get arrested," she said. "Why are you passing the buck in this case and putting it on prosecutors to make a determination on whether he should be arrested?"

"Because it is the proper thing to do," Chief Bill Lee responded. "By statute if someone makes a statement of self-defense, unless we have probable cause to dispute that, we cannot make an arrest."

Ms. Oliver watched as the confrontation grew, well, if not heated, at least tense.

"Hang in there, Chief, hang in there," Ms. Oliver said she told Bill Lee after he completed his press conference.

"Thank you, Ms. Oliver," she said he replied.

. . .

On Wednesday, March 14, the protest moved to Sanford's Allen Chapel, the old NAACP-affiliated church in the Goldsboro community. An overflow crowd of four hundred–plus citizens and members of the media packed the pews, rafters, even the "Amen Corner," where the deacons and other dignitaries usually sit.

Jamal Bryant, the young and eloquent pastor in Baltimore's megachurch called the Empowerment Temple, was the first of many national black leaders to make the pilgrimage to Sanford, and he was picked to speak at the rally. He began promoting his visit long before his arrival.

"Headed to Orlando Florida to help mobilize community for #trayvon justice," he alerted his 745,000 followers on Facebook and 225,000 on Twitter. "Meet at Allen Church in Sanford at 12:30. Come! . . . Don't meet me there, beat me there!"

People started arriving at the church early that Wednesday evening. Outside, there were protesters with signs—"No Rest Until Arrest!"—men wearing symbolic hoodies, vendors selling unauthorized Trayvon T-shirts, and a steady stream of supporters.

"We come together today in the name of justice," Pastor Valerie Henry told the congregation at the outset. "We stand as his voice," meaning Trayvon's voice.

"I will stand, even if I stand alone," said Ms. Velma Williams, the city commissioner, who told the crowd she'd asked Police Chief Bill Lee to step aside.

Then Jamal Bryant, in his dark suit, colorful tie, and big, black glasses—looking more like a stylish professor than a pastor—walked onto the pulpit and up to the podium.

"We call for an immediate arrest," he said. "We want him behind bars. This is a wake-up call for the state of Florida!"

Four hundred voices thundered in agreement throughout the church.

"We are going to shut Florida down until justice weighs down!" he said. He then asked everyone to take out a pen and paper, and he gave them the phone number of the Seminole County state attorney's office. "Call the number and *demand* criminal charges and an arrest," he said.

Four hundred hands wrote down the number.

"No justice," said Jamal Bryant.

"No peace," responded the congregation.

He would say more later that evening, and even more at other rallies, among which were some of the fieriest benedictions on the case, including what he said before the church rally on the *Michael Baisden Show*:

> I feel like I'm in a time zone. Just three weeks ago, we were in the march from Selma to Montgomery, and it feels like we are back to Selma all over again . . .
>
> If you've got Skittles, everybody better eat Snickers because it's really a wake-up call that racism is still alive and our children have to be educated about the process. . . .
>
> Thinking about justice and mercy and grace, Frederick Douglass said, "I prayed for twenty years. Nothing happened until I got off my knees and started marching with my feet." And that's the role of the church. We already prayed about it. Now let's take action on it.
>
> You've come to worship! Now, leave to serve. It's not just about shouting. . . . But what are you doing after the benediction? . . . We're asking everybody who can't make it to Sanford . . . to send a bag of Skittles to the sheriff's department, and we're going to keep inundating them until he understands that this is something that is not sweet to us.

Four hundred voices screamed "Amen!" People were crying, shouting, ready for action, eager for justice. A congregation of individuals had become one.

Sanford's mayor, Jeff Triplett, had come to the rally, too. He soon stood, saying that his two young sons attended school not far from the church.

"Today, when I drove over here, I thought to myself, *What if . . . ?*"

He promised a thorough investigation—even if he had to pay for it himself. Local NAACP president Turner Clayton called for a US Justice Department investigation.

People left that church knowing that this was just the beginning.

"It's important and essential that we get the release of the 911 tapes," Congresswoman Corrine Brown told my sister and me as we sat in a restaurant in Sanford after she had met with the mayor, the city manager, and the police chief of Sanford. The nine-term African American congresswoman was as bold as her look: big hair, big glasses, colorful business suits—often red—and a voice that booms. But she also gave off a powerful aura of compassion. She reminded us of a fiery and undeniable aunt who was looking out for us—a fighter, but fighting for us. We were lucky to have her on our side. If anyone could convince them to release the tapes, I felt, Corrine Brown could. "I'm going to do whatever I need to do to try to help you and make sure you get those tapes," she said. "It's not something they should be trying to conceal."

The media coverage multiplied, and direct-action protests followed. On March 15, the computer servers at State Attorney Norman Wolfinger's offices were overwhelmed by a hundred thousand emails from citizens demanding the arrest and prosecution of the killer, and there was no telling how many bags of Skittles rained down on the police station and sheriff's office in Sanford after Pastor Jamal Bryant asked supporters to mail them in as a sign of protest. And Corrine Brown and other officials joined our chorus, hammering away on our demand for the tapes.

That same day, the killer's father delivered a one-page letter to the *Orlando Sentinel,* in which he claimed that the media's portrayal of his son had been "false and extremely misleading," accused "some individuals and organizations" of using "this tragedy to further their own causes," and insisted "at no time did George follow or confront Mr. Martin."

That last statement, at least the part about following our son, could be tested only once we had the tapes. The killer was starting to build his own story about what happened, which he could do only because the key piece of evidence that would clarify exactly what happened was being kept from the public. We needed those tapes.

I was working now, every day, pushing hard, and sometimes I'd take a moment to wonder at the events swirling around us—in those moments, I felt Trayvon's presence, guiding us and giving us the strength to fight. But inside I was still numb. My body was in motion, but my soul felt stunned into stillness and broken into a thousand pieces.

On the morning of March 16, nineteen days after our son's death, we held another press conference on the front porch of Attorney Natalie Jackson's Orlando office. The day was cloudy, and our faith in getting answers from the Sanford Police Department was gone. It was one of those days that despair threatened to swallow me, but once again I was saved by the compassion of strangers. I remember the hugs I received that day from these strangers—and the voices of two young women, witnesses from that awful night. And with those women came a glimmer of hope that the true story might finally be told.

Each of these women told a far different story than the official versions or anything we'd heard before. They were both single mothers who lived together at the Retreat at Twin Lakes, Mary Cutcher and Selma Mora Lamilla, and they'd come to that press conference to offer their testimony.

Crump spoke first, introducing the two young women, who stood with us in front of attorney Jackson's office. "We are here with these individuals who bravely came forward after making several attempts to contact the Sanford Police Department to tell them what they saw on the night that Trayvon Martin was killed," he said.

He looked over at Tracy and me.

"Trayvon's mother and father thought it was important to drive to

Central Florida to stand shoulder-to-shoulder with these courageous women, especially in light of the attempt yesterday to intimidate them and discredit them by the Sanford Police Department," Crump said.

This was a reference to a press release from the police department the previous day, saying the women had made statements on local television that were "inconsistent" with their previous statements to police, which to Crump meant the police were calling these witnesses liars.

"The attack of the character of these witnesses by the Sanford Police Department is further evidence of the conspiracy to cover up the killing of Trayvon Martin by only releasing parts of their investigation that are beneficial to George Zimmerman," he said. "The Sanford Police Department can't have it both ways."

As he continued, Crump began waving his hands and shouting in disbelief. "They ran a background check on Trayvon Martin! The young man who was dead on the ground. But did not run a background check on George Michael Zimmerman, the man who had just shot this teenager in cold blood. *What kind of police work is that?* . . . Next, a drug and alcohol analysis on Trayvon Martin. But no drug and alcohol analysis on George Michael Zimmerman?"

He stood back and stared at the media in shock. "So you're gonna do a drug and blood alcohol analysis on the dead kid. But not on the shooter?"

He looked over at the two women who were ready to speak about what they saw and heard on the night Trayvon was shot. "We now have two witnesses who have come forward to say that it was Trayvon Martin who was the one who was [yelling] for help" on the 911 tape as Zimmerman pursued him.

Before introducing the witnesses, Crump turned to Tracy and then me. Tracy offered some heartfelt words about how we missed our son and felt betrayed by the authorities. I always appreciated his direct demeanor—he was a truck driver, and as gregarious as he was, he was never a big public speaker. But he didn't hesitate to lay open his heart to the public for the sake of our son. I wanted to do the same, but it was so hard.

I stepped forward.

I had a lot going on inside me at that moment. Crump was right about everything he'd just said. It was clear that people in Sanford were trying to intimidate these women into silence. The police and others hadn't hidden their unhappiness about them coming forward. From the outside looking in, it certainly seemed like the killer was receiving favors from the Sanford Police Department, like they were on his side. Everyone who stood up for Trayvon was setting themselves against these powerful people—and against the police force. I felt a surge of gratitude that anyone would even try.

"I stand before you today to publicly thank these ladies . . ." I said, and even as I tried to steady myself inside, I could feel myself breaking down. ". . . for helping in this investigation," I went on, and then my voice caught in my throat. Crump put his hand on my shoulder for support. "And just to know that regardless of what happens, there are still good people in this world." I was sobbing again. "I'm so very hurt by this whole situation. It's a nightmare. And I don't understand why this man has not been arrested. At least charged. And let a judge and jury decide if he's guilty. Thank you."

I stepped back. Jahvaris hugged me. Crump came back to the microphone and introduced Mary Cutcher and Selma Mora Lamilla. I composed myself and watched them step up to the lectern.

Mary Cutcher was a single mother and full-time student whose child had been playing near the crime scene only a short time before the shooting. Mary and her roommate, Selma, were making coffee that Sunday evening when they heard the screams, then a gunshot, followed by silence. They looked outside to see the killer crouching over Trayvon's body.

They told police what they'd experienced: a quiet Sunday night torn apart by the loud "whining" of a kid's voice, then the single gunshot. They looked outside. Trayvon was "facedown in the grass and not moving." The killer was "pacing," "thinking," Mary said at the press conference. Three times they asked him if everything was okay, before he finally, "nonchalantly," said, "Call the police."

"Common sense would tell you immediately he's going to be arrested," Mary Cutcher said to the assembled reporters. "And the following day is when we found out he was released without being arrested. That evening I took the flyer from the door they had passed out [in which police alerted residents of the Retreat about the shooting] and called the number on the bottom. Four times I called him [the police], repeatedly telling him, 'You guys have let him go. We verbally spoke with the shooter; he's seen our faces; he knows where we live. We're worried. For our safety. We know it's not self-defense.'"

She said the police officer told her, "You have nothing to worry about." Still concerned for her safety and the safety of her children, she called again later that day and was told again not to worry. "He's harmless," she said the officer told her. "He's not going to hurt you." She said she called back again. "I said, 'I firmly believe this was not self-defense,' and he finally says, 'If you feel that strongly about it, I can give you the number of the lead detective.'"

Finally, she was given the number of Detective Chris Serino. "I made multiple calls on Monday, left a message for Chris [Serino]," she said. An appointment was eventually made for nine P.M. that Thursday, March 1, but instead of going by her house in the evening, as they had planned, Serino called to take their statements by phone, and then suggested that Mary and her roommate come in to the station for a recorded statement, which they did on Friday, March 2.

She told him how shaken up they were, noting that she lived at the end of the row of townhouses where Trayvon had fallen dead. "We only heard one gunshot. . . . There was no physical fighting going on. . . . I heard nothing but a little kid, scared to death and crying. I feel in my heart, and I wouldn't say this if I honestly didn't believe it. . . . I honestly do believe that he intended for this kid to die.

"Multiple people had my phone number, and not one person

called me back," Mary continued at the press conference. "My point was that I feel it was not self-defense, because I heard the crying and if it was Zimmerman that was crying, Zimmerman would have continued crying after the shot went off."

Selma Mora Lamilla added that she was in the kitchen making coffee when she heard the night explode with violence right outside her window on what would have normally been a quiet Sunday night. "I heard the whine of a kid," she said. "I ran to my back porch and I look at this guy on top of the body, and I ask him, 'What's going on?' " she said, adding that the killer didn't answer her until after the third time she asked and then only replied, flatly, "Just call the police."

"That's exactly what we told the police five days after this happened," said Selma Mora Lamilla, beginning to cry. "I'm just trying to help. This is not something that you see every single day. To me it has been so hard realizing that it was a body. I have never seen a [dead] body in my life."

I stood behind these two women, mothers who'd bravely joined our cause. I was moved by their courage, but every detail of the shooting, every mention of my son's last cries, tore at me. I stood up but felt like collapsing.

That same day, three days before our demand for the release of the 911 tapes was supposed to be decided upon by a judge, the city manager, Norton Bonaparte, called Crump and told him that the city was going to release the tapes voluntarily. The mayor would later say he did it to keep the peace and avoid any violence that might come from protesters or others who were feeling anger around the city's stonewalling—although violence had already been unleashed and blood spilled in his city. We were upset and angry. But the talk of violence seemed premature to me. We hadn't heard any talk of violence at this point, and if we had, we certainly wouldn't have encouraged it.

Our press conference had just ended. I felt empty, drained, suddenly very tired. It was getting dark, and we were preparing to drive back to Miami. Then one of the attorneys' cellphones rang. It was the city manager.

"Come to the mayor's office to listen to the tapes," he said.

We immediately drove over to Sanford's City Hall, which houses the mayor's and city manager's offices. City Manager Norton Bonaparte met us at the back door and took us to the mayor's office. We were told that Chief Lee wanted to say something to us. We said we would rather not speak to him, and we asked that the uniformed police that were in the building keep clear of the area where we would be listening to the tapes. We didn't want to see them, either. These were the men who allowed the killer of our son to go home and sleep in his own bed while Trayvon left the crime scene in a body bag headed for the morgue.

It was somewhere between six and seven P.M. when we walked into the mayor's office: Tracy, Jahvaris, and I and other family members, our attorneys Crump and Jackson, and our media consultant, Ryan Julison. We met Mayor Jeff Triplett and City Manager Norton Bonaparte for the first time.

"Hello, I'm Mayor Jeff Triplett," he said, greeting us. He seemed sincere and aware of how difficult this was going to be for us. "Everybody come in and have a seat."

We filed into a row of chairs set up behind his desk, facing his desktop computer. The mayor expressed his condolences and told us that he was going to play the tapes for us and then allow us to rewind and listen to them for ourselves. "I will personally play the tapes through my computer for you and you can listen as many times as you want in my office and take as much time as you need," he told us.

"You know, I'm a father. I can't imagine the pain and anguish of what you are getting ready to hear," he said.

The mayor hit PLAY and we began listening. My heart felt heavy, and I braced myself as if for a hurricane of pain. But I had to listen. The 911 recordings were on his computer, so we could easily play them as many times as we wanted. As soon as the first recording started, I thought even one time might be more than I could handle.

"Sanford Police Department," said the male dispatcher.

"Hey, we've had some break-ins in my neighborhood, and there's a real suspicious guy, uh, it's Retreat View Circle," came the voice of the neighborhood watch volunteer. "The best address I can give you is one-eleven Retreat View Circle. This guy looks like he's up to no good, or he's on drugs or something. It's raining, and he is just walking around, looking about."

"Okay, and this guy, is he white, black, or Hispanic?" the dispatcher asked.

"He looks black."

"Did you see what he was wearing?"

"Yeah, a dark hoodie, like a gray hoodie, and either jeans or sweatpants, and white tennis shoes. He's here now, he's just staring."

"Okay, he is just walking around the area?" asked the dispatcher.

"Looking at all the houses," said the watchman. "Now he's just staring at me."

"It's one-one-one-one Retreat View or one-eleven?" asked the dispatcher.

"That's the clubhouse," said the watchman.

"He is near the clubhouse right now?"

"Yeah. Now he's coming towards me," he said. "He's got his hand in his waistband. And he's a black male."

The dispatcher asked, "How old would you say he looks?"

"Late teens. . . . Something is wrong with him. Yup, he's coming to check me out; he's got something in his hands. I don't know what his deal is."

"Just let me know if he does anything, okay?" said the dispatcher.

"How long until you get an officer over here?"

"Yeah, we've got 'em on the way; just let me know if this guy does anything else."

"Okay," said the watchman. "These assholes, they always get away."

I could feel the blood rising to my face and something roiling in the pit of my stomach. *These assholes*. The words stung. The watchman began giving directions to the dispatcher: "When you come to the clubhouse . . . you go in straight through the entrance and then you make a left . . ."

After giving more directions, he suddenly said, "Shit, he's running."

"He's running?" asked the dispatcher. "Which way is he running?"

"Down towards the, uhhh, other entrance of the neighborhood . . . ," said the watchman.

We could hear the neighborhood watch captain breathing heavily on the tape and the wind whistling through his cellphone, and we could imagine Trayvon. *Running*. For his life.

"Which entrance is that that he's heading towards?"

"The back entrance . . . Fucking punks," he said under his breath.

"Are you following him?" asked the dispatcher.

"Yeah," said the neighborhood watchman.

"Okay, we don't need you to do that," said the dispatcher.

"Okay," he said.

"All right, sir, what is your name?" asked the dispatcher.

"George . . . He ran."

"All right, George, what's your last name?"

"Zimmerman."

I'd heard his name before, of course, and I had seen his picture. But now, hearing his voice in those final moments of my son's life, I could finally really see the man, and imagined him following Trayvon.

"All right, George," the dispatcher said, "we do have them on the way. Do you want to meet with the officer when they get out there?"

"Yeah," he replied, and more directions followed. The dispatcher asked the watchman if he lived in the area, and he said, "Yeah . . ."

"What's your apartment number?"

"It's a home. It's 1950. Oh, crap. I don't want to give it all out. I don't know where this kid is."

Back and forth we went on the opening section of the recording—playing it again and again as if we might be able to rewind the tape all the way back to the beginning and, through some miracle, bring Trayvon back.

It was agonizing, but I knew it was important. We were finally able to hear *exactly* what happened on that rainy night in Sanford. So we all leaned in close to the computer speaker: my family, our attorneys, Tracy, and I, all huddled around the mayor's desk, bracing ourselves—and praying for God to give us the strength—to listen to Trayvon die.

At the same time, I kept an eye on the mayor's office door, knowing that if things got too intense, if hearing my son's voice in the final seconds before the bullet ended everything became too much to bear, I could get out of that office, into the hallway, out of the building, out of Sanford if I had to.

What came next were the 911 calls from the neighbors, the calls where we could hear in the background the truth and the terror of what happened that night.

"911," the female dispatcher said on the first tape. "Do you need police, fire, or medical?"

A woman's voice came on the line. "Um, maybe both," she said. "I'm not sure. There's just someone screaming outside."

"Okay, what's the address that they're near?" asked the dispatcher. But the address couldn't be heard on the tape. "And is it a male or female?"

"It sounds like a male," said the neighbor.

"And you don't know why?" asked the dispatcher.

"I don't know why; I think they're yelling 'help,' but I don't know. Just send someone quick, please."

"Does he look hurt to you?" asked the dispatcher, and we could hear the screams in the background.

"I can't see him. I don't want to go out there. I don't know what's going on, so . . ."

"Tell them to come now!" a male voice said in the background.

"They're sending," said the caller. The scream was louder now. A shriek.

"So you think he's yelling 'help'?" asked the dispatcher.

"Yes," she said.

"All right, what is your—"

I heard Trayvon's last, long agonizing cries, loud and raspy, the voice of a teenage boy in despair. The voice of Trayvon. We knew without a doubt. It was Trayvon.

Then we heard the gunshot. A single, loud, echoing *pop* from the neighborhood watch volunteer's pistol that went through my baby's hoodie, his chest, and his heart.

"Just, there's gunshots," said the neighbor.

Now Tracy had taken over the controls of the computer. He began playing the tape over and over again, the scream, again and again. Each time it became clearer. We could hear someone yelling, shrieking, howling, and calling out what sounded like a long, drawn-out cry: "Help!" I knew it was Trayvon. *I was 100 percent sure that it was Trayvon.* I don't care who claimed it wasn't, and lots of people would say it was the killer's voice, and not my son's voice on that tape. A mother knows her son's voice; a mother knows her son's screams; a mother listens to her baby's voice every day of his life. A mother *knows.* And I knew: that was Trayvon, and I didn't have to tell everybody who was in that room that it was Trayvon's voice. They knew it was Trayvon's voice, too. And I started crying, bawling, big tears rolling down my face in uncontrollable sobs. I eyed that door, that escape. But before I ran out, I looked around the room. And I could see that everybody else in the mayor's office was crying, too. My sister, crying. My cousin, crying. Tracy, crying.

Even the mayor of Sanford, Florida, was very emotional. He was really shaken, almost as shaken as we were. From his reaction, it seemed like he was just hearing the tapes for the very first time. I could tell that what he'd heard had not only touched him; it had shaken him. *He knows something is wrong, that something is not right with this case,* I thought.

"Did you just say gunshots?" asked the dispatcher.

"Yes."

"How many?"

"Just one . . ."

The neighbor, also a mother, then apparently turned to her son, saying, "Get in here now," and I felt my heart break again at the sound of a mother instinctively protecting her son. Because with that single, static-muffled, echoing *pop*, I knew that my own son was dead.

"I don't hear him yelling anymore; do you hear anything?" the dispatcher asked.

And that was it for me. I screamed. I sobbed. I ran. Through the mayor's door and into the hallway, as if I could run all the way back into that night at the Retreat at Twin Lakes, and tell my son to "get down," save him from that *pop*, that bullet, that gun. Save him from the killer. But I couldn't, of course. So instead I collapsed on a couch in Sanford's City Hall.

Crump came out to console me. My sister came out to comfort me. Even the mayor came out to check on me. Jeff Triplett was working for the city. He had to stand with his team. But the kindness he showed us made a big difference at that time. He'd not only let us listen to the tapes, he'd gone one step further. He saw the human side of our loss. He saw our case through the eyes of a parent. Not as a white parent, or a black parent. Just a parent.

"I'm so very sorry for your family," he said. "I'm sorry for what happened to your son."

Tracy came outside to check on me, too, but then he returned to the mayor's office, where he, Jahvaris, and the others continued to listen to the tapes, which, they started to notice, seemed to have been altered in some way. Phone numbers and addresses were redacted. There were gaps. It was obvious that somebody had edited the tapes. We would never know for sure what was missing. But at that moment, it was our best and maybe only evidence of what happened to Trayvon that night. So the others kept listening, hanging on to every word. Play, rewind, and then play again, listening to our son die again and again, determined to find the truth.

That night I couldn't sleep, just like most nights. But this night, as I prayed before going to bed, as I always did, I asked: "How could an adult shoot and kill an unarmed teenager, claim self-defense, and go home and sleep in their own bed?" Who could be so heartless?

Tracy

∽

March 16, 2012–March 21, 2012

The mayor's office turned quiet for a moment. Sybrina had run out of the room, crying, and her sister and Jahvaris had followed her. I was alone with the lawyers, the mayor, Sybrina's brother, and those 911 tapes. I wanted to take my time and listen to them, *really* listen to them. At that point, I knew that Tray was gone. I wanted to know why. So I sat at the mayor's computer, playing the tapes, back and forth, back and forth, listening to every word.

I moved from one tape to another, each one more heartbreaking than the last.

I was now listening to a woman, frantic, like the other neighbors, about the gunshots that had erupted right outside her back porch. "There's someone screaming outside . . . ," she said. "Yes, I heard a gunshot. Hurry up. There's someone screaming—I just heard gun-shots. . . . Hurry up, they're right outside my house. . . ."

Another tape, another frantic caller: "I think someone's been shot!"

"Where at?" asked the dispatcher.

"Oh, my God!" was all she said back.

"Where?" asked the dispatcher. "Why do you think someone's been shot?"

"Because they're out in the backyard and a gun just went off and they said, 'Call 911.' Now there's people coming with flashlights."

I could hear her speaking to what were surely her children, trying to protect them from the violence taking place right outside their back door, telling them, "Get inside, get inside, get inside."

Another neighbor, another female, came on the tape. "I'm looking out my back of my townhome and someone's screaming 'help' and, I don't know, I heard, like, a bang," she said. "I'm looking out my window, like my backyard, and someone is yelling and screaming 'help,' and I heard like a *pop* noise and they're both still out there right now, and I don't know what's going on."

"Well, I can tell you right now, you're not the only person that's calling," the dispatcher reassured the caller. "We already have one officer on the scene and another on the way . . ."

"Oh, my God!" she continued. "I see the person right now. I see him like walking. . . . I don't know what he did to this person. I can't see, there's a man walking with a flashlight right now. . . . I don't know what's happening. Someone's on the ground."

"You see someone laying on the ground?"

"I don't know, someone's been shot," said the neighbor. "I don't know what's going on."

"Calm down, stay on the line with me. Like I said, we have an officer on scene . . ."

"Oh, my God, they better hurry up. I don't know if someone's dead on the ground or something. . . . I see out my back window, and . . . a sidewalk and grass and stuff . . . There's a man who's out there with a flashlight with a man who's been wrestling . . . People are coming. I can see another gentleman with a flashlight. I don't know if they're police or not. Oh, my God, he shot the person. He just said he shot the person."

"Who is saying they shot who?"

"The people out there—um—a guy is raising his hands up, he's saying he shot a person. I think it's a police officer that's with him right now. Oh, my God."

The neighbor seemed as distraught as we were as we listened to her cries.

"I can see somebody's killed!"

"Listen, we don't know if they've been killed . . . ," the dispatcher said.

"The person is dead, laying on the grass!" said the caller.

"Just because he's laying on the ground doesn't mean he's passed," said the dispatcher. "We have an ambulance on the way, as well. We're gonna probably pick him up and take him to the hospital."

At first tears had been running down my face, and the faces of everyone who had stayed in that room. But soon, as we listened to recording after recording, my sadness turned to anger. *How did this happen?* I thought. *Why did this man kill my son? And why is he walking around free?*

The neighbor kept talking, almost as if she were speaking to herself. "I didn't see it because it was too dark and I just heard people screaming, 'Help me, help me.' And this person shot him. He was like wrestling with him, you know what I mean? On the ground, from what I could see. It was very dark . . ."

"You don't have to worry right now. We have many officers on the way and I think about two officers on scene at least right now. So we are on scene, okay?"

One more neighbor called that night on the 911 tapes.

"Sir, what exactly did you see?" the dispatcher asked.

"I saw a man laying on the ground that needed help that was screaming and I was gonna go over there and try to help him but my dog got off the leash so I went and got my dog and then I heard a loud sound and then the screaming stopped," he said.

"Okay, did you see the person get shot?" he was asked.

"No," he replied. "I just heard a loud gunshot sound and then the screaming stopped."

The screaming stopped for the neighbors.

It would never stop for us.

Now, however, we knew much more than we had before. We knew the shooting was heard by at least seven neighbors. We knew that the cries for help came from our son. And we knew that even the 911 police dispatcher felt sure they had the man who shot our son in police custody. I also knew with more clarity than before that someone needed to be held accountable for this crime.

When we finished listening to the tapes, I was enraged. I wanted an arrest right then. Those tapes needed to be released so that the public could hear what happened that night.

But to release or not to release the tapes would be decided by Mayor Triplett.

The mayor had a decision to make because the media was waiting outside Sanford City Hall at that very moment.

The media had been following us all day, all week long. From the press conference on the courthouse steps, when Crump filed the public-records lawsuit, to our press conference outside Natalie Jackson's office. Everywhere we went, the media was there.

He asked our attorney Natalie Jackson, who was born and raised in Sanford, and others their opinions.

Meaning, *What should we do about the tapes? Should we release the tapes or not release the tapes?*

The mayor, to his credit, and against the urging of his police chief and others who did not want the tapes released, decided to release them anyway.

Soon the media played the tapes to the public—and, like everything in this case, we were totally unprepared for what came next.

Out in the parking lot, on the night we heard the 911 tapes, our attorney Jasmine Rand shared the reaction had by many. She had arrived later than the rest of the legal team, so she didn't have time to make it inside the mayor's office to hear the tapes with us. But someone brought her a copy outside, and she and the journalist Trymaine Lee, who would write many insightful columns about our case, sat in his car. He popped the CD into the player, and they listened to the sounds of the night Trayvon died for the first time. Jasmine Rand is a lawyer; she doesn't cry easily. But as she listened, tears began rolling down her face. "It turned into an uncontrollable sob, my whole body was shaking," she would later tell us. "I was embarrassed to cry in front of Trymaine. I have never heard a client cry for 'help' before. To hear his pleas and cries and know that I was already too late because the shots had already been fired, well, for a moment I wondered about the purpose of the legal system. I realized that there was no winning in this case. I could never give our clients what they wanted most in the world: their son. The best we could ever do would be to bring them justice, honor to his legacy, and to try to save other people's children from the same fate."

The 911 recordings ricocheted around the world. It was still too real and raw for us. Sybrina refused to read the newspapers or watch the news. But I followed it closely, reading the articles and watching the news reports that dominated the media over the next several days.

Rock Center with Brian Williams featured several NBC anchors and commentators describing how they felt when they first heard the 911 tapes.

"The first time I heard the 911 tape I was actually at home," said anchorwoman Tamron Hall. "And I clicked on the audio."

She took a deep breath.

"I couldn't believe what I was hearing," she continued.

The TV segment cut to the 911 tapes, with the screams and the neighbor saying, "There's just someone screaming outside."

Then the scream and the shot rang out.

"To hear the gunfire, the shot, and to know that at that moment or soon after that sound, a boy the same age as my nephew had *died*," Tamron Hall said, and I could see the grief on the elegant anchorwoman's face.

Next came Tony Dungy, the NBC Sports analyst and former NFL head coach: "You see a young man, and to me, that's the tragedy of this, a young man who could have been any of the guys that I coach, could have been any of my sons. Just to see that life taken away, it's stunning."

"Listening to the 911 tape, you heard somebody applying all the stereotypes that you were afraid that people out there are applying to us: on drugs, violent, up to no good," MSNBC contributor Touré said. "All these sort of things that we fear people are seeing at a distance and [saying about] a boy who's just walking down the street on the phone."

We began seeing Michael Skolnik, a young man living in New York City, speaking about Trayvon on television. First a few shows, then more, then he was everywhere, talking about justice for Trayvon. Soon, he was with us in Sanford, for marches and rallies, at our side, both physically and spiritually, writing about our case, appearing on television, doing whatever he could, as, he would later say, our actions for justice for Trayvon began to grow into something bigger, a movement: Black Lives Matter.

But at the time, I had something else on my mind.

It was Saturday, March 17, two days after we'd heard the 911 tapes, and I was at home. I kept thinking about Trayvon's last night. There were so many unanswered questions bothering me. By then, we knew the timeline of when everything happened. But though we knew when our son died, we certainly didn't know everything about why he had died, or even exactly *what* had taken place on the last night of our son's life. So I kept thinking, *What could Trayvon have been doing just before he was shot?*

Then it hit me: *Trayvon was on his phone.*

I knew that my son, like almost every seventeen-year-old, stayed on his phone. But who was the last person Trayvon talked to on the night that he was killed? And what might that person know that we didn't? Trayvon's phone bill was on the same T-Mobile plan as mine. So I called T-Mobile and asked them to set up my account so I could view my call records on my computer.

Text messages couldn't be viewed, but calls could. And Trayvon's calls scrolled down seven or eight pages of my T-Mobile bill. There were incoming calls, outgoing calls, with both the time of the call and how long the call lasted. Several of the calls dated February 26, 2012, stood out: more than a dozen incoming and outgoing calls of around thirty minutes all to the same number. Especially interesting was a call at 7:12 P.M. The police put Trayvon's time of death at 7:17, which would mean this call happened a few minutes before he died.

The person with the number on the T-Mobile bill was the last person Trayvon spoke to by phone right before he died.

I dialed the phone number.

"Hello?"

It was the voice of a young woman, a deep, sad, somber voice. I explained that I was Tracy Martin, the father of Trayvon Martin, and I was looking over his phone records.

"I noticed that you were the last person who talked to my son," I said. "I was hoping that you could shed some insight into what happened to Trayvon the night he was murdered."

There were a few seconds of silence.

"Who am I speaking with?" I asked.

"This is Diamond," she said after some time.

She sounded hesitant. I could tell it wasn't an upbeat time for her. She almost sounded like she was grieving as much as I was.

"Did you hear anything?" I asked, trying to lead her into a conversation. And pretty much the first thing that came out of her mouth was, "A man was following Trayvon."

She said that she and Trayvon had been on the phone all day, talking back and forth. They were talking that night as he was returning to the Retreat, and he told her that there was a man following him.

"I asked him, 'Who's following you?' And he said, 'This creepy-ass cracker.' I told him to *run*.

"And he told me he hadn't did anything, so he wasn't going to run," she continued. "He said it had started drizzling and that he was going to put his hoodie up on his head and he was going to walk fast back to the house."

She said she then heard Trayvon asking somebody, "Why are you following me?"

"And I started yelling into the phone, 'Run! Run, Trayvon, run!' And then I heard a scuffle and then the phone went dead."

"I never heard from him again," she said. I thought I heard her crying on the other end of the line.

I kept asking her, "Are you sure? Is that all you remember?"

And she said, "That's all I know. That's all I heard."

I finally told her that she was the last person to speak with Tray while he was alive, other than his killer. She told me that she had heard that Trayvon had been killed. But she didn't know he had been killed while she was talking to him. She didn't know she was the last person to speak to him.

She got real quiet and she didn't say anything else. I told her I'd call her back. I hung up and immediately called Crump and then Sybrina. I gave them her contact information, and they started trying to reach her.

Diamond was a young girl who would quickly become caught up in somebody else's tragedy. We couldn't have known at the time that she would play an extremely important role in understanding what had happened to our son. There were other things we didn't yet know about Diamond. Like her age. She said she was sixteen, but she was actually eighteen. We would also learn that her name wasn't Diamond.

It was Rachel Jeantel.

Rachel spoke English, Creole, and Spanish, but her English poured out in a slang that was all her own.

She first said she hadn't attended Trayvon's funeral because she was in the hospital, but later admitted that she had lied about the hospital part. She didn't go to the funeral, not because she was sick or scared, but because she felt guilty.

"I could have [done] something," she would later say in her deposition in the case. "I kept calling Trayvon when the phone hung up. I kept calling him. I should have called 911 after I heard the bump, really. And I should have talked earlier to her [meaning Sybrina] about what happened. . . . I found out that Trayvon's killer did not get charged, really on that Saturday when the dad called me. I thought he was in jail. And I felt guilty."

Rachel was hurt. She had known my son since elementary school. Later we found out that people used to pick on her at school. They teased Rachel about how she spoke, how she dressed, and more. But Trayvon befriended and defended her. He tried to help her through her feelings of insecurity. He saw how people treated her, and he wanted to let her know that there were people who cared about her. They had reconnected only that February, less than a month before his death, when he rode over to her house on his bicycle. It was February 1, her birthday, and their friendship was reignited.

It might have gone further than friendship. "It was getting there," she would later say, meaning a relationship might have blossomed. But for now, they were friends. "For fun," she said. And conversation. Endlessly long telephone conversations. On the last day of Trayvon's life, they spoke on the phone at noon, throughout the day, and into the night, on and off for about five hours total.

"That morning, he had text me," Rachel said of February 26, 2012. Since it was a Sunday, she was in church. "I told him I'd call him later," she said. "And I had called him on the afternoon. . . . That was the whole day I was talking to him."

"Do you remember what happened?" she was asked by the attorney after an extended discussion of other things.

"Yes," she said, and she went into great detail, opening a window onto that dark, rainy night.

"This what happened," she said in the distinctive way that Rachel spoke. "He told me the dude was now following him. Now the following start . . . He, he said, 'Oh, oh shit, oh, he following me. . . . I was shocked, and I said, 'Okay, *run*.' He said nah, he gonna try to lose him. And then . . . I think a second or a minute later, he say he gonna run from back, and then I said okay. And then, as I know, he ran, 'cause I heard the wind, and then . . . I lost contact with him again."

I heard the wind. I thought about that for a long time. She heard the wind rushing through the phone as Trayvon ran from this man, this stranger with the gun, following him.

Still, Trayvon didn't seem worried. Once Trayvon felt he had lost the man who had been following him, he felt safe enough that he asked Rachel to check on the All-Star basketball game, which was starting any minute. And Trayvon talked about her devotion to her hair. Rachel later told the author Lisa Bloom that he found the time to say, "You're gonna die with those hot rollers on, Rachel!"

Trayvon wasn't looking for trouble.

He was only trying to get home.

Then his pursuer reappeared.

The rain was falling, and Rachel said, "He told me he gonna put the hoodie on so he can lose the dude." She lost contact with him as he ran.

"I had [to] call him back, he had answered and he was breathing hard. And I say, 'Where you at?' He say he in back of his daddy girlfriend house . . . And I told him *keep running,* he say nah, he lost the dude and he just walk fast, to his daddy, his daddy at the house. It's just right there. That's where I thought, *Okay, he's close to his house. Okay, he's safe.* . . . Then, then a second later I hear Trayvon come and say, 'What you following me for?' Then the dude come and say, 'What you doing around here?' I was saying 'Trayvon, Trayvon, what happen, what happen, what's going on, what's going on?' . . . Then I heard a bump. . . .

"Somebody . . . had to hit Trayvon, for the headset to fell. 'Cause all I was hearing, in the background, grass, somebody saying, 'Get off.' And I was calling Trayvon. 'What's going on?' And then the phone just"—at this she clapped her hands once—"hang up."

Rachel knew it was Trayvon's voice saying "Get off," she would say, because Trayvon had a high-pitched voice—she called it a "baby's voice," which is what the voice screaming on the 911 tapes sounded like: a high-pitched wail. And, after all, Rachel had been speaking to Trayvon for five hours on the phone that Sunday.

"I was still saying, 'Trayvon, what's going on?'"

But Trayvon didn't answer. His phone went dead.

Trayvon was dead.

At first, Rachel didn't know it, never heard about it, not from the news, because she never watched television news, except for the weather. "To make sure I don't get wet," she said.

She found out about Trayvon's death when she went to his Facebook page many days after that Sunday, and saw a long line of messages from Trayvon's friends scrolling down his wall.

"RIP, Trayvon."

Rest in peace, Trayvon. Rest in power.

A day or two after I called her, Sybrina tried to reach out to her. But Rachel didn't answer. She was in school. Then Sybrina texted her, asking to speak with her and her mother, saying, "All I want to know is what happened to my son." Rachel texted back: she'd have to speak to her mother about it. And while her mother approved, Rachel wasn't sure about getting involved, especially when it came to speaking to Sybrina—she later said that she didn't "like to see people get emotional." And, of course, she was still feeling guilty. So instead she decided to write a letter and drop it off at Sybrina's house. But she was too nervous to do that—she told us her hands shook when she tried to write. So she dictated a letter to a friend who worked as a nurse. The nurse knew Sybrina—she had been to her house when she cared for Sybrina's brother Ronnie. Once she'd dictated the letter, Rachel asked a friend to drive her over to Sybrina's house, where she planned to drop off the letter and leave.

I first saw Rachel when she came to deliver the letter to Sybrina, a young woman visibly stressed-out and so nervous that she didn't even want to come inside the house. You couldn't blame her. The house was full of family, lawyers, mourners, people with questions, and Rachel was terrified. So she sat in her friend's car parked by the curb outside Sybrina's house with that letter, a first account of what she heard just before Trayvon died.

Sybrina went outside to talk with her.

"I have a letter for you," Rachel said, and she handed her a neatly folded piece of lined notebook paper, on which her friend had written Rachel's words about Trayvon's last night.

Sybrina invited her inside the house, and I went into the kitchen so that they could speak alone. Sybrina told me that Rachel was a nervous wreck and didn't seem to want to talk at all. She was afraid and uncomfortable. But she wanted to help.

Sybrina reassured Rachel that she would be okay, and that no harm was going to come to her by coming forward and meeting with us.

Then Sybrina began reading the letter, which was written in a neat cursive script:

I was on the phone when Trayvon decided to go to the corner store. It started to rain so he decided to walk through another complex because it was raining too hard. He started walking, then noticed someone was following him. Then he decided to find a shortcut 'cause the man wouldn't follow him. Then he said the man didn't follow him again. Then he looked back and saw the man again. The man started getting closer, then Trayvon turned around and said, "Why are you following me!!" Then I heard him fall, then the phone hung up. I called back and text. No response. In my mind I thought it was just a fight. Then I found out this tragic story.

The letter was signed "Diamond Eugene."

In the kitchen I could hear Sybrina start to cry, a sound that crushed me every time I heard it. I knew whatever Rachel had told her had brought her back to the night of the killing.

Rachel left the house, but it was just the beginning of our journey with Rachel Jeantel. Attorney Crump and I called her that evening in a three-way call. The call was recorded, and the next day parts of the call would be broadcast on ABC News—without revealing Rachel's identity, because we were concerned about identifying her. The show said that she was his "girlfriend," which wasn't true, and that she was sixteen, which, again, wasn't accurate. But what Rachel said in that nighttime phone call, which she took while standing in the closet of a friend's house she was visiting, speaking over her Bluetooth, was 100 percent true. And the world would hear it on March 20, 2012, on ABC News:

> Trayvon said, "What are you following me for?" And the man said, "What are you doing here?" Next thing I hear is somebody pushing, and somebody pushed Trayvon because the headset just fell. I called him again, and he didn't answer the phone.
>
> The line then went dead. Besides screams heard on 911 calls that night as Martin and Zimmerman scuffled, those were the last words he said.
>
> Trayvon's phone logs, also obtained exclusively by ABC News, show the conversation occurred five minutes before police first arrived on the scene. Crump said the girl's identity was being withheld because "her parents are gravely concerned about her health and her safety." Her parents asked that only an attorney be allowed to ask her questions.
>
> Martin's father, Tracy Martin, and mother, Sybrina Fulton, listened to the call, along with ABC News, ashen-faced.
>
> "He knew he was being followed, and tried to get away from the guy, and the guy still caught up with him," Tracy Martin said. "And that's the most disturbing part. He thought he had got away from the guy, and the guy backtracked for him. . . ."

Sybrina kept Rachel's letter in her Bible from that day forward. "Because it came from the last person to talk to Trayvon," she told me. Months later, when Sybrina was called to give a deposition in the case, the prosecutor asked her, "Regarding the letter, did you bring here today the original?"

She had it in her Bible. Because she brought her Bible everywhere, to all of the important moments in our case for justice for Trayvon, including that deposition. When the defense lawyers were questioning her, Sybrina showed them her Bible with the letter from Rachel Jeantel folded up inside it.

In that Bible was the truth. Still, the truth was taking a long time to come to light.

Fittingly, the words that came to summarize our fight for justice came from the mouths of students.

Our attorney, Jasmine Rand, was also a first-semester law professor at Florida A&M University in Tallahassee. Twice a week she left Parks and Crump's law office and rushed to FAMU's campus to teach at night. In her very first semester teaching, Jasmine had given the students in her Legal Problems of the Poor class an assignment: to apply what they were learning and provide services to homeless people. But when she got involved in Trayvon's case, she switched gears. She told her class the basics of our case: "A seventeen-year-old student was shot by a neighborhood watch volunteer while walking home with a can of iced tea and a bag of Skittles. We don't know exactly what happened, but the neighborhood watch volunteer had a gun, Trayvon had Skittles, and he ended up dead and his killer has not even been arrested.

"You have a new assignment," she continued. "I am going to teach you how to write press releases and hold press conferences. I am going to teach you how to use the media to forward a social justice issue and be a voice for the voiceless. Trayvon Martin doesn't have a voice, so now our job is to speak for him. We're going to hold a press conference outside the courthouse in Sanford." Class didn't end until about 9:00 P.M., but the next morning she turned on her BlackBerry to discover that her students had been working throughout the night and had already messaged her a video, in which each student told the story of Trayvon Martin and his shooting in their own voices, becoming his voice beyond the grave and calling for justice.

Ben Crump had been trying to get a meeting with Norman Wolfinger, the longtime state attorney for the Eighteenth Judicial Circuit Court of Florida. But Wolfinger wouldn't—or perhaps couldn't—meet directly with Crump or our family. He agreed to meet with Jasmine Rand, as both a citizen and a professor, along with some of her students. And he agreed to have them meet with his assistant state attorney, Pat Whitaker, at the Seminole County courthouse in Sanford.

Jasmine and her students wouldn't just meet with the assistant state attorney; they would hold a press conference outside after their meeting. To prepare for that, Jasmine taught her students how to write a press release, how to develop media sound bites, and how to lead a mini-protest and mini-movement.

Jasmine got chills and later shared the video with us. When we saw it, we got chills, too. So many young people—fresh, smart, of different nationalities and backgrounds, optimistic and with their lives ahead of them—saying the name of our son and directing that youthful, idealistic energy to his cause. For the first time, we felt that kind of direct connection with people, especially young people, who didn't just share our pain, but were moved to action, to changing things—that was the beginning of a new feeling for me, the sense that Trayvon's spirit was still with us, but not just us. His spirit was motivating a movement.

The day after the video was uploaded, Jasmine took her students to the store, where they bought poster board and markers. That night, in the Parks and Crump law office over pizza and Cokes they made posters. One I remember said "Gun Versus Skittles." Another said "Justice for Trayvon Martin." They finished writing the press release to alert the media of their activities and they prepared the sound bites. They pooled their money, rented a car, reserved two hotel rooms, one for male students and one for female students, and drove to Sanford for their meeting with Assistant State Attorney Pat Whitaker, and to hold their press conference to tell local media what the state attorney planned to do in the case of Trayvon's killer.

Soon into the hour-long meeting it became apparent to Jasmine Rand and her students that the state attorney still didn't seem to have any intention to press charges. The assistant state attorney told them that the investigation by the Sanford Police Department was not as thorough as he would have liked, and that the state attorney's office would launch an investigation that would be "greatly supplemented." But it was what he didn't say that concerned Attorney Rand and her students: the state attorney's investigation seemed to be centering on whether or not the killer's self-defense claim could be proven—instead of whether or not charges of manslaughter, or even murder, would be brought. Attorney Rand and her students felt that the state attorneys, who were supposed to represent the people, still seemed to be on the side of Trayvon's killer. Later, she told us and the legal team that you can't always place a finger on racism, but she and her students felt that the way the state attorney received them and communicated with them led them to think that Trayvon's race was the unspoken X factor in the decision that was already apparent: he had no intention of arresting George Zimmerman.

Attorney Rand and her students were frustrated when they left the meeting, but she pulled them into a private room before they emerged from the courthouse to meet the media. She reminded them that despite what the state attorney just said or how he treated them, they had the ability to walk out of the courthouse and become a voice for Trayvon and advocates for change. Channeling frustration into passion for justice, her students were ready to be our voice in the media. When they emerged from the courthouse, there were around seventy-five other protesters gathered along with the media, singing "We Shall Overcome" and chanting for an immediate arrest.

Jasmine spoke first, then passed the microphone off to her students.

"Are we satisfied? No," said one student of the meeting with the assistant state attorney. "We appreciate the gesture."

"It seems all the people are on Trayvon's side," said another. "The government is on [the killer's] side."

"This is not acceptable," said another student. "There was a time when this was acceptable. That time is not now."

One student, Kendra Neal, said, "He had dreams like we did. But because of this travesty, we'll never know what great successes he would have shared with the world."

After each student expressed their thoughts, they repeated slogans from their posters:

What happened to him could happen to anyone.

No justice for Trayvon, no peace for Sanford.

My skin is not my sin.

Finally, one of the students said: "I am Trayvon Martin." *I am Trayvon Martin,* a phrase that became a rallying cry for people united to fight for justice for our son.

Even in all this darkness, with the screams from those death tapes still echoing in my mind, a light appeared, the possibility that there was some salvation in all of this pain. In the voices of these young people, we began to hear a redemption song for Trayvon that would spread to languages and countries around the world.

"I am Trayvon Martin."

My son's spirit lived.

If the local authorities weren't interested in pursuing charges against the killer of our son, we thought maybe a higher authority would help, and our attorneys began to petition the FBI to step in. By March 21, the FBI and the US Justice Department announced they were investigating Trayvon's death and sending officials to Sanford "to address tension in the community."

A meeting was scheduled between the FBI, members of the U.S. Department of Justice, and us.

Attorney Daryl Parks drove us to the FBI's field office near Orlando, in his rental car. It was the first time we'd met Parks, Crump's partner, who heads the Parks and Crump office. Parks had done some civil rights work in the past, but he said a lawyer would "die trying to do this work exclusively." So when we first signed on with his firm, he was out helping other clients in less controversial circumstances. Eventually, however, he decided he needed to get involved and lend a hand—the case was turning into something larger than any one or two people could handle. We needed a team of attorneys, and we were lucky to have them led by Crump and his partner, Daryl Parks.

Their young associate Jasmine Rand was right when she told us in the beginning that Parks and Crump would fight harder than anybody to have the man who killed our son arrested.

The moment we met Daryl Parks we immediately knew why he and Benjamin Crump had been such a successful team. We also knew we had the best lawyers to find justice for our son. They met as undergraduates at Florida A&M in Tallahassee, where Parks was the president of the student body and Crump was president of the Black Student Union. They ended up at the Florida State University College of Law together, and there they became fast friends and, as legend has it, printed their Parks & Crump business cards before they even graduated.

When they first began practicing law they couldn't afford money for hotels, so if they had court appearances out of town they slept on the sofas of friends and relatives. Neither came from a wealthy family; both were first-generation college students; both had the drive and ingenuity that only struggle can bestow. As Parks and Crump fought tirelessly for their clients in courtrooms across the state, word of the "dynamic duo" and their success spread.

Along with their success in the courtroom came financial success. But Parks and Crump didn't keep the money for themselves; they immediately began giving back to their community, funding scholarships and hosting community events in the beautiful building they purchased in downtown Tallahassee.

By the time we met them, Parks & Crump was more than a law firm; it was a family, and we were lucky to become part of it. Our attorneys—Parks, Crump, Natalie Jackson, and Jasmine Rand—all believed they could make the world a more just place for people like my son. And while they all shared the same vision, Attorney Parks's role was more practical. As the firm's managing partner, he oversaw the legal team. Before major events in our case, and before each court session, we all prayed together. In between, we shared meals together, stayed in the same hotel together. As our bond and love for one another grew, so too did our strength to fight together for Trayvon.

From the moment we met him, Daryl Parks was with us, literally by our side and at our backs, every step of the way. Driving us, counseling us, crying with us, praying with us, staying in hotel rooms down the hallway from us, and guiding us through a legal process that we didn't know anything about.

"The feds play their cards close to their vest," Parks told us on the drive up. "They know everything that's going on, but they don't tell you everything. They invite you to a meeting and you don't necessarily know who is going to be there."

We met the rest of our legal team outside the building: Ben Crump and Natalie Jackson.

We walked inside. When we found the right conference room, I counted at least eighteen feds, including officials from the U.S. Department of Justice, local FBI agents, and a number of armed officers. I didn't know what to make of such a large, intimidating crowd. Were they here to help?

We were told that the U.S. Attorney's Office was going to launch an investigation into what happened the night that Trayvon was killed. We were assured that the federal government was closely watching the case, and would provide whatever resources it had available. They didn't think there was much that could be done from a civil rights standpoint, but if something was found during their investigation they would do all they could to pursue it.

We could feel the weight of the federal government examining the death of our son, and we left the meeting feeling hopeful. But Crump and Parks said we couldn't afford to relax. We had to keep applying the pressure.

At some point during this period, I was walking with Sybrina and our attorneys into Logan's Roadhouse, a casual restaurant in Sanford, when we all started receiving calls, texts, and emails: "Chief Bill Lee stepped down!" He'd only been on the job for ten months, but said he was now temporarily stepping down after a three-to-two no-confidence vote by the Sanford City Commission.

Later that day, we watched the chief's press conference on television—he was standing behind a lectern surrounded by the media. He wore his uniform, with his big brass badge on his chest and four golden stars on his collar, surrounded by microphones, cameras, and reporters in front of the Sanford Police Department, preparing to do what would have been unthinkable less than a month ago, when we were strangers to Sanford: leave the police department because of the shooting of my son.

"My role as the leader of this agency has become a distraction from the investigation," the chief told the media that day. "While I stand by the Sanford Police Department, its personnel, and the investigation that was conducted in regards to the Trayvon Martin case, it is apparent that my involvement in this matter is overshadowing the process. Therefore, I have come to the decision that I must temporarily remove myself from the position as police chief for the City of Sanford. I do this in hopes of restoring some semblance of calm to the city, which has been in turmoil for several weeks."

Later that night, the television was filled with commentary on the chief's resignation. Once again, we weren't sure what to make of the news. But we knew it was the first crack in the Sanford Police Department's wall—the first time they acknowledged that there might be a problem with its investigation.

Crump, as always, rallied us all to use the event to raise the stakes and bring the media heat to a boil. His strategy was always to be relentless, to spot a weakness and exploit it, to find your talking point and drill it over and over and over again. Sybrina and I both went on local news shows the next day. I said that we needed a "permanent solution," not a temporary removal. We needed the immediate arrest of the killer of our son and a full investigation into the Sanford Police Department.

"[I] just felt like the Sanford police department decided on the scene to be judge and jury," Sybrina would say on the *Today* show, where she and I were interviewed side by side with Crump. Earlier she had said, "I just want this guy arrested so he can be brought to justice."

As I had said before, "We aren't looking for revenge, we're looking for justice—the same justice anyone would expect if their son were shot and killed for no reason."

Around this same time, the state attorney, Norman Wolfinger, announced that he was going to convene a grand jury, which sounded to me like a good thing. Crump told us otherwise: "If you take it to a grand jury, that's where cases go to die," he said. "If the case goes to a grand jury, there's a ninety-nine percent chance that they're not going to indict."

He took a breath.

"Lawyers like to say, 'A prosecutor can get an indictment on a ham sandwich if they want to,'" he said. "Because ninety-nine percent of the time the grand jury is going to do what the state attorney or the district attorney wants them to do." But if the prosecutor didn't want an indictment, the case would go away.

So our strategy became to keep our case out of the grand jury and in the public eye. We had to make the pressure to arrest so high in the public that doing anything but making an arrest would seem like an injustice. So on the evening of March 20, we flew to New York for our largest media blitz yet, one television show after another. Sybrina, Crump, and I crisscrossed the city in a black SUV. It was mid-March but still bitter cold. And Sybrina was starting to get run-down physically. She was still a mother in mourning for her child, of course, which would knock anyone out. But she was also now constantly on the move in high-pressure, public situations that were completely new to her. And now she had the flu. She must have gone through three boxes of Kleenex that day. Her body ached, her head hurt, her nose ran, and her heart was broken. But we remained grounded in our faith.

We kept telling our story, with a singular refrain: *Why hasn't the man who shot our son been arrested?*

Our last stop on Wednesday, March 21, was with the Reverend Al Sharpton's show, *Politics Nation,* in his studio at MSNBC.

Before the show, we met "the Rev," as we would soon call him, in his New York office, a small room with a desk and two chairs, the walls lined with plaques and pictures of him with famous faces and families.

He turned to Crump and said, "I'd like to speak with Sybrina and Tracy alone for a moment."

After Crump left, we sat down with Reverend Sharpton, who looked regal in his elegant suit and tie, gray hair, and mustache. He was smaller than I expected, but as he spoke he seemed to grow to match the power of his words.

"I have children and I sympathize with your loss," he said. "Whatever you want me to do, I'm going to do. I'll help you in any way I can and support you. I'm not going to be here now and then I'm gone tomorrow. I'm going to be a longtime supporter."

Reverend Sharpton was as good as his word. He is still fighting with us every day.

He led us into the MSNBC television studio. Sybrina, Crump, and I sat across from the reverend's chair.

The cameras rolled, and Reverend Sharpton stood and started to speak in his big, booming voice, pointing his finger at the camera, demanding justice for the killing of our son. We were all run-down by then, but the interview energized us.

Reverend Sharpton asked Sybrina if she was "determined to hang in there no matter what until this is over."

"Until the day I die," she said. "I'm a mother. And I want justice for my son, and I won't stop until I receive that."

It was getting dark and cold when we left the television studio. Reverend Al walked us outside, and before we climbed back into the SUV, he told us that our day wasn't done. A rally had been planned in Trayvon's honor, the reverend said.

"It would be great if you guys could drive straight over to Union Square, so they can see the parents of Trayvon Martin and you can thank them for their support," he said. "There's going to be a lot of people there. They're calling it the Million Hoodie March."

He added, "Prepare yourself to be amazed."

Once again, strangers descended on our cause like angels. This time, it was Daniel Maree, a clean-cut young black writer, speaker, filmmaker, and activist. After graduating magna cum laude from American University in 2008 he worked as a digital strategist at Interpublic Group, an advertising and communications agency, in New York. Maree had grown up in Johannesburg, South Africa, but had lived in Gainesville, Florida, for three years when he was Trayvon's age. He'd had experiences of being stopped by police as he walked through gated communities, "for no reason other than being a young African American," he said. He saw our story and thought, *That could've been me.*

Outraged, Maree founded what he called Million Hoodies Movement for Justice, and began posting on Twitter with the hashtag #millionhoodies and made a YouTube video, asking people to post pictures of themselves in hoodies and sign the petition on Change .org, whose numbers were still growing at a record rate.

Along with the Twitter posts and the YouTube video, Maree asked supporters to march on Union Square on Wednesday, March 21. In two days' time, Maree, his friends, and his ad agency colleagues had not only organized the rally but had also created a poster, which looked like a poster for a professional boxing match, with a picture of Trayvon in his hoodie and the words:

1,000,000

HOODIE MARCH

FOR

TRAYVON MARTIN

MARCH 21, NYC

6 P.M. TILL 9 P.M., UNION SQUARE

We had been up since before dawn. It had been a long and exhausting day, and we were beat. All of our energy had been spent on the television shows. But we pulled it together and rode over to Union Square in the SUV.

We had always been big believers in the NAACP, the Urban League, and other organizations, and proud of the deeper history of the civil rights movement. But we were private people, far from activists, busy raising a family and keeping food on the table. We didn't know what it meant to be on the front lines of a protest; we didn't even know what a protest looked like before, to be honest, and only had a vague idea of what they were for or how they accomplished anything. Now the logic of protest became clear. It's about numbers.

What we saw as we got closer to Union Square took our breath away: a sea of hoodies stretched across the historic public park. Too many hoodies to count. As far as I knew there could have really been a million hoodies in Union Square that night, representing a million Trayvons, a million young kids at risk of falling dead to gunfire, a million lives already lost and unmourned by the world but still calling out for justice.

The crowd was black and white and everything else, men and women, young and old. There were too many signs, banners, and flags to count. I tried to pick out individuals in the crowd—I saw one young kid, no more than twelve, wearing a red hoodie and holding a sign: "Am I Next?"

I looked over at Sybrina, who I imagined was exhausted and wrung out from the day, from the weeks. I tried to find the words that would help—and I knew that if anything motivated Sybrina, it was a chance to direct her energy toward helping someone else. "We have to stay strong for all of the people who are supporting us," I said.

We got out of the car and were engulfed in that sea of people, all of them trying to get close to us. The New York City police were literally pushing them back until, suddenly, a path cleared. We held onto each other and pushed our way through the thick, cheering crowd.

Sybrina was still sick, but I could feel her strength growing along with mine. Here we were, thousands of miles from home, and so many people beside us. Our spirits were energized.

We were led up to a makeshift stage, a small opening in the crowd, with people still pressing all around us. Daniel Maree was also onstage, looking studious in his black-framed eyeglasses but also wearing a dark hoodie. The hoodies began to cheer and shout.

"We are one! We are one!" they said.

Crump handed me a microphone, and I tried to find more words. I just pulled them from my heart. "Trayvon Martin *did* matter," I said. "I just want New York to know that we're not going to stop until we get justice for Trayvon."

The hoodies cheered.

"Trayvon was your typical teenager. Trayvon did typical teenage things," I continued. "Trayvon was, I repeat, Trayvon was not a bad person. George Zimmerman took Trayvon's life for nothing. George Zimmerman took Trayvon's life, profiling him. Our son did not deserve to die. There's nothing that we can say that will bring him back. But I'm here today to ensure that justice is served and that no other parent has to go through this again."

"We want justice!" I could hear chants surging out from the crowd. "We want peace."

I handed the mic back to Crump.

"Now we will hear from Sybrina Fulton, Trayvon's mother," said Crump.

Sybrina had spoken in public before. But nothing like this. I could feel the emotion rising in her, but had no idea what she'd say.

"My heart is in pain," Sybrina began, her voice shaking. "But to see the support of all of you really makes a difference."

"We love you!" screamed someone in the audience.

She seemed to gain strength from the support of that enthusiastic crowd.

"You probably don't understand how much you guys mean to us," she continued. "But it's the support that we need. We need this kind of support. Our son was not committing any crime."

More cheering.

Then the words arrived, the right words, and I was staggered, like everyone else, by what Sybrina said.

"Our son is your son," she said, and I could see her tremble and shake, but her voice gained power.

"We're going to stand up for justice, and stand up for what's right," she said. "This is not a black and white thing. This is about a right and wrong thing."

The hoodies erupted.

"I am Trayvon Martin!" people chanted. "I *am* Trayvon Martin!"

"Justice for Trayvon! Justice for Trayvon!"

The rally closed with a prayer. "Pray that this happens to no other child," Daniel Maree told the crowd before they left Union Square, thousands strong, and marched through the streets of New York, waving flags and carrying posters that read "Justice 4 Trayvon" and "A Million Hoodies for Trayvon."

On the day that I found out my son died, I was alone in Sanford, feeling a pain I never before imagined, and a helplessness I'd never known. The pain lingered. But the helplessness was gone.

Because now it wasn't just Sybrina and me fighting for answers and justice.

Now it was a nation.

CHAPTER 9

Sybrina

∽

March 22, 2012–March 26, 2012

"Hi, Sweet Candy," attorney Crump began on the phone, which is what he—and everyone else who is close to me—has called me since my grandmother, whom we all called "Nana," gave me the nickname.

"I want to apologize," Crump continued. "I told you that you were going to be free for the next couple of days, but there's this rally . . ."

If he said it once, he said it a million times. *There's this rally. There's this press conference. There's this media appearance.*

In the beginning, I would say, "Crump, you're working me too hard." Because I was still grieving and just wanted to withdraw from the world that killed my son, instead of confronting it.

"Sweet Candy," Crump would say in his most persuasive drawl, "the most important people in defending the legacy of your child are you and Tracy. People *have* to hear from you."

And since it was for Trayvon, Tracy and I never hesitated. We always did as Crump and his partner, Parks, asked us.

. . .

In the days following the Million Hoodie March, rallies supporting Trayvon began popping up across the country. From Sanford to Seattle, San Francisco to New York, thousands upon thousands of Trayvon Martin supporters gathered and gave their prayers, their time, their energy, their anger, and their voices to demanding an immediate arrest and criminal prosecution.

What began as a family tragedy had turned into a national movement. We had a goal, a platform, and supporters from coast to coast all clamoring for justice for Trayvon.

We were constantly on the road, traveling from one media appearance, rally, or event to another, from congressional hearings in Washington, D.C., to town hall events back in Sanford. We could feel the momentum growing everywhere we went.

We kept our bags packed. I had all of my personal things—lotion, toothbrush, and carry-on toiletries—stored in my suitcase; I never took them out. When we did finally come home, it was never for long, just enough time to switch whatever clothes were in the suitcase for a fresh set I kept ready in my closet, and then we were off again, always going. If we couldn't get a flight on time, we drove wherever we needed to.

Soon, I had to buy extra business clothes and suits. The sales people at Dillard's, New York & Company, and Macy's in the Pembroke Lakes Mall near Fort Lauderdale began recognizing me, and, bless them, they sympathized with my loss and treated me with extra care. Before my son's death, I had a few business suits, but not nearly enough to keep up with our nonstop appearances.

Then there were the mirrors. They were everywhere: on planes, in hotel rooms, and in television studios. Sometimes, I would stare into those mirrors and look at myself. My smile had disappeared. I had also lost a lot of weight, which would soon add up to nearly forty pounds and four dress sizes. I chalked it up to grief and depression. Because whenever I wasn't on the road, I just lay around the house.

My mom noticed a strange swelling on one side of my neck, which I ignored at first: *Justice for Trayvon; worry about your health later*, I told myself. Everything was just moving so fast. At night, both at home and in a never-ending series of hotel rooms, I would lie in bed trying to sleep, but my heart was racing like I had run a marathon. *Let me sleep, please let me go to sleep,* I would tell myself. But I couldn't relax. Some nights, my heart pounded so fast I thought I might have a heart attack.

Thank goodness for my family, my friends, and my church community, people I had known since I was a kid. My sister handled the physical logistics: meetings, traveling, getting me where I needed to go. And my best friend, who I've known since grade school, handled the technical details: keeping watch over the Internet and alerting me whenever Trayvon's name or case was mentioned, and handling my Twitter, Facebook, and email accounts.

This enabled Tracy and me to keep going. Our job was to turn these protests into a real movement—one that would lead to an arrest and a prosecution, although it was starting to get even bigger than that. Through our advocacy for Trayvon, we were also shining light on the issues that brought us to this point—profiling, gun violence, and a broken criminal justice system—which helped us engage more and more people in our mission. While we stood in front of the cameras, our attorneys were working behind the scenes—and often right alongside us in front of the media—supporting us and our cause, and trying to get traction on the case.

Of course, along with the incredible outpouring of support came the inevitable backlash of opposition. Hate mail was flooding in, all kinds of hate mail: bundles of letters to Crump's offices and uncountable emails and Web postings expressing hatred toward us and our dead son, making threats. I found it interesting that some of these people threatened to kill Tracy and Crump and used the N-word against them. But with me, and our women attorneys, Natalie Jackson and Jasmine Rand, the threats were sexual in nature: threats of rape and other sexual violence. We did our best to brush it off, but the sheer volume of hateful and violent messages was getting hard to ignore.

We found strength in the endless letters and emails of support from people of different races and from all over the country, including mothers and fathers who identified with us as parents who had lost a child. Donations began to come in to help us pursue the case. Along with the letters and emails came postings on social media— Trayvon was now almost always trending at or near the top of every social media site, driven by the nonstop media coverage, rallies, and protests nationwide.

On March 22, another rally was scheduled in Sanford in Fort Mellon Park. A press conference was scheduled for five P.M., two hours before the seven P.M. rally, which we would attend with our family, friends, Martin Luther King III, and Reverend Sharpton.

Less than an hour before the rally was to begin, we were at our hotel in Lake Mary, a town a comfortable distance away from Sanford. We felt somewhat safe there, away from the media and the city where emotions were running high. People were literally pouring into Sanford for the rally, along with media, both local and national.

Just as we were preparing to leave our hotel, Crump's phone rang. He answered it and came back with what we thought was incredible news: the governor wanted to see us. *Finally,* we thought, *someone with the power to launch a thorough investigation is paying attention.*

We knew that Florida governor Rick Scott had publicly taken an interest in our case. On March 20, he held a press conference, saying, "I'm confident that with FDLE [Florida Department of Law Enforcement], the local law enforcement, and the FBI, that we will find out what happened." Still, we had become skeptical that anyone in Florida government would come to our aid. But now, with media heat intensifying, the governor seemed ready to do something more than give lip service to the case.

We all piled into Attorney Parks's Toyota rental car—me, Tracy, Crump, Parks, and Natalie Jackson—and drove from our hotel to a small city-government building near the park where the rally would be held in Sanford.

On the short ride over, Crump talked a blue streak. "We'll tell the governor why we are so passionate and certain that this is bigger than a Sanford, Florida, issue," he said. "That it's certainly a national issue, and that the government of Florida needs to do something because this case is shameful."

We got out of the car, entered the building, and walked into an office. And there he was, the tall, thin, bald governor, surrounded by his support staff and at least ten uniformed Florida Department of Law Enforcement officers.

"I'm so sorry for the loss of your child," the governor began. He told us that he was a father and that he couldn't imagine our grief, and would do his best to make sure we got some relief. I don't remember him saying that we would get justice, but he did say that he wanted to put all of the resources of his office to make sure that everyone knew that he took our case seriously.

I told the governor that I didn't feel anything was going to be done: no arrest, no trial, no justice. Tracy told him that the Sanford Police Department didn't even look to see if Trayvon lived in the gated community where he was shot and seemed to just take the killer's word—and his side—about everything.

Crump was, of course, always eager to speak, especially to the governor. He told him that everyone knew that the state attorney for Sanford, Norman Wolfinger, wanted to send the case to the grand jury—"where cases go to die," as he repeatedly told us—and didn't seem to want to prosecute the killer of our son.

The governor told us he had already contacted Wolfinger, who would be stepping down from our case. In his place, the governor was appointing by an executive order a special prosecutor: Angela Corey, a veteran of thirty years in the state attorney's office, where, we read, she had tried several hundred cases, including more than fifty homicides, and had built a reputation as a fearless prosecutor. Soon, we would meet her, a medium-built, middle-aged woman with a friendly smile. She told us from the beginning that she was sorry for our loss and would do her best to bring justice for our family. And now she was handling our case.

"This is good," I whispered to Crump.

It was maybe the second victory we'd managed to win—the first being getting the tapes released—in our almost monthlong fight for justice.

"Wow," said Crump, expressing what all of us felt as we left the governor and his team. But we were under no illusions about what had happened. This was only happening because of the media.

That same day, March 22, the governor announced that he was creating a task force to investigate how to make sure a tragedy like this does not happen in the future. The task force would "thoroughly review Florida's 'Stand Your Ground' law and any other laws, rules, regulations, or programs that relate to public safety and citizen protection," according to the governor's news release that day. He would ask Florida Lieutenant Governor Jennifer Carroll to lead the task force, and conduct public hearings and recommend actions—legislation and otherwise—to both protect our citizens and safeguard our rights.

We knew that the Stand Your Ground law would loom large in our fight for justice—and, if the shooter was ever arrested, it could be the law that could lead a jury to let him go free. But the law is unfairly applied by some. Could Trayvon have used Stand Your Ground if he shot the killer? Would he have walked free? I'm sure it would not have been applied had it been Trayvon that did the shooting.

In the research I'd done, I discovered that advocates for Stand Your Ground laws included the powerful National Rifle Association and the secretive American Legislative Exchange Council. It was first pushed, in part, as a measure to help women suffering from domestic violence, to give them legal protection in cases where they defended themselves. But a report by the *Tampa Bay Times* that analyzed 237 Stand Your Ground cases in Florida between 2005 and 2013 found that only 33 were related to domestic disputes. In most cases it was men who claimed the law in defense.

We kept hearing that Stand Your Ground was a bad law, because it was not applied fairly. It was a law that gave someone the right to do bodily harm to a person, even shoot a person dead, and say that the shooting was justified because he felt threatened. That's how it was explained to us in the beginning. Our attorneys told us that Stand Your Ground would be used during the trial. But two months before the trial started, we were told that Stand Your Ground would *not* be used as a defense—although the law would be much discussed outside of the court.

A review of the Stand Your Ground law not only sounded good, it sounded essential for our case.

I almost had to pinch myself. It seemed too good to be true. And it was—nothing really came of that task force.

But we couldn't stop now.

From there, we drove straight to Fort Mellon Park, a big, green lakeside park with playgrounds, tennis courts, picnic tables, and fountains. When we arrived I saw a mini-skyline of thirty-foot satellite antennas rising from a caravan of news vans. Police and news helicopters hovered overhead. The crowd would later be estimated at eight thousand people, but it definitely felt like more than that—they were bused in from Central Florida and Georgia, and some came from as far away as Las Vegas. They lined the streets, waving signs and screaming for justice and crowding in front of the stage where folding chairs and a lectern had been set up for us to speak.

Reverend Sharpton was waiting for us at the park. We had met him before, of course, on his show, but seeing him at a rally was really seeing him in his natural habitat. Seeing him in Sanford, for our son, wearing his beautiful suit and tie, his slick salt-and-pepper hair, vibrating with a righteous anger that always seemed to be on the verge of exploding into words, was an emotional moment.

We gathered together just before we went onstage. Reverend Sharpton hugged me, like he always would when we met, and gave his usual greeting: "Good evening. I am here for you now and until the end."

Shortly before boarding the plane to Florida from New York at six that morning, Reverend Sharpton received word that his mother, Ada Richards Sharpton, had died at eighty-seven. He could have—and most people would have—canceled his appearance at the rally.

"My mother, Ada Sharpton, passed away in the early hours of this morning," Reverend Sharpton tweeted just after learning of his mother's death. "She was my all. I hope God will give her now, PEACE. I love you, Mom."

Then, shortly after that, he tweeted again: "I am on the flight to Florida and will move forward with our plans to protest the killing of Trayvon Martin. My MOM would have wanted me to."

He came to our rally mourning his mother, whose funeral he would plan that night after our rally in Sanford. The emotion of that weighed heavily on all of us, but it also proved to us the meaning of true devotion to a cause.

The rally began and we stood upon a little stage alongside the legends of the civil rights movement, including activist and comedian Dick Gregory, Martin Luther King III, and family members of Rosa Parks, known as "the mother of the freedom movement." Reverend Sharpton was one of the first to speak, and listening to him I felt a dam breaking inside me, inside all of us—all the grief, sorrow, and emotion that we had been feeling finally given its most eloquent, passionate, loudest voice.

"Twenty-six days ago this young man, Trayvon Martin, did nothing criminal, did nothing unethical, went to the store," he said. "He came back and lost his life. Trayvon could have been any one of us. Trayvon represents a reckless disregard for our lives. . . . We come to tell you tonight, 'Enough is enough.' We are tired of going to jail for nothing and others going home for something. Zimmerman should have been arrested that night. Zimmerman had no probable cause that night. You cannot defend yourself against a pack of Skittles and iced tea. Don't talk to us like we're stupid. Don't talk to us like we're ignorant. We love our children like you love yours. Lock him up. . . ."

The crowed erupted in cheers.

"Some people say to me in the media, they say, 'Reverend, seems like a lot of people are angry. Are you afraid of violence?' I say, 'No. I'm afraid of the violence you already have!' Violence is killing Trayvon. Don't act like we are the ones who are violent! . . . We didn't shoot nobody!

"Don't let them trick you," he continued. "They gonna send provocateurs in, talking bad. They are working for the other side. The Trayvon side, we're gonna win this. . . .

"Just you gathering, just what you've done on a grassroots level, we've seen today: the governor put a new prosecutor in. We met with the justice department. The chief said he did a temporary leave. No. We want permanent justice! But though it is good what the governor did . . . we don't just want good. We want to see Zimmerman in handcuffs behind his back charged with the death of this young man, Trayvon Martin. . . ."

The crowd hung on his words.

I could feel the emotion of the crowd welling up, along with my own.

As the cheers grew louder and louder, Reverend Sharpton went on.

He mentioned Tracy and me, as well as his own personal grief. "I got a call at two o'clock this morning from my sister that my mother had died," he said. "One mind said, 'Don't come tonight,' but another mind said that my mother would be ashamed of me if I didn't have the strength to stand up for this man and this woman and their son. My mother didn't raise me to duck a fight; she raised me to stand up and fight."

On Tuesday, he added, he would fly to Alabama. "To bury my mother," he said. "It'll be painful but not as painful as it is for a man and a woman to bury their son. Sons are supposed to bury their mothers. Mothers are not supposed to bury their sons."

Then he mentioned us again. "If they can bear the pain to stand up for us, then we can take the pain to stand up with them. They have woke America up. And they have shown something that this world needs to see. And that is we love our children, like everyone else loves their children. We may not have as much as others have, but we have each other, and we are not going to let anyone take our children from us."

Now we were like family, united in the grief of loss: our son, his mother.

I was, of course, teary-eyed by then. And now I had to speak.

"May we welcome to the platform, welcome to the microphone, the parents of Trayvon," said Reverend Sharpton. "Those that have fought the fight, let us hear from them and give them our love."

Tracy and I came forward, both of us teary-eyed now at what the reverend had said and sad for the loss of his mother. I had gained strength from what Reverend Sharpton had said, and his decision to come to Sanford on this mournful day. Tracy and I thanked the thousands of supporters that showed up for the rally. We told them we loved them and, once again, said that for us, justice meant nothing short of an arrest, followed by a trial and a conviction for the murder of our son.

When I stepped up to the microphone, my voice was still trembling. Just a few weeks ago I was an average mother grieving the loss of a child. Now I was speaking to eight thousand people. I did what I have always done in times of trouble and uncertainty. I took a deep breath, said a short silent prayer, and turned to scripture.

"The Lord is my shepherd," I began, looking out at that sea of people. "Proverbs, the third verse, the fifth and sixth chapters, tells me, 'Trust in the Lord with all your heart, and lean not on your own understanding.' I stand before you today not knowing how I'm talking right now, because my heart hurts for my son. Trayvon is *my* son. Trayvon is *your* son. I just want to say thank you. Thank you for all of your support. . . . We want justice for Trayvon."

The crowd cheered, and with that, I left the podium.

When Tracy finished his comments, syndicated radio and television host Michael Baisden spoke. He had been with us practically from the beginning, one of the first public figures to share our story with his audience on his program, *The Michael Baisden Show*.

"Unarmed 17-year-old boy shot by neighborhood watch captain in Sanford, FL outside of Orlando," Baisden tweeted shortly after Trayvon's death, which was surely the first time many had heard my son's name, and provided a link to a local news story. Baisden then took up Trayvon's death as his personal cause on his radio program, demanding an arrest.

"Sybrina Fulton was right: it's about what's wrong," he said. "And what happened here was wrong. How do you have a black child, or any child, lying in the dirt and nobody even takes a statement from the man who shot him? That ain't right! Tell me that ain't right!"

"That ain't right!" the crowd screamed, raising fists and protest signs high into the Florida night sky.

"Don't even knock on a single door to find out if this child belonged to anybody," Baisden said. "That ain't right!"

"That ain't right!" the crowd chanted back.

"We got a black man in the White House, but we can't get one white man arrested for killing a black child. That ain't right!"

"That ain't right!"

"You can lock up Michael Vick for killing a dog, and we can't get justice for a young black boy! That ain't right!"

"That ain't right!"

The Justice for Trayvon movement was growing stronger by the minute, the hour, and the day.

At Dr. Michael M. Krop Senior High School in Miami, which Trayvon was attending at the time of his death, between three hundred and four hundred students planned to walk out of classes, demanding an arrest.

I was traveling at the time, but immediately called the superintendent of Miami schools and told him that my family and I deeply appreciated the support, but we didn't want kids to miss school. "We don't want them to get in any trouble, and don't want anyone to get hurt," I said.

At Miami Carol City Senior High School, which Trayvon once

attended, the kids marched into the middle of the streets, tying up traffic around the school for blocks—carrying signs and chanting for justice. They also protested at North Miami High School, and many others.

At Miami Southridge Senior High School in Cutler Bay, Florida, administrators and students came up with an imaginative form of protest: the students fanned out onto the football field and organized themselves in a "TM" formation, for Trayvon Martin, that could be seen, and was photographed, from the air. The photograph was seen in newspapers and other media nationwide.

The center of the movement, however, seemed to be my living room. At the time of the shooting, I lived in a split-level, three-bedroom, two-bathroom house in the suburb of Miami Gardens. It was cozy and clean, and I'd carefully decorated it in a way that reflected my own style back to me; it felt like home, a place for family.

But that was all gone now. Now it was a meeting place, a head-quarters, a nexus for the Justice for Trayvon movement. Reverend Al would later tell us, "Movements are not about what you can project. Movements are about what is right. And if you've come together in what is right, God will bless you and the rest will follow."

I was happy to give over my home to the Justice for Trayvon movement. But with that came the realization that it would not be a home again for a very long time. Again, as Reverend Al said, "Anybody can be mad for ninety days. They calculate, 'They'll be mad a couple weeks and go home.' You've got to learn how to organize when the momentum is going against you. You have to learn how to get in the trenches when they disparage you. You have to learn how to be there when the cameras are *not* there, when the newspapers ignore you. That's when you see who you really are. . . ."

The trenches of our movement ran straight through my home.

There was constant traffic in and out of the house. People at all hours of the day and night. My living room television, once devoted to my favorite shows, was now feeding us the latest news on our tragedy. I tried not to watch, and when Tracy would come over and watch the news, it would just upset him. All day, every day, commentators would give their opinions about our son and what had happened to him.

But I wasn't worried about that. All I cared about was an arrest and finding justice, which meant getting the word out to as many people as possible.

Then, seemingly out of the blue, came a supporter who would startle us all.

On March 23, the day after the first big Sanford rally and almost one month after Trayvon's death, Tracy, Jahvaris, and I were in Tracy's truck driving down the turnpike between Sanford and Miami, somewhere near Fort Pierce, when our cellphones began ringing in unison: calls, emails, Facebook messages, tweets, everything at once. Jahvaris and I picked up our phones, and everybody was saying the same thing: *President Obama is talking about Trayvon! Trayvon's name is being mentioned in the White House!*

"The White House?" we all said at once.

Jahvaris pulled up one of hundreds of immediately posted articles on his phone and read it out loud. During a press conference in the Rose Garden, President Obama was asked about Trayvon. Gun violence had become one of the president's highest domestic priorities, and when he spoke of Trayvon his body language and his tone made it clear our case had affected him as a parent.

"Mr. President, can I ask you about the current case in Florida?" a reporter asked at that day's press conference. "Very controversial allegations of lingering racism within our society and of the so-called Stand Your Ground law and the justice in that. Can you comment on the Trayvon Martin case, sir?"

The president paused a moment before speaking. The press conference was not supposed to be about Trayvon, but that is what it would come to be remembered for. President Obama took a breath.

"I'm the head of the executive branch, and the attorney general reports to me, so I've got to be careful about my statements to make sure that we're not impairing any investigation that's taking place right now," he said. "But obviously, this is a tragedy. I can only imagine what these parents are going through. And when I think about this boy, I think about my own kids. And I think every parent in America should be able to understand why it is absolutely imperative that we investigate every aspect of this and that everybody pulls together, federal, state, and local, to figure out exactly how this tragedy happened."

Like the mayor of Sanford, the president was a father. And for a father, or a mother, the Trayvon Martin case was a simple case of right and wrong. I felt that the president was saying, *This could happen to anyone.*

He continued: "So I'm glad that not only is the Justice Department looking into it, I understand now that the governor of the state of Florida has formed a task force to investigate what's taking place. I think all of us have to do some soul-searching to figure out how does something like this happen. And that means that we examine the laws and the context for what happened as well as the specifics of the incident."

I felt he was speaking not only as a parent but as an African American parent of African American children in a country where black children are still so vulnerable to violence of all kinds. Our children can't just be kids; they have to be so much more. Our children don't always feel safe in their own communities.

"My main message is to the parents of Trayvon Martin," the president continued. "You know, if I had a son, he would look like Trayvon. And, I think they are right to expect that all of us as Americans are going to take this with the seriousness it deserves, and that we're going to get to the bottom of exactly what happened."

We were overwhelmed that our tragedy, and our son's name, had reached the White House. We sat in the car stunned. The president of the United States was talking about Trayvon Martin.

By the time Tracy pulled his truck into my driveway, the news was on every television set in my home. Meanwhile, homes across America and around the world were hearing about our case being discussed at the highest possible level.

It took others to put what the president had said in perspective. Once again, as it had been from the start, the media was our best ally.

In the *Washington Post,* Jonathan Capehart would later call President Obama's comments about Trayvon the "most powerful remarks on race since his speech on the subject that saved his presidential campaign in 2008."

Later, President Obama would speak again about Trayvon's death, at another press conference: "You know, when Trayvon Martin was first shot I said that this could have been my son. Another way of saying that is Trayvon Martin could have been me thirty-five years ago."

In saying this, "the President reached past one man and one boy and one case in one small Florida town, across centuries of slavery and oppression and discrimination and self-destructive behavior, and sought to place this charged case in a cultural context . . . ," wrote Charles M. Blow in the *New York Times,* who also noted, "And while words are not actions or solutions, giving voice to a people's pain from The People's house has power."

The president's words unleashed a deluge of support. In Miami, Dwyane Wade, then a shooting guard for the Miami Heat, and his future wife, actress Gabrielle Union, apparently spent several days talking to each other about Trayvon, wondering how they could best join the growing demand for justice. Eventually they decided that Wade could make a bigger statement with his team than he could as an individual.

When the Heat players hit the court in Detroit on March 23, 2012, against the Pistons, several players, including LeBron James, Udonis Haslem, and Dwyane Wade, ran out with messages written on their sneakers: "RIP Trayvon Martin" and "We Want Justice," which they later gave to me as a memorial to my son.

A few hours later, James posted a picture on Twitter and Facebook, encouraged by Wade and Union's idea to make a strong statement about Trayvon. Wade and Union had gathered other Miami Heat players at their hotel in Detroit. Thirteen members of the team were wearing hoodies, their hands in their pockets and their heads bowed.

The post was tagged #WeWantJustice, and it quickly went viral.

"Last Christmas all my oldest son wanted as a gift was hoodies," Wade told the Associated Press, lamenting a world in which an article of clothing worn by a young black man can immediately raise suspicion and guilt. "So when I heard about this a week ago, I thought of my sons. I'm speaking up because I feel it's necessary that we get past the stereotype of young black men and especially with our youth."

"It really is a tragic story," Heat coach Erik Spoelstra told a local newspaper after Twitter and Facebook posts about the team's actions began flooding the Internet. "And the more you learn about it, the more confused you get. But for them to come together, to draw more light on the subject, I think is a powerful move, and we all stand behind them, not only the staff, but the Miami Heat organization."

In Toronto, the New York Knicks' star player, Carmelo Anthony, tweeted a picture of himself head down in a gray hoodie before his game against the Raptors. Across the front of the photo he wrote, "I Am TRAYVON MARTIN!!!!!" in red letters.

Anthony's teammate at the time, Amar'e Stoudemire, who was born and raised less than an hour from Orlando, arrived at Air Canada Centre in a hoodie sweatshirt and wore it, both in solidarity and as a protest, during warm-up.

The National Basketball Players Association, the labor union that represents NBA players, sanctioned these actions. They stood with my family and me, calling for not only an arrest but also an investigation into the Sanford Police Department.

The hoodie had become an instrument of protest. But not for everyone. For some, the hoodie was the root cause of Trayvon's shooting—and therefore the shooting was Trayvon's fault for wearing it. But we all know that this is ridiculous because people from all walks of life wear hoodies. Trayvon's only crime was the color of his skin. The theory that a hoodie could have led to my son's shooting was most prominently presented by Fox News's Geraldo Rivera. "I think the hoodie is as much responsible for Trayvon Martin's death as George Zimmerman was," he said on the *Fox & Friends* show.

"Trayvon Martin, God bless him, an innocent kid, a wonderful kid, a box of Skittles in his hand. He didn't deserve to die," Rivera continued. "But I'll bet you money if he didn't have that hoodie on, that nutty neighborhood watch guy wouldn't have responded in that violent and aggressive way.

"You cannot rehabilitate the hoodie," Rivera concluded.

To which I would say: Trayvon could have taken off the hoodie, but he wouldn't be safe unless he could also have taken off the color of his skin.

Geraldo Rivera's words triggered another explosion in our case. Rivera's own son wrote him to say he was "ashamed" of his father's comments. But Rivera didn't back off. He tweeted, "Parents must do whatever they can to keep their kids safe," meaning make them take off the hoodie.

The reaction was immediate—and fierce.

"What I gotta stroll around rocking a tux 24/7 so I can put others who are ignorant at ease? What about the OTHER side of that coin?" the Roots drummer Questlove tweeted to Rivera. The comedian Aziz Ansari was more direct. "It's really appropriate to tweet this any day, but seriously, F--k you Geraldo," he wrote.

MSNBC's Melissa Harris-Perry opened her weekend morning show with a mock news segment called "Dress Code for Black Safety," which poked fun at legislation banning excessively saggy pants and suggesting black men dress like Steve Urkel, the nerd next door from the 1990s sitcom *Family Matters*. She also held up always elegantly dressed Harvard professor Henry Louis Gates, Jr., as an example of safe attire before showing a 2009 picture of him being arrested for attempting to enter his own home.

. . .

But people like Geraldo Rivera were not relevant in our progress. On March 23, Change.org announced that a petition on its site calling for an arrest had become the fastest-growing petition in its history, with more than 1.5 million signatures.

The movement was growing stronger.

∽⟳∼

March 26, 2012, was the one-month anniversary of my son's death.

One month!

It seemed like a lifetime. But it had only been thirty days.

We had a number of events scheduled to commemorate the day, including a Sanford City Commission meeting to address some of our concerns. The day before would turn out to be a pivotal day in our fight for justice. It began as so many things would begin in our quest for justice: with prayer.

On Sunday, March 25, several prayer vigils were held in Sanford, mostly in the black community of Goldsboro, one of which was attended by Sanford mayor Jeff Triplett along with his two sons. Just south of Sanford, in Eatonville, Florida, the legendary civil rights leader Jesse Jackson, who had come to Florida to attend our rally the next day, spoke with the congregation at Macedonia Missionary Baptist Church, which had been founded in 1882 by newly freed slaves in search of their own place to worship.

That same Sunday, Tracy and I rushed from one media event to another, running between churches, cameras, and microphones, from one end of Sanford to the other.

But we weren't the only ones talking to the media. As it turned out, the death and rape threats and the misguided news segments by people like Geraldo Rivera were only the tip of an ugly iceberg. There were people who wanted us to fail, and who would do anything they could to undermine our case. We were not just demanding justice for Trayvon; we were now also forced to *defend* Trayvon's name against what we believed were leaks to the media, possibly by those in the Sanford Police Department, perhaps also by the killer's supporters and representatives, to discredit Trayvon and cast doubt upon his character and his actions.

We had heard that the police department had split into pro-Zimmerman and pro-Trayvon factions. Leaks to the media seemed to be coming from both sides. There would be a leaked video of the killer arriving at the police station with no apparent injuries. In the weeks and months to come, other photos of him would leak and he would have a swollen and bloody nose, and blood on the back of his head.

Then leaks that focused on Trayvon's character began appearing in the news.

While Bill Lee was still police chief, he had supposedly tried to put an end to the leaks and put his station on lockdown. Our attorney Natalie Jackson told us that one of the reasons Lee lost control was he had originally blamed leaks that were favorable to Trayvon on Sanford's black police officers. So black officers were understandably offended. In fact, there was a sentiment among Sanford's black officers that it would not be advisable for one of them to leak any information since there were so few of them, elevating the risk of being caught.

But the leaks on all sides continued, most of them negative toward Trayvon. First, his school records, which we were told weren't supposed to be released. Not when the student is a minor with no prior police record. But a school administrator released his records to the media.

Then there were the drug and alcohol tests, and background checks, which the authorities felt necessary to do on Trayvon, while not doing drug or alcohol tests on the killer. Trayvon's background check came back clean because he had never been arrested for anything. Once again we felt the sickening prejudice against the victim and toward the killer.

The tests showed traces of THC in Trayvon's system at the time of his death. I didn't know what THC was, but the story of the THC in Trayvon's system became the media story of the day. And so as soon as I came out of the hotel we were staying in, a dozen reporters rushed us, asking, "What do you think of Trayvon being on drugs?"

But he wasn't "on drugs"; he had trace amounts of THC, which I came to learn was the chemical term for marijuana, in his system. Was that a reason to kill him? Hell, no.

On March 26, after a noontime forum hosted by CNN's Roland Martin to discuss the case, we had to confirm reports that one of the reasons for Trayvon's ten-day suspension from school just before his death was for possessing a small bag that contained marijuana residue. We didn't see how it was relevant to the killing of our son.

"They killed my son and now they're trying to kill his reputation," I told a group of reporters, fighting back tears and a growing sense of rage.

I have to admit, I was no good for the rest of the day. I retreated to the hotel room, where I knocked everything off the desk and dresser until it was all over the floor.

"Sybrina, are you all right?" I heard someone say from the hallway. The person had surely heard the crashing commotion.

I wouldn't let anybody in the room. I just cried and cried and cried. And I said, *What is this? THC?* Whatever. I didn't know what it was—until it was leaked and all over the news. I just couldn't believe people were on the news justifying a seventeen-year-old teenager being killed by a twenty-eight-year-old man because he had traces of THC in his blood.

Next, the *Orlando Sentinel* reported that law enforcement officials said that after the killer lost sight of Trayvon and he headed back to his truck, "Trayvon approached him from behind, the two exchanged words and then Trayvon punched him in the nose, sending him to the ground and began beating him." They said Trayvon then climbed on top of him, slamming his pursuer's head into the sidewalk before my son was shot.

We weren't buying it, and neither were some of the most influential columnists in America.

"To believe Zimmerman's scenario," wrote Charles M. Blow in the *New York Times,* "you have to believe that Trayvon, an unarmed boy, a boy so thin that people called him Slimm, a boy whose mother said that he had not had a fight since he was a preschooler, chose that night and that man to attack. You have to believe that Trayvon chose to attack a man who outweighed him by 100 pounds."

City Manager Norton Bonaparte, Jr., said the acting police chief would conduct an internal affairs investigation into the leaks and threatened disciplinary action and possibly termination for those who leaked the reports.

But we never heard of anyone ever being identified, much less disciplined.

So the stories rolled on in the media: every day, every hour, all the time.

What they didn't ask, and what I wanted to know, was this: Why was this information, whether true or false, being leaked out? Before an arrest, much less a trial? We knew that it wasn't coming from our side. I came from government, my career of over twenty years was with Miami-Dade County, so I knew there were rules and processes for handling confidential material. You abide by policies and procedures or you get fired.

But now too many things were being leaked. Things the media— and the public—shouldn't have known if there was an open investigation. Soon they knew things about Trayvon and about the crime scene that even we didn't know—things that we didn't even know were true or not.

In this supercharged atmosphere came the biggest Sanford rally yet, on March 26, 2012, one month after Trayvon's killing.

It began with a meeting with the Sanford City Commission, where we, along with the civil rights leaders and other dignitaries who had flown to Sanford to support us, would be allowed to speak to the commissioners. They all came to support us. There was Reverend

Jackson, Pastor Jamal Bryant, Judge Greg Mathis, NFL star Ray Lewis, and, as always, Reverend Sharpton.

When the word got out about the list of speakers, the city of Sanford was basically shut down. Traffic was at a historic high. Police lined the streets. And everyone was headed toward the Sanford Civic Center, which could hold about 850 people in its auditorium, annex, and lobby.

Tracy and I led a march to the civic center from the First United Methodist Church. We called it the National Trayvon Martin March for Justice, and marching alongside us was our attorney Crump, Reverend Sharpton, Pastor Bryant, and Reverend Jackson, and many other clergy and supporters.

We began at the corner of Fourth Street and Park Avenue, where three churches converge: First United Methodist, Holy Cross Episcopal, and First Presbyterian. Tracy and I and our well-known allies stood at the front in a line of banners and solidarity. And behind us, unbelievably, were thousands. We marched north along Park Avenue for three blocks until we reached First Street, Sanford's main drag, with its restaurants and nearby performing arts theater. We turned right and continued toward the Sanford Chamber of Commerce and continued past the Historic Sanford Welcome Center. At the Chamber, we turned up Sanford Avenue and marched until we reached Seminole Boulevard and the civic center.

"Justice for Trayvon!" we shouted until our throats were raw and our voices raspy.

Soon we arrived at the Sanford Civic Center, which sits on the southern shore of Lake Monroe. A large shade tree guards the entrance, and an overhang runs along the building's front to a small patio with an atrium to the south.

The crowd that marched with us was too large for the civic center auditorium. For the hundreds who were unable to enter the hall, the city had constructed a large closed-circuit TV screen at Fort Mellon Park, which sits adjacent to the civic center, to broadcast the meeting live.

The crowd inside the civic center was large and buzzing with anger, but not violent. As Reverend Sharpton said in our first big Sanford rally, the only shot fired in all of this was the one that killed our son. We were loud in our demands for justice, but there was an understanding that everything was to be done in peace. Violence would only hinder our mission. People filled the hall with chants and cheers. The tension was high, and the speeches would be heated. But it was important to us that everything remain peaceful.

Shortly after five P.M. the town hall meeting began with a welcome from Sanford mayor Jeff Triplett.

"I just want to let everyone know where we've gone over the last week," the mayor said after the benediction and the pledge of allegiance, sitting at a long table with four city commissioners and the city manager. "The city manager, Mr. Bonaparte, and I have flown up to Washington, D.C., to meet with Congresswoman Brown and her congressional delegates and the Department of Justice, and openly asked them to come in and review what we've done, how we've done it, and if we have made a mistake, help us correct it. We've reached out to the FBI and . . . several organizations within the United States Department of Justice, to help us out and take us down the right path.

"I just want to reaffirm from us sitting up here that we truly are in pursuit of truth and justice, and we've looked outside our walls to help people deliver that to us," said the mayor. "And we will take swift and decisive action when that happens."

The mayor surveyed the overstuffed auditorium, his eyes darting quickly back and forth across the expanse of the crowd. I could tell the weight of the moment affected him as both a mayor and as a man. He was a good man caught in a bad situation. He had spoken only four days ago at our rally. But now the city he presided over had become the epicenter of what was fast becoming a new civil rights movement, becoming known not for all the city's progress and beauty, but for what it had failed to do in a racially charged murder that brought a lot of people back to the darkest days of the South.

Velma Williams, the only African American member of the city commission, spoke next, presenting a motion to allow presentations from our group, which the commissioners approved unanimously.

Then Reverend Sharpton spoke. He sternly stared directly at each commissioner, and then introduced perhaps the most powerful symbol in our case: the boxes from Change.org filled with two million signed petitions. Boxes upon boxes of the actual paper petitions stretched in front of the commissioners, representing *two million* signatures, all demanding an arrest, all calling for justice.

I looked over at the commissioners. They didn't seem to react; they just sat with neutral expressions.

"To the commissioners, we come tonight, many from around the country, many from your own community, to bring with the family two million signatures of people petitioning you to execute the immediate arrest of the killer of Trayvon Martin," said Reverend Sharpton.

"We do not need a trial and a jury to make an arrest," he continued once the applause, cheers, and shouting over the dramatic display of the boxes finally quieted down. "An arrest is based on probable cause. Any time you have an unarmed man killed and you have a man on tape saying he was pursuing him . . ."

He paused to let the weight of that sink in. "A man *not* authorized. A man *not* on the national register. A man that has a record of assault. A man who had violence against law enforcement. You have probable cause to make an *arrest*."

The crowd roared and the reverend paused again. He moved on to mention recent talks over Trayvon's issues at school.

"None of that was known or unknown to Mr. Zimmerman," he said. "Because Mr. Zimmerman didn't interview him. *He shot him!*"

Another roar from the crowd.

"You voted no-confidence in the police chief!" he continued, after stating a few facts of the case. "How can you have confidence then in the lack of police action?"

Reverend Sharpton mentioned how our case was conflicting with the world's view of Sanford, a beautiful city on the water with great potential for tourism. "You are risking going down as the Birmingham and Selma of the twenty-first century!" he said. "You are making the world know you as a place of racial intolerance and double standards.

"For one man, would you risk the reputation of a whole city? Zimmerman is not worth the history of this city."

Now the reverend's words became inaudible as the crowd leaped to its feet, in cheers and praise. "You need to arrest him and redeem this city right now!"

The commissioners sat silently, their faces still stern, unmoving.

"As you said, Mr. Mayor, we don't need violence!" the reverend continued. "Let me tell you, we marched, tens of thousands, the other night. Reverend Bryant has marched thousands today. The only violence that has occurred is a month ago when Zimmerman killed this young man. . . . *Do the right thing!* Do the right thing and arrest Zimmerman *now!*"

The crowd erupted in its loudest uproar yet. They stood and shouted Reverend Sharpton's refrain, fists pumping in the air: *"Do the right thing! Do the right thing!"*

Crump, Tracy, and I were next. We followed Crump to the podium, and I could see the commissioners staring back at us. The standard rules of the meeting were to give each commenter five minutes, but under the circumstances Mayor Triplett yielded as much time to Tracy and me as needed. The crowd had started to chant again. "Justice for Trayvon! Justice for Trayvon!"

They quieted as Crump stepped to the lectern.

"Ms. Fulton and Mr. Martin want to say something to you all," Crump said, directing his words at the commissioners. "As I stand here, we want to dialogue with you about a lot of things that went wrong with this investigation. But at the crux of the matter, we would implore you to tell us . . ." and his demand to the commissioners was simple: Why had the Sanford Police Department refused to do "what over two million people thought was the simple performance of their job duty? We want to know as their supervisor . . . what are you going to do about it as Police Chief Lee's employer?"

"The parents are going to talk to you . . . ," Crump continued. "What we want to know, real simple, is, what are you going to do because they did not do their job?"

I was next, and my emotions, as usual, were running high. I had so many breakdowns. Behind the scenes, away from the attorneys and the cameras, I felt so broken. I would go from leading a march or speaking to a crowd or a television audience of hundreds of thousands back to the woman who couldn't get out of her room. Grief would overcome me, and I would sob, scream, fall down on the ground, and think about all of the should-haves, could-haves, and whys. Each time this happened, I would pray and ask God for strength. But I still questioned what happened to my son.

Why wasn't I there for my child on the night he was shot?

He needed his mom. Every child needs their mom.

And I wasn't there to help him.

Everything was a reminder of him. It could be a group of teenagers. A hoodie. A mother with two children, holding each of their hands, reminding me that I was missing one of mine, one of my hands now empty. It could be a song on the radio. And it would plunge me back into that loss, grief, and brokenness, and I would relive his passing all over again.

No one saw this, other than, sometimes, my family. In public, I looked strong—"dignified," so many people said. I wasn't sure that I was. I was determined not to let people see these broken pieces, as Bishop T. D. Jakes calls them, when I would return to my purple bedroom and my grief. When people saw Tracy and me, we were always sitting upright, speaking clearly, standing strong for Trayvon.

"I want to try to get through this without tears," I said, pausing to gather my thoughts and still my nerves.

"My heart is broken," I was finally able to say. "That's first and foremost. That was my baby. And I just want to appeal to you all, if you have kids, if you have children and something happens to your children, you want to know what happened.

"You want some answers to your questions as a parent. So I'm not asking for anything special, any extra favors. I'm just asking for what you would ask for *as a parent*. I know I cannot bring my baby back. But I'm sure going to make changes so that this does not happen to another family."

The crowd cheered. I was near the end of my comments, but I had one more thing to say. As I waited for quiet, I felt a flood of sadness and grief rush through my heart. My voice was still strong, but now it was shaking. I thought of Trayvon and all the pain. I took a deep breath, blinked, and held back the tears.

"Lastly," I added, "I just want to say that God is in control."

Tracy spoke next.

"The greatest gift that God can give to a man is a son," he said, his voice, as always, stern and unshakable. "For the Sanford Police Department to feel as though they were going to sweep another young, black minority death under the rug, it's an atrocity. This family *is hurt*. This family *is torn*, and the Sanford Police Department needs to be held accountable. George Michael Zimmerman needs to be arrested. He needs to be put on trial. He needs to be given a sentence by a jury of his peers. We're not asking for an eye for an eye, we're asking for justice, justice, justice.

"We consider ourselves strong black parents. We take pride in our kids," he said sadly. I watched him speaking and saw that his brow had furrowed and he was starting to clinch the bridge of his nose between his thumb and index finger. A tear dropped as he continued to say, "It tears me apart to sit here and listen to slander they are giving to my son and not arresting the [killer] of my son . . ."

"No justice, no peace! No justice, no peace!" the crowd chanted, louder and louder. Crump tried to speak, but he couldn't be heard, even over the PA system. He raised his hand and turned toward the crowd, pleading with them for quiet.

"We have some important things to talk about," Crump said. "Mr. Mayor, I'm here with Trayvon's mother and father, and they are very, very emotional. Because when we hear those 911 tapes we know where the end is and they know where that tape went. They lost their child at the end of that 911 tape. But as lawyers and as the legal team here, we are going to attempt to divorce ourselves from emotion for a few minutes to ask some questions that we implore you to ponder and use your leadership to make the decisions. We ask that you let your heart be your guide."

Crump went on to list the questions that had still gone unanswered:

Who was the officer who made the decision for whatever reason to not do a background check on George Zimmerman, who had just shot and killed Trayvon Benjamin Martin? But yet saw fit to do a background check on this dead child on the ground?

Number two, who was the officer who made the determination not to do a drug and alcohol analysis on George Zimmerman, who had just shot an unarmed teenager with a bag of Skittles, but yet found it appropriate to order a drug and alcohol analysis of Sybrina and Tracy's son?

Who was the officer who made the determination that we're just going to question Mr. Zimmerman and take his statement as the gospel and let him go home . . . with the clothes and the evidence that he had on his body?

"You all have to hold him accountable," Crump told the commissioners. "Nobody else can do it here this evening. You all have to ask these questions, take the names, and if they did not do their job, would they lose their job?"

The mayor broke in.

"I've stated several times that's the path we are going down," Mayor Triplett responded. "That's the only path. I can't change what transpired. But I swear to you. I swear to you—"

Crump took a moment to silence the crowd again.

"And, Mr. Mayor, we do owe you a debt of gratitude," he told the mayor. "Because it was your leadership to release the 911 tapes.

This family wants to have faith in the system. My God, they've been waiting for so long for them to get simple answers. We don't want anything extra . . . just equal justice. . . . It is hard to ask them to trust you and to have patience. . . . There has to be something where you all have to take a stand to let us know we can believe in you, that you will do the right thing, that you won't sweep it under the rug when the cameras go and when everybody goes home. *Because they're never getting Trayvon Martin back!* And they are depending on you all to do your job, just as we would have prayed that Chief Lee and the Sanford Police Department would have done their jobs."

Crump paused and asked, "Can't you understand that none of this would be going on if they simply would have treated George Zimmerman like they would have treated Trayvon Martin . . ."

He was again interrupted by chants and cheers.

"In conclusion, I would only ask that you consider *your* children when you make these decisions that you have to make," Crump told the commissioners. "And imagine if you can," he said, pausing for a moment to address the commissioners and the city manager, "if that was your child and the police refused to make an arrest. You let your heart and your conscience be your guide and you determine what would you do to your employee who refused to arrest the person that killed your unarmed child. It's as simple as that."

He sat down to thunderous applause.

Still, the commissioners appeared unmoved. I didn't understand what was happening.

The meeting stretched on, as a number of notables spoke, from Reverend Jesse Jackson to political leaders like Marc Morial, former mayor of New Orleans and president of the National Urban League.

Pastor Jamal Bryant, the young, fiery minister from Baltimore who would become one of our most ardent supporters, spoke next, loudly, passionately, and angrily.

"The justice system in Florida is sick," he said. "Thirty days after a young man was brutally and innocently killed, and after the 911 tapes have been released, and after we know exactly who the culprit is, there still is not an arrest. Around the world, people are looking into Sanford trying to figure out how sick is a system that would allow a young boy to be killed and no one is arrested.

"The balance is off in the justice system," he continued. "Today while we are speaking, there are 635,000 black men behind bars, when we are only 12 percent of the US population but 56 percent of the prison population. . . . The reality is that all of us realize that if Mr. Zimmerman happened to have a darker hue of melanin, we would not be waiting for a thorough investigation.

"Trayvon Martin found himself splattered just blocks away from his father's house," he continued. "But that's not the first time we've seen a Martin killed. Just a few years ago on the balcony of the Lorraine Motel we saw another dreamer who was walking toward justice. And because some insecure sniper who couldn't get a real job stood in the bushes and shot down that dreamer so racists believed they could kill the dream. But I stand on behalf of these two million people to tell you the dreamers are still coming."

With that, Jamal Bryant left the podium.

Reverend Jackson spoke next, comparing our tragedy to others, and saying, "If a black vigilante shot a seventeen-year-old white child, he would be in jail today. And maybe he should be. All we really want is one set of rules."

Congresswoman Corrine Brown thanked the mayor for releasing the 911 tapes, then said fifty members of Congress "sent a letter to the United States Justice Department asking that this be investigated as a hate crime." Former New Orleans mayor Marc Morial, president of the National Urban League, encouraged the commissioners to "go on record for the arrest of George Zimmerman. Number two, to repeal the so-called Stand Your Ground, what we call the Shoot to Kill, ordinance. And number three, initiate the effort today to clean up your own police department."

The meeting ended with Congresswoman Sheila Jackson Lee, who said, "The law is on the side for arresting Mr. Zimmerman now."

It was a powerful event, but I worried that it would all be for nothing. We were left uncertain about what would happen next as far as the commissioners were concerned. But at least they had listened, and that was something.

As soon as the commissioners' meeting came to a close, we all made our way across the street to Fort Mellon Park, only a few hundred feet from the Sanford Civic Center, to address our supporters who had watched the event from there. Original police estimates expected ten thousand people. But the newspapers would later report that at least *eight thousand* showed up that day, and some believed it could have been more. It was our biggest rally yet. Despite police concerns, there was no violence, no looting, no arrests, even with so many people in the park. Like us, the people were angry. But also like us they were there for justice, and the route to that, we believed, was through peaceful protest.

"If you're not here in peace, you're not welcome," said Reverend Jackson so many times that day it became a refrain.

Fort Mellon Park has a small stage, which on the night of the rally was positioned between two trucks with large television screens hoisted up high in the air so that everyone could see the stage and hear the speakers. But the stage was so rickety that once we got up there with all the dignitaries—Crump, Reverend Sharpton, Jamal Bryant, Reverend Jackson, and a dozen others—it seemed to be on the verge of collapse.

Once again, we all spoke on that swaying stage, touching on many of the things we had said to the commissioners and reaffirming our stand to fight until justice was served, until an arrest was made. We thanked those who came and reminded them that Trayvon was our son, but he was also their son, too.

All the while my thoughts were swirling. Would the commission do anything? Would Trayvon simply go down as another lost life in a series of lost lives, another injustice in a country filled with them? I would go from despair, thinking *Oh, my God,* to euphoria, thinking *Thank you, God!* Maybe our meeting before the city commissioners would only lead, as we had been told, to more meetings. But looking out on the crowd, I realized, something was already happening. This was immediate. This was powerful. This was thousands upon thousands of people who could not be dismissed or denied. And it would be broadcast to the world.

More affirmation came in the halls of Congress, where three powerful representatives voiced support for our journey to justice: Congresswomen Frederica Wilson, Maxine Waters, and Sheila Jackson Lee. On March 27, thirty days after Trayvon's death, Representative Wilson said in an interview that Trayvon was "hunted down like a rabid dog, he was shot in the street. . . . He was racially profiled. Mr. Zimmerman should be arrested immediately for his own safety."

"I really, personally believe this was a hate crime," Congresswoman Waters told CNN, calling for an end to the Stand Your Ground law. These three brave and outspoken congresswomen would continue to support us, in both their words and their actions.

Around this same time, I received extraordinary support from a more local source: my coworkers at the job I had left a month before. For twenty-four years I worked for the Miami-Dade County Housing Agency. When Trayvon was killed, time off from work under normal circumstances would have been expected, but given the extremity of our situation a few days of funeral leave fell woefully short.

By this time, I had already used up my four weeks of leave and sixty hours of vacation. Then I learned that 192 of my fellow Miami-Dade County colleagues donated 1,362 hours—more than eight months of vacation time worth $40,825—so that I could continue the fight for Trayvon. The donation was made possible by a resolution passed that allowed county employees to donate up to $50,000 in vacation time to any member of my family employed by Miami-Dade County. (One of Trayvon's aunts, who worked as a water and sewer customer service representative, also received nine weeks of donated vacation time from seventy county employees.)

County Commissioner Jose "Pepe" Diaz, who sponsored the resolution with fellow commissioners Bruno Barreiro and, of course, Barbara Jordan, said it was a reaction to "generous county employees [who] have expressed a desire to contribute their earned holiday and annual leave" to Trayvon's aunt and me. I was grateful to all the co-workers who showed me so much love and support.

I was still working, although I would never return to my good county job that I loved at the Miami-Dade Housing Agency. Now, I was in the Justice for Trayvon movement full-time, 24/7.

CHAPTER 10

Tracy

March 27, 2012–July 6, 2012

After the rallies and speeches were over, things started happening. A series of damning dominoes began falling for the man who shot our son.

MARCH 27

The Justice for Trayvon movement moved on to Washington, D.C., where on Capitol Hill we addressed the issue of racial profiling with the House Judiciary Committee.

Before we even went into the chamber, we met with Congresswomen Eleanor Holmes Norton, Sheila Jackson Lee, Frederica Wilson, Maxine Waters, and others to discuss how important our message would be to begin the movement to better protect and value the lives of our nation's young people of color.

Then we walked inside. The chamber was packed. There were important figures from civil rights history in the room, including, right in the front row, former Little Rock Nine member Ernest Gideon

Green, who made history in 1957 by integrating Little Rock Central High School. But more important, maybe, were the young people. A line of teenagers lined up outside the hearing room, hoping to get a spot inside for the hearing. I was starting to believe that Trayvon had inspired his peers to find their place in our long history of activism. I could sense that this generation was ready to take its stand—to fight for their own rights.

There were many speakers: me, Sybrina, Crump, Congresswoman Corrine Brown, even House Speaker John Boehner, who called the shooting of our son a "tragedy."

But the person who might have had the biggest impact spoke the following day: Bobby Rush, then sixty-five, a senior Democratic congressman representing Illinois's First District. Apparently, he was so moved by our story that he wore a gray hoodie beneath his pin-striped suit jacket into the Congressional Chamber. The presiding speaker, Gregg Harper, a Republican from Mississippi's Third District, gave Rush the floor.

He began speaking, and shortly into his remarks, he removed his suit jacket, revealing the sweatshirt and pulling its hood over his head while continuing his speech.

"Racial profiling has to stop, Mr. Speaker," he continued. "Just because someone wears a hoodie does not make them a hoodlum."

Now he replaced his eyeglasses with a pair of sunglasses.

As he began reading from the Bible, reminding us that the Lord requires us to do justly, love mercifully, and walk humbly with your God, Speaker Harper began pounding his gavel, calling on Rush to stop speaking. But Bobby Rush raised his voice higher, and moved on to another passage as he hung his jacket on the podium—while Harper banged his gavel incessantly, louder and louder, demanding for Rush to stop speaking.

"May God bless Trayvon Martin's soul, his family, and . . ." Rush's words trailed off as the microphone at the podium was disconnected and he was escorted out of the room, calling for justice until he was on the other side of the House doors.

Harper requested that the sergeant at arms "enforce the prohibition on decorum," reminding House members of a rule that prohibited them from wearing hats in the chamber—although a hoodie is not a hat. "The chair finds the donning of a hood is not consistent with this rule," he said. "Members need to remove their hoods or leave the floor."

We reached out to Bobby Rush and gave him a big thanks.

MARCH 31

Another big rally in Sanford, this one beginning in Goldsboro, the African American community in Sanford. A thousand people were led through the historic streets by Reverend Al Sharpton, Reverend Jesse Jackson, and NAACP president Benjamin Jealous. More people lined the sidewalks and watched from porches and balconies as the demonstration marched through the neighborhood to the front of the Sanford Police Department, where an NAACP meeting would be held.

In these early rallies, and the larger ones that followed, we felt our best chance for justice was peaceful demonstration, as opposed to violence, even though we personally felt as much anger as the people in Ferguson, Missouri, did, where the police killing of Michael Brown, in August 2014, would turn into violence that raged for days and nights. We had to think strategically. We were being advised by veterans of the civil rights movement as well as the new activists. What good would it have done to tear up our own neighborhood? Whether it's Miami Gardens outside Miami or the African American community of Goldsboro in Sanford? It wasn't about people over property—we didn't just care about depreciating the value of where we lived, we were concerned with no one else being killed.

Others saw things differently. People wanted to get involved but didn't know how, didn't know what to do. People were doing things that we couldn't control: like putting a $10,000 bounty "for the capture" of the killer. We prayed that things didn't explode, which, we knew, could happen slowly—and then quickly. It could be something as simple as burning a garbage can. And then someone else throws that garbage can through a store window. And the spark lights the fire and burns the neighborhood down, leaving—what?—ashes, more rage, and no progress.

People were ready to burn, loot, destroy. I understood the anger myself, but I had my own brushes with anger and the damage it can cause earlier in my life and had always taught Tray and my other kids to find better ways to deal with conflict, with rage, even when it's justifiable rage. It would be hypocritical to promote violence now, in my son's name. If we promoted that, what would it do? We weren't here to express our rage and then go home; we were trying to seek justice.

As Sybrina would later say, "We know that Trayvon won't be able to rest in peace until there is peace." If we held our heads and our mission high, we felt sure that justice would prevail.

When the rally arrived at the Sanford police station on March 31, the crowd gathered around a temporary stage set up by the NAACP with their seal on either side, a podium in the middle, and a huge picture of Trayvon in his hoodie as a backdrop.

Benjamin Jealous spoke and so did Reverend Jackson. By the time they were done, with their rousing remarks, the crowd had reached a fever pitch, chanting and cheering, crowding closer to the stage. Now a member of the NAACP introduced Reverend Sharpton. As he listed Sharpton's past achievements, the crowd began shouting, "Bring him on! Bring him on!"

Reverend Sharpton took the stage, absorbing the applause, and before it completely died down, he spoke into the microphone. "No justice!" he said.

And the crowd roared back, "No peace!"

"No justice," said the reverend.

"No peace!"

"What do we want?" he asked.

"Justice!"

"When do we want it?"

"Now!"

"I am," Reverend Sharpton said to end his electric entrance.

"Trayvon!" responded the crowd.

"I am!"

"Trayvon!"

"I am!"

"Trayvon!"

"I am!"

"Trayvon!"

"All right," Sharpton said as he quieted the crowd and began his speech, another passionate exhortation for justice. He finished it with these words:

> We are living in the middle of an American paradox. We've made great progress, and at the same time in some areas we haven't moved at all. The American paradox, that we can put a black man in the White House but we can't walk a black child through a gated neighborhood. . . . We are not selling out, bowing out or backing down until there is justice for Trayvon Martin.

APRIL 6

Enter the Dream Defenders, a group of forty activists, including college students, graduates, and organizers, banded together by Umi Selah (formerly Phillip Agnew), a twenty-seven-year-old former pharmaceutical salesman from Chicago, now living in Miami. Selah was so moved by our story that he quit his job and created the group, named for their mission to defend the "dream" of Dr. Martin Luther King, Jr. Most were from Florida colleges, but others came from as far away as Atlanta to participate in a march "against racial profiling, institutional racism, and the legacy of violence," according to the group's leaders.

The group marched for three days and forty miles, from Daytona Beach to Sanford. What made the march so beautiful to me, was that the young people were going beyond just demanding justice for Trayvon and for an arrest. They were also using this moment to move civil rights forward and maintain the energy and enthusiasm surrounding Trayvon's death to create long-lasting change. I once again felt my son's presence in these people, proud that even though he was gone and would never be able to go to college or become an activist, his spirit lived on in the actions of young people.

On the march's final day the Dream Defenders entered the city of Sanford, led by two students holding a banner that read "We Are Trayvon Martin." They knelt in front of the Sanford police station, blocking its doors, and preventing people from entering or exiting.

The next morning the Sanford Police Department was shut down, closing its doors to the public for the day. The Dream Defenders had shut down the Sanford police station! They remained kneeling in front of the building, praying for Trayvon and our family, praying for justice, praying for this country. They also met with city leaders, hoping their voices were heard but knowing either way they would keep fighting for what's right, in the hope that, as the Defenders' leader, Umi Selah, said, their struggle would awaken the country.

APRIL 10

The strangest thing yet: the killer had *disappeared*.

At least from his attorneys, who held a surreal press conference in front of the Seminole County Courthouse in Sanford. The attorneys, Craig Sonner and Hal Uhrig, announced they would be withdrawing as his legal counsel. Their reason? They had lost control of and contact with their client.

They could not find him.

Although they had never met him in person, they had been communicating with him daily via phone and email. Now they had lost track of him and hadn't been able to reach him for two days, although they seemed certain he was still in the United States.

Meanwhile, the killer made an off-the-record phone call to Fox News commentator Sean Hannity and even tried to contact special prosecutor Angela Corey. But the attorney said that she had refused to speak with him without counsel.

The killer had even set up his own website called The Real George Zimmerman, where he was collecting money and communicating electronically with supporters.

"As a result of the incident and subsequent media coverage, I have been forced to leave my home, my school, my employer, my family and ultimately, my entire life," he wrote on his website. "This website's sole purpose is to ensure my supporters they are receiving my full attention without any intermediaries."

He was asking for people to take care of him, and people crawled out of the woodwork to actually do it! I was sickened by it.

The news of his disappearance was surprising. We knew he had been in hiding, and we would later learn that he was wearing a bulletproof vest, but we had been under the impression he was still in Florida. When his attorneys further announced that he had likely left the state, we became concerned that he had become a flight risk. Crump issued a statement on our behalf. Some experts wondered if these developments would force Angela Corey's hand in issuing a warrant for his arrest sooner than she would have liked.

But as far as the state was concerned, this was a nonissue. The fact remained that until there was a warrant he was free to go wherever he wanted.

APRIL 11

The biggest and most important domino dropped thus far.

We were in Washington at Reverend Sharpton's National Action Network's annual convention, with Pastor Jamal Bryant, Reverend Sharpton, and our attorneys Parks and Crump. The conference room was filled with representatives from the NAACP and the Urban League, all working on strategies for our case, when word came that Angela Corey was going to hold a press conference.

It had been forty-five agonizing and crazy-busy days since our son's shooting. Before going on television for the press conference, Angela Corey had called Ben Crump and said something to this effect: she and her team had met and believed they had enough evidence to charge and arrest the killer, whose story, they came to believe, didn't add up. The charges would reflect the state attorney's belief that the killer had, for all intents and purposes, stalked Trayvon before he shot him. Just as we'd felt all along.

Then she called me. My heart was pounding uncontrollably from all the tension of the moment, and I barely heard anything she said until she got to these words: "We are charging him for the death of Trayvon."

She then spoke to Sybrina, and when they were done, a small group met in a side room in front of a television and waited for the press conference to begin.

Finally, there she was, wearing a red jacket and standing between two American flags on a stage in Sanford, members of the police department and her legal team beside her.

"Just moments ago, we spoke by phone with Sybrina Fulton and Tracy Martin," she began. "It was less than three weeks ago that we told those sweet parents that we would get answers to all their questions, no matter where our quest for the truth led us. And it is the search for justice for Trayvon that has brought us to this moment. The team here with me has worked tirelessly, looking for answers in Trayvon Martin's death."

She introduced the prosecutors, John Guy and Bernie de la Rionda, and gave some acknowledgments to those who had assisted in the investigation. She said they didn't take anything in the case—or the arrest—lightly, and offered some details of their investigation. She said that they were trying to seal out the public clamor around the case; she and her office's mission was to seek the truth.

"Today, we filed an information charging George Zimmerman with murder in the second degree," she said. "A capias has been issued for his arrest. With the filing of that information and the issuance of a capias, he will have the right to appear in front of a magistrate in Seminole County within twenty-four hours of his arrest, and thus formal prosecution will begin.

"We thank all of those people across this country who have sent positive energy and prayers our way. We ask you to continue to pray for Trayvon's family as well as for our prosecution team. I want to especially thank Mr. Crump and Mr. Parks, who have stayed in touch daily with us on behalf of our victim's family. Remember it is Trayvon's family that are our constitutional victims and who have the right to know the critical stages of these proceedings." Corey then confirmed that the killer had already turned himself in.

It felt like the weight of the world had been lifted from us.

We thanked God. We prayed. This was what we had been waiting forty-five days to happen. All the long hours of traveling, all the time away from our families, all the strain of watching Trayvon criticized by strangers, all of that had brought us here. Our voices, voices they had tried to silence through inaction, were being heard. Our son might yet rest in peace.

After Angela Corey finished speaking at the press conference, I turned to Sybrina. Tears were running down both of our faces.

"I told you we were going to get justice," I said.

I can't say I always believed this would happen, because in the beginning it didn't look like it would. But we kept our faith and had been waiting for this moment. We knew this wasn't the end, but just another beginning. There was still much more work to do.

But we finally had a chance at justice.

At last, we had proof that our belief in the American system of justice was justified.

Sybrina was overcome with emotion, immediately reverting from activist to mother in mourning, and she cried and cried, with grief and gratitude, and finally relief. We would have our day in court.

I took Sybrina's hand.

She took Jahvaris's hand.

And we silently took Trayvon's hand.

"We're going to get justice," I said. "We're going to get justice for Trayvon."

The killer had turned himself in to the state police in Jacksonville and was then driven to the John E. Polk Correctional Facility in Sanford, where he was photographed entering the building with a black coat hiding his head.

After the arrest we were amazed at, and grateful for, the legions of people, some of them famous, who were still coming to our side. Some came through social media, others in person at marches, rallies, and personal appearances.

APRIL 12

The next day, the killer appeared in court in a gray prison jumpsuit, beside his attorney, Mark O'Mara, who said Zimmerman had no money and that he would be providing representation without charge.

We weren't there, but we saw the media coverage and heard from prosecutors. The killer, in shackles with his hair cut close to his scalp and wearing a few days' growth of beard, kept his composure during his first court appearance, but he appeared shocked and dazed as he stood beside O'Mara, who would represent the killer with his co-counsel Don West.

I first saw them on the television news and read about them in newspapers. They were two middle-aged Orlando lawyers in suits, and while I was told they had impressive law school educations and résumés, they were now representing the killer of my son. So we were adversaries from the start.

The team would be led by O'Mara, a tall, redheaded longtime trial lawyer, originally from Queens, New York, who was soon all over the media, including in this account from NBC:

"The central Florida defense attorney and former prosecutor has nearly 30 years of experience under his belt, representing clients in criminal cases ranging from drunk driving to the death penalty. He also has clocked time in front of the television cameras, serving as a legal analyst for local station WKMG Channel 6, where he commented on high-profile cases, including the Casey Anthony case and even the Martin one— before he was hired to represent Zimmerman."

Don West, a pale, bald longtime Orlando defense attorney, had come to Florida to start a private law practice in the 1980s.

"Before he joined the Zimmerman team, West had already handled some of the most high-profile criminal cases in the Orlando area in the past 20 years," reported *The Orlando Sentinel*. "In 1998, he served as co-counsel and helped Joseph 'Crazy Joe' Spaziano get off death row. Spaziano is the former motorcycle gang member who was convicted of raping and murdering an Orlando teenager, whose body was found in an Altamonte Springs dump. West also represented Orlando music mogul Lou Pearlman on bank-, mail- and wire-fraud charges . . ."

Orlando attorneys would reap national exposure from the case.

Compared to the defense, our team was low-key but solid. Overseen by Angela Corey, the prosecutors were Bernardo "Bernie" de la Rionda, John Guy, and Richard Mantei.

Bernie was born in Cuba but came to the United States at four years old, when his parents put him onto a cargo plane to escape the Castro regime. Raised by his grandparents in Miami, "he never saw his parents again," according to the *Orlando Sentinel*.

As the lead prosecutor, he had a reputation for being tough on crime, sometimes emotional in his court presentations, and aiming for the most severe punishments: his county accounted for a quarter of the death sentences in the state, even though by population it was only five percent of the state according to media reports. Assistant State Attorney John Guy had tried what the media estimated at a hundred cases since becoming a prosecutor in 1993. Richard Mantei had also prosecuted a number of high-profile murder cases.

O'Mara assured Judge Jessica Recksiedler, as well as the media, that his client would plead not guilty, a move we more than expected. And although O'Mara stressed he would attempt to get his client out of jail as soon as possible, we knew he would remain behind bars at least until the bond hearing.

APRIL 18

Two days before the scheduled bond hearing, Judge Recksiedler announced she was removing herself from the case due to an apparent conflict of interest—a move requested by O'Mara. Recksiedler's husband, Jason Recksiedler, was a partner at the firm of Mark NeJame, who had recommended O'Mara to the killer and his family. Judge Kenneth Lester, Jr., was immediately tapped as her replacement—a good development, our attorney Natalie Jackson told us.

"He's one of the smartest judges on the bench, but also one who makes up his own mind," she told us. "You know Judge Lester is going to read the file and know all of the information in that file."

She gave us a quick rundown on his background. He was a fifteen-year veteran of the court. He'd served in combat in Vietnam. He went by the book—he addressed lawyers formally using their full names.

APRIL 20

The first time we came face-to-face with the man who killed our son was at his April 20 bond hearing in the Seminole County Courthouse in Sanford, Florida. It was about nine in the morning, and Sybrina, our attorneys, Jahvaris, and I stood in a little side room in the court's hallway, and we prayed.

We did this before every major event—we'd ask for strength, composure, and guidance, so that we could keep ourselves together. But the prayer was also an affirmation that no matter what we did, our faith was in God's ultimate authority to render justice, no matter what happened in the court that day.

"Keep cool, Tracy," Crump said as we took our seats in the courtroom. He could tell that I was on edge, he told me, because he noticed my legs were bouncing up and down even when I was sitting still. My whole body seemed to be shaking.

The hearing was to determine if Judge Lester would allow the defendant to be released on bond. The only people in court were the defense lawyers, the prosecutors, and us. And of course the defendant. The killer's family did not attend. They would testify by phone due to alleged threats to their life and safety.

The killer entered the courtroom from the left wing, escorted by two police officers. He wore a dark suit and a gray tie with restraints around his wrists that were chained to his waist, instead of the traditional handcuffs that would have bound his hands together. And there were no cuffs on his ankles. So he was able to walk into court like a regular citizen, which Crump later told me would have been unusual had a jury been present. The shock appeared to have worn off since his first court appearance. He was clean-shaven. He took a seat at the defense table next to Mark O'Mara, where he sat quietly with a neutral expression, aware but not engaged.

And inside I raged.

The man who killed my son was now sitting only twenty feet away from me. Sybrina sat beside me, and Crump was nearby at the end of the bench in the first row. There was a wooden divider between my son's killer and me, designed to block people in the audience from the counsel tables. And the man who killed my son was sitting right there.

Before he was called to take the stand, I sat there looking at him as he stared blankly ahead, and once again I could feel my body starting to shake.

"Keep your cool, keep your composure," Crump whispered. "Tracy, please make sure that we don't do anything inappropriate here."

Crump always reminded Sybrina and me to keep our emotions under control no matter what happened. Because we would be judged as much as—if not more than—the man who had been arrested and was about to stand trial. We were parents of the victim, but we were black parents of a black teenager—whatever sympathy the general public had for us would vanish if we ever truly showed all the anger and frustration we felt. But I felt tested like never before in the presence of the killer. My neck tingled. My hands shook. All I could think of was destroying the man who took my son's life.

"God is in control, and we don't need to help God," Crump whispered in my ear. "God is going to make sure that this wrong is made right; we don't have to do anything more at this point."

But I wanted more; I wanted revenge.

As these thoughts bubbled up inside me, I tried my best to keep them at bay. I looked over at Sybrina, who was beside me. She seemed calm, just rocking back and forth quietly. She held her Bible, silently praying.

Judge Lester began speaking.

"Good morning," he said. "Let's call case number 2012-1083, *State of Florida versus George Zimmerman.*"

Attorney Mark O'Mara was allowed to speak first. He handed over his client's passport to the court and then called his first character witness, the defendant's wife, Shellie.

Testifying by phone, Shellie Zimmerman's voice could be heard on the court's loudspeakers as she was sworn in. After receiving her promise that she'd do everything in her power to guarantee that her husband made his court appearances, O'Mara began asking Shellie questions about her family's financial status in order to determine the bond amount.

"Are you working presently?" O'Mara asked.

"No, I'm not," Shellie said.

". . . What do you do with your time?"

"I'm a nursing student."

"Is that a full-time endeavor presently?"

"Yes it is . . ."

"So you're not earning any income presently?"

"Correct."

O'Mara continued asking questions: Did they own their home? ("No, sir.") Did they have assets that could be sold to pay for a bond?

"None that I know of," she said.

"Are you of any financial means where you could assist in those costs?"

"Not that I'm aware of."

Shellie Zimmerman again confirmed that she and her husband's family would take on the responsibility "to scrape up anything that we possible can" to meet the conditions of his bond. She also discussed the family's fear that some harm might come to her or her husband should information about where he would be released be made public. She maintained that George Zimmerman was not a danger to the community.

I held my raging thoughts in my head, but I felt like destruction.

Then, Bernie de la Rionda began his cross-examination of the defendant's wife.

"You stated that you don't believe your husband is a danger to the community. Is that correct?" de la Rionda asked.

"That is correct," Shellie replied.

"You are aware of what he's been charged with, that is, second-degree murder. Correct?"

"Yes, I'm aware of that."

"That is a crime of violence. Would you not agree?"

"I agree . . ."

"And, ma'am, would you not agree that your husband had a violent history?"

"No, I do not agree with that."

"So, were you not aware when he got arrested for a violent crime in Orange County?"

"I'm aware of that situation."

"And did that not involve him striking or in some way battering a law enforcement officer?"

"No."

"Did you talk to him about it?"

"Yes, I have."

"Did he tell you that he was arrested and charged with various crimes, battery to a law enforcement officer and obstructing justice?"

"Yes, he has informed me of those charges . . ."

"Did you read the arrest document to that charge, ma'am?"

"No."

De la Rionda then submitted the arrest document to the court and to O'Mara, and read the pertinent parts to Shellie.

" 'I identified myself as a state police officer and showed Zimmerman my badge and asked him to leave the area,' " de la Rionda read. " 'He stated, "I don't care who you are." I again asked Zimmerman to leave. He stated the F-word and he said "you." At that time I attempted to escort Zimmerman from the interview room and he shrugged away from me and pushed my arms away with his hands. After a short struggle he was placed in handcuffs and detained.' "

Shellie said she had discussed the incident with her husband, but continued to deny it proved a history of violence. De la Rionda then asked about an injunction filed against the killer by another woman, reading from the injunction: " 'He picked me up and threw me on the bed. . . . I got up to leave and he grabbed me again . . .' "

"You weren't aware of that incident?" de la Rionda asked.

"I am aware he had to protect himself from being attacked from her," Shellie said. "And there was blood drawn on him from her, and he also filed an injunction against her."

De la Rionda asked, "Now, so despite those two incidents, the prior arrest involving a law enforcement officer and the incident involving the injunction, you still assess or determine or tell the court that he is not a violent person or a threat to the community?"

"Absolutely, he is not a violent person, nor a threat to the community," said Shellie Zimmerman, of the same man who, she would later claim during a 911 call on September 9, 2013, accosted her father.

After O'Mara questioned Shellie Zimmerman, the next witness was called: the killer's father, Robert. He also testified by phone, answering the same questions about ensuring that his son would show up to court and stated that he would take out a second mortgage on his home if the court required it for his son's release.

"Do you believe that your son is a violent person?" O'Mara asked.

"Absolutely not," Robert answered.

"Can you expound on that?"

"I have never known him to be violent at all, unless he was provoked, and then he would turn the other cheek."

We couldn't believe what we were hearing. This man who shot our son was the type to "turn his cheek" when provoked?

De la Rionda soon stood to cross-examine Robert Zimmerman.

"You mentioned your son was not a violent person, is that correct?" de la Rionda asked.

"Absolutely," Robert said.

"In fact, if I wrote it correctly, you said that you've never seen him be violent unless he's provoked, and even then, you say, he turned the other cheek, is that correct?"

"That's correct."

"You're aware of what he's charged with in terms of murder, correct? And you were not a witness . . . there to see what happened, correct?"

"No, I was not."

"You are aware of his prior arrests involving violence, are you not?"

"I am aware of an incident involving alcoholic beverage control officers in plain clothes . . ."

"Did you discuss that matter of his prior arrest with your son?"

"Yes, I did."

"And did he tell you in that particular case he turned the other cheek?"

"Well, he did. A friend of his was grabbed and thrown up against a wall by some people in civilian clothes."

De la Rionda had already established Robert's past as a magistrate before continuing with questions about the killer's prior arrest.

"Did he tell you that they asked him to leave and he told them 'I don't care who you are' when the officer identified himself as a law enforcement officer?"

"No."

"Did you ever read the actual arrest file?"

"No, I did not."

"Were you not curious out of being a magistrate in terms of whether your son was telling you the truth or just for curiosity's sake?"

"I never questioned whether my son was telling me the truth."

Next to take the stand, again by phone, was the defendant's mother, Gladys.

"Did he discuss with you his arrest at the hands of Alcohol, Firearms and Tobacco officers?" O'Mara asked.

"Yes, he did. That was a long time ago," Gladys answered.

And she said the same thing as the others: George was pushed, and merely wanted to defend a friend.

Hearing the killer's family members speak about him in positive ways was sickening and disturbing. My stomach churned. Again I wanted to stand up and scream, and the only thing that kept me in my chair were Crump's words: "You will be judged as much as—if not more than—George Zimmerman."

Bernie de la Rionda cross-examined Gladys Zimmerman briefly before dismissing her.

O'Mara called his next witness: Dale Gilbreath, the bearded lead investigator with the state attorney's office with thirty-five years' experience. He signed the probable-cause affidavit with co-investigator T. C. O'Steen that said Trayvon "was profiled by George Zimmerman," who "assumed Martin was a criminal."

"Disregarding the dispatcher's request not to pursue Trayvon, the shooter, who said, 'These assholes, they always get away,' and also said 'These fucking punks . . . confronted Martin and a struggle ensued,' read the affidavit."

"Witnesses heard people arguing and what sounded like a struggle," the affidavit continued. "During this time period witnesses heard numerous calls for help and some of these were recorded in 911 calls to police. Trayvon Martin's mother has reviewed the 911 calls and identified the voice crying for help as Trayvon Martin's voice."

"If I say to you the word 'peanut butter,' what do you think?" O'Mara asked Dale Gilbreath on the witness stand.

"Jelly."

"Okay, Moe, Larry, and—"

"Curly."

"When I say the word 'profiling,' what do you think?"

"I believe you're applying a predetermined thought pattern to a set of circumstances."

"No other word comes to mind when I say 'profiled' to you?"

"I gave you my answer, sir . . ."

For some reason, it seemed, O'Mara wanted to get the investigator to introduce the idea of racial profiling. I didn't understand why.

O'Mara continued to pull apart the affidavit, down to its smallest details.

De la Rionda cross-examined Gilbreath, recounting many of the events the night Trayvon was killed before also parsing through the affidavit.

"Why did you use the word 'confronted,' sir?" de la Rionda asked Gilbreath.

"Because Zimmerman met with Martin and it was compiling the facts that we had along with the witness statements of the argumentative voices and the authoritative voice being given from one of the witnesses and then the struggle that ensued that came from several witnesses."

De la Rionda soon rested, but O'Mara had one counterattack.

"So do you know who started the fight," he asked.

"Do I know?"

"Right."

"No."

"Do you have any evidence that supports who may have started the fight?"

"No."

"Mr. Zimmerman gave a statement that very night, did he not?"

"Yes."

"And within that statement, he said that he saw somebody, he was concerned, he got out of his car, he called nonemergency, and began to go towards the person. Is that paraphrasing but pretty correct so far?"

"Paraphrasing, yes."

O'Mara continued to question Gilbreath, getting him to admit that although he had no evidence as to who started the fight, and while he had never spoken with George Zimmerman himself, Zimmerman did claim that he was the victim and that it was Trayvon who had "confronted him and assaulted him" in the initial interview conducted by the Sanford Police Department within an hour and a half of my son's death.

"Do you have any evidence to contradict or that conflicts with his contention given before he knew any of the evidence that would conflict with the fact that he stated 'I walked back to my car'?"

"No. . . ."

"Any evidence that conflicts any eyewitnesses, anything that conflicts with the contention that Mr. Martin assaulted first?"

"That contention that was given to us by him, other than filling in the figures being one following or chasing the other one, as to who threw the first blow, no."

"Now, you know, as one of the chief investigators, that is the primary focus in this case, is it not?"

"There are many focuses in this case . . . ," he said.

"Nothing further."

The confrontational back-and-forth took me by surprise. De la Rionda then stood. "Mr. Gilbreath, I didn't know we were going to be trying the case," he said. "I apologize. I want to add some questions. You had reviewed or other members of the team had reviewed [the defendant's] interviews, is that not true?"

"That is . . . ," Gilbreath said.

"And isn't it true that a lot of statements that he made do not make sense in terms of the injuries that he described? Did he not describe to the police that Mr. Martin had him on the ground and kept bashing his head on the concrete over and over and just physically beating him with his hands?"

"He has said that, yes."

"And isn't it true that there is evidence that indicates that's not true?"

"Yes."

"Did he not state or claim that the victim in this case, Mr. Martin, put both hands one over his mouth and one over his nose so that he couldn't breathe?"

"Yes."

"And all of a sudden that's when he was able to get free and grab the gun? Or, I'm sorry, Martin was grabbing for the gun, did he not claim that, too, at some point?"

"Yes."

"But, and I'm not going to get into every little contradiction, but wouldn't you agree that a lot of his statements can be contradicted by the evidence, either witnesses, or just based on what he says himself?"

"Yes."

De la Rionda had no further questions. After a few more questions from O'Mara, Gilbreath was dismissed and O'Mara stood to address Judge Lester.

"My client wants to make a statement to the court, Your Honor," he said.

The defendant was going to take the stand? Another surprise. I braced myself. The killer approached the bench to be sworn in. Because he was in shackles, he was only able to raise his right hand halfway as he took the oath. He then sat down at the witness stand. He seemed to be looking somewhere into the distance, but he addressed Sybrina and me, although not by name.

"I wanted to say I am sorry for the loss of your son," he said. "I did not know how old he was. I thought he was a little bit younger than I am, and I did not know if he was armed or not."

He's admitting his guilt!

I was speechless. So was Sybrina. She just shook her head and refused to look at the defendant.

O'Mara had no more questions, but de la Rionda was eager to cross-examine.

"Okay, and tell me, after you committed this crime and you spoke to the police, did you ever make that statement to the police, sir? That you were sorry for what you'd done or their loss?" de la Rionda asked.

"No, sir," the killer responded.

"You never stated that, did you?"

"I don't remember what I said. I believe I did say that."

"You told that to the police?"

"In one of the statements, I said that I felt sorry for the family . . ."

"And you're sure you said that?"

"I'm fairly certain."

"And so which officer did you tell that to? You made five statements, I believe, total."

"Yes, sir. I'm sorry, all the names run together . . ."

"And let me make sure the record's clear—you stated exactly what to those detectives?"

"I don't remember exactly what verbatim."

"But you're saying you expressed concern for the loss of Mr. Martin, or that you had shot Mr. Martin, that you actually felt sorry for him."

"I felt sorry that they lost their child, yes . . ."

"Why did you wait fifty-something days to tell them—that is, the parents?"

"I don't understand the question, sir."

"Why did you wait so long to tell Mr. Martin and the victim's mother, the father and mother, why did you wait so long to tell them?"

"I was told not to communicate with them."

"Okay, so even through your attorney, you didn't ask to do it right away? Your former attorneys or anything?"

"I did ask them to express that to them, and they said that they were going to . . ."

After some back-and-forth regarding the killer's statements to the police, de la Rionda asked, "Would you agree you changed your story as it went along?"

"Absolutely not."

After a few more questions, the defendant was allowed to step down. It was now time for Judge Lester to either set bail or to keep him in jail for the duration of the trial without bail.

O'Mara of course asked the judge to release his client on bail; de la Rionda asked the judge to consider the charges the killer was facing: ". . . life in prison . . . a life felony, and that obviously makes it different . . .

"You also have the fact that it is an unarmed seventeen-year-old boy . . ." de la Rionda continued, "an innocent young man whose life is no longer among us.

"He has violence in the past and obviously he committed this crime, or he's charged with committing this crime.

"Our position is that he still will be a danger to the community, and, based on the crime, he should be kept on no bond or the bond should be one million dollars, quite frankly. . . . What it boils down to, he shot somebody."

Not only shot; he killed someone.

Judge Lester leaned forward and stroked his goatee as he considered the facts. He said he considered the defendant's prior resisting-arrest charge "a run-of-the-mill-type run-in with the alcohol and beverage agents." He felt the injunction against his ex-girlfriend was "mild" compared to others he had seen.

He set bond at $150,000, under certain conditions: electronic GPS monitoring, abstinence from alcohol and possession of firearms, as well as a curfew.

JUNE 1

The judge's ruling on April 20 seemed final. But six weeks later, on June 1, Judge Lester would revoke the original bond and order the killer to turn himself in to the court after the prosecution discovered that Shellie had lied about their family's finances. It turned out that Shellie and her husband had access to $135,000 raised through a Pay-Pal account on their website for his defense. Yet Shellie had told the court, under oath, that she and her husband were indigent and without any available funds.

This lie was discovered through phone conversations between George and Shellie Zimmerman while he was still in custody in the Seminole County Jail.

"This court was led to believe they didn't have a single penny," de la Rionda said in the motion to revoke the bond. "It was misleading, and I don't know what other words to use other than it was a blatant lie."

According to the prosecutors, the couple knew their conversations were being recorded and devised a code designed to cover up the exact amounts they had raised. Money raised on the website was then deposited into the killer's credit union account, then transferred to his wife's account and various other accounts. Transfers never exceeded $10,000, which would have required the bank to report the transactions to the IRS.

"Judge Lester's finding that George Zimmerman was dishonest is very important," Crump told reporters when the news broke. "His credibility is the most important thing in this entire case."

The killer had also failed to hand over his passport, instead surrendering a passport he had reported as stolen eight years earlier. The old passport that was given over to the court was set to expire shortly after the initial bond hearing. But the newer passport, which he had held on to, was valid until 2014.

Judge Lester lashed out at the defendant and his attorney over the lies.

"Does your client get to sit there like a potted palm and let you lead me down the primrose path?" he asked. "That's the issue. He can't sit back and obtain the benefit of a lower bond based upon those material falsehoods."

Judge Lester was tough, and we felt lucky to have him presiding over the case. But that luck wouldn't last for long.

CODA

On June 12, Shellie was arrested on one count of perjury. As for her husband, on July 5, he was given a new bond—$1 million—and ordered to stay away from airports, among other conditions.

After posting bail, the killer was once again released from jail.

And we braced ourselves to see what would come next.

We didn't have to wait for long. On July 13, the killer's attorneys filed a motion on his behalf to disqualify Judge Lester, writing that the court, meaning the judge, "makes gratuitous, disparaging remarks about Mr. Zimmerman's character; advocates for Mr. Zimmerman to be prosecuted for additional crimes; offers a personal opinion about the evidence for said prosecution; and continues to hold over Mr. Zimmerman's head the threat of future contempt proceedings."

Six weeks later, on August 29, an appeals court granted the motion for a new judge, agreeing with O'Mara that Judge Lester had "created reasonable fear in Mr. Zimmerman that the court is biased against him."

Now we had yet another judge presiding over the case, this one being the third: Judge Debra Nelson.

CHAPTER 11

Sybrina

⤽

March 12, 2013–July 27, 2013

Almost a year had passed since the April 11 arrest of the man who killed our son. We continued to get the word out, doing media interviews, traveling to rallies and events, and telling the world how we felt, in the hope that as many people as possible would be aware that the case of the man who killed our son was finally going to trial. Supporters continued to come to our side. Our constant ally Michael Skolnik and the music producer Russell Simmons brought our social injustice to social media and broadening the platform. Then the Oscar-winning actor Jamie Foxx came to our side in support. It began at the forty-fourth annual NAACP Image Awards on February 1, 2013, where, from the stage, the legendary entertainer and civil rights activist Harry Belafonte called upon celebrities and leaders of the entertainment industry to channel the power of their fame into standing up for the rights of others, as he had stood by Dr. Martin Luther King, Jr., during the civil rights movement. When Jamie Foxx stood up to accept an award that evening, he gave an impromptu speech, accepting the mantle from Harry Belafonte and the responsibility of his power to help bring about change. From that moment on, Jamie joined us in our fight for justice for Trayvon. Two weeks after the NAACP awards, he joined us on February 26, 2013, for our peace walk on the first anniversary of Trayvon's death. He was instrumental in galvanizing the support of other celebrities and bringing our fight for justice to a far wider audience. During award ceremonies he traded in his tuxedos for shirts that he had specially made with Trayvon's image to show solidarity with our family and our cause. "I'm absolutely committed to all you out there who have young kids," he told the media at one point. "I hope you never have to go through anything like this." We also had invaluable support from the national radio star Tom Joyner, who played an enormous role in getting the word out about our cause on his show. We also wanted people to know how we felt as parents about how our son was killed and the unfairness of the justice system.

It was important for us to stay focused.

Parks and Crump told us that we all—Tracy, Jahvaris, and I—would have to provide depositions about a month before the trial, which was now scheduled to begin with jury selection on Monday, June 10, 2013. I knew a little about depositions. I had given a deposition before, when I was pregnant with Trayvon. It was over a confrontation at my workplace: I was a dispatcher at the time, and I saw two employees go into an office for a meeting over a dispute they had a few days before, and they came out of the office with what we thought was a resolution. As they were leaving the meeting, one employee shot the other in the back.

The employees' union brought people in to try to iron things out. Several months later, along with other witnesses, I was called in for a deposition on that case. This was many years before our tragedy.

So for our son's case, I knew I'd be drilled with questions and that the defense would be looking for contradictions, uncertainties, or weakness to take advantage of during the trial. I knew I would tell the truth in the deposition, just as I always did, but I was still nervous.

Although it wasn't the State of Florida versus Trayvon Martin, it certainly felt like he was on trial.

My deposition was scheduled for March 15, 2013.

I dressed in one of the business suits I'd bought at the mall for our media appearances and drove alone to a state office building by the Miami International Airport. I walked into a conference room scattered with chairs and people in business suits, divided by a long table. Lawyers against lawyers. Us against them.

They asked me to sit at the head of the table, across from a court reporter, who would type my every word, and a video camera, which would record my every word and movement. More than a year after losing my son, our road to what we hoped would be justice had arrived in this cold, gray conference room, with bright camera lights bearing down on me and the lens fixed on my face, an interrogation. As if I'd committed a crime.

Of course, I expected this. I expected to be grilled with questions about things most people don't remember. *What did you do seven months ago and what did you have on?* Seven months ago I was doing well if I could get up, comb my hair, and eat something.

At 9:29 A.M. I was sworn in, and Zimmerman's attorney O'Mara asked me to state basic facts about myself for the record: my name, birthdate, children's names and birthdays, where I lived, with whom and when.

"We are under a court order that certain information that we gather through depositions will be held confidential," O'Mara explained. "That includes such matters as your address and other demographic information. So I'm gonna ask you those questions but with the understanding that we understand that should reports be identified, such as a transcript, that it would similarly be redacted or maintained confidential. You know what I mean by that?"

"I understand what you're saying, yes," I said, even though I knew that information had consistently been leaked out for over a year about the case, including our home addresses. But now we were supposed to believe that our addresses would be kept confidential if we revealed them? It was a joke. I also knew that State Attorney Angela Corey and her prosecutors had to do everything by the book, while the other side, the killer's attorneys, could be more aggressive.

"Can I make just one statement?" Crump interjected. "Like Mr. Martin, she [Sybrina] is reluctantly giving her personal address because she does feel that her home and her mother's home have already been posted on Internet sites along with very racist comments and blogs and threats to her family, so she is majorly concerned about the safety of her family." It was true: we had been under siege with direct threats, threatening posts online, and more.

"Sure, and we certainly understand and agree with it," said O'Mara. "The Zimmerman family has had similar attacks on them with their privacy as well, so we know, not only from the desire to keep your information private, but we maintain the same requirement for the Zimmerman family, so I certainly understand the concern."

Reluctantly, I gave them my home address and told them I had lived there nearly two years, with my son Jahvaris and my brother.

Then Mark O'Mara asked me a series of questions about my life.

"Tell me about your employment. What type of work do you do?" he asked.

"I'm a program coordinator for the Miami-Dade Housing Agency," I explained. "I help low-income residents with housing-related issues. I work with a program called Hope VI. I manage the grant, and with that grant money I was able to provide services, program services, to the residents of Miami-Dade County."

I told him I had been with the housing agency for ten years, and worked as a code-enforcement officer for Miami-Dade County Solid Waste Management for about twelve years before that.

"So, for most of your adult career, you've been working in the governmental system?" O'Mara asked. "Miami-Dade, one way, one place or the other?"

"Yes," I confirmed.

"Okay. Presently, what is your approximate salary, at the housing agency?" he continued.

I told them the amount of salary I received, while thinking, *What did this have to do with the killing of my son?*

"And I understand that you're presently on sort of a hiatus or break from that actual employment," he said.

"Leave, yes," I said.

"A leave," he repeated. "And that began just after Trayvon's passing?"

"Yes," I said.

"Are you still being compensated . . . ?" he asked.

"No I am not," I said.

"Okay," he said. "And I understand just from my general knowledge from the case that you're spending a lot of time working with foundations that have been set up since [Trayvon's] passing."

"Yes," I said, and when he asked me to tell him about them, I added, "Particularly the Trayvon Martin Foundation."

I explained that the Trayvon Martin Foundation was set up six months after Trayvon's death, in August 2012. "The Trayvon Martin Foundation will provide advocacy for families of victims of gun violence," I told Mark O'Mara. "We are also going to offer a mentoring program to help young adults with conflict resolution and their rights as a teenager. We're also going to have a . . . scholarship program component, which will help young adults pursue a higher education . . ."

"Who is in charge of that?" O'Mara asked.

"Right now the Miami Foundation handles our finances," I said, "and we have put together a board. Most of the work we have been doing is on a volunteer basis, but we've been pretty successful trying to get people to help us out . . ."

"Who's on the board now?" he asked.

"Tracy and I . . ." I answered. "We do have a person acting as [an] executive director to try to just get us on the right track. So she's been helping a lot.

"However, right now we're just getting established," I added. He asked the source of the money and I told him, "Only from donations."

The word "donations" caused the attorney to drill in deeper.

"Okay. Do you have an approximate amount?" he asked.

"No, I don't," I repeated.

"Okay, less than ten thousand dollars, more than ten thousand dollars?" he pressed.

I shook my head, no. "I'm not sure," I said. "I don't know how much came in." I explained that we had produced two events—a sit-down candlelight dinner in remembrance of Trayvon and a Peace Walk (and a Peace Talk) to let youth in the community and around the country know that they have a right to walk in peace without being followed, profiled, chased, or shot and killed.

"As we go through this," he said, "I'm certain that it is going to bring to the forefront memories of Trayvon's passing. We as lawyers are sort of trained to stay distanced from the emotions of what's going on around us. Sort of like doctors with blood, I guess. I don't mean to be insensitive when I ask you questions about Trayvon, his passing, what you've done about it, and things like that. But I know it's very emotional for you, so as we go through this, again, if there's a time you want to take a break, I'd rather we take a break, let you gather your thoughts, and even if you say to me that you'd rather talk about that some other time . . . 'cause it's going to sound somewhat insensitive as I go through this, but I'm trying to balance that insensitivity, the way it presents itself, with my job, as getting some information, okay?"

Very soon, I would become aggravated that they kept asking me the same things over and over again. They would ask once, then go on to something else, and then go back to the same thing. But I tried to hang in there, stay calm. I believed that if I answered their questions, the justice system would work and the man who shot my son would be held accountable.

"How much of your time is spent dealing with the Trayvon Martin Foundation?" O'Mara asked.

"Twenty-four hours," I replied.

How did I spend that time? he asked after a while.

I tried to explain my work, which involved research, contacting other families whose children had died from gun violence, speaking engagements, and the events I attended to get the word out about my son, his death, and the upcoming trial of his killer. I explained that after the trial, we wanted to help families of victims of gun violence through community outreach and to revise the Stand Your Ground law, to create a "Trayvon Martin amendment."

"The Trayvon Martin amendment would just simply say that you cannot pursue or follow anyone, be the aggressor, and then get in a fight and shoot and kill 'em and say you [were] standing your ground," I added.

I thought he might ask me more about that. But O'Mara kept returning to a single theme: fundraising and what we did with the money.

Crump objected to some of these questions.

"Are you paid any salary from the foundation for your work on behalf of it?" Mark O'Mara asked.

"No," I said.

"Okay. How are you making your daily bills and monthly bills?" he asked.

"Friends and family," I replied.

"I'm gonna ask you first, how are things going financially?" he asked.

"Financially, I have friends and family that's been helping me out," I said.

He asked about the Trayvon Martin Trust, the Trayvon Martin Foundation, how donations worked and who benefited from them. He asked about my coworkers' generosity in donating their vacation time to me, how I stayed afloat financially without working following Trayvon's death—and I answered: my friends and family, my own built-up annual leave, and eight or so months of annual/donated time, which would end a few months after the deposition, in December 2013. I'd spent my time working to spread the word about the tragedy, but we were never paid to speak or appear on any television show. He asked me to recall the largest deposit into the foundation ($1,000 to $2,000) and the largest withdrawal ($5,500, which was transferred to the Miami foundation, which was the entity handling our foundation). He asked who owned my home, had I purchased real estate within the past year, had any real estate been purchased on my behalf in the past year.

After practically every penny, nickel, and dime were accounted for, O'Mara turned the questioning toward Trayvon, beginning with his academic history, including—especially—his trouble in school.

"Trayvon was just a month into his seventeenth year when he passed? Is that correct?" O'Mara asked.

"Not even a month," I replied.

Then: questions about his character, his transfer from Carol City High School to Michael M. Krop for his eleventh-grade year, his falling grades, his truancy, his suspensions, and our parent–teacher conferences.

"I don't remember who contacted me from the school, but one of the things they told me was that although we were actually in walking distance of the school, they said that he was late to school a lot," I said at one point. "So what I did was, [I] started taking him to school."

They had a student case management referral, which they called Exhibit D, from the school, which listed all of Trayvon's problems, something that I, as a parent, had never seen.

O'Mara handed it to me.

I read from the report, dated September 26, 2011, five months before his death. "The concern is excessive tardiness and failure to comply with school rules," it read, and indicated a recommendation in a comment: "Indoor suspension."

"I've never seen this before," I said.

When asked about Trayvon's tardiness, I again told the attorney that once the school had contacted me about it, "that's when I decided to start taking him to school.

"That continued until his death," I added.

They had the records to reflect the precise number of times Trayvon had been tardy, the number of times he had been absent, and other information from various reports that, again, I had never seen.

"In your mind, as his mother, do you think that Trayvon was going through any type of—my mom used to call it 'growing pains,' I think," he asked. "Not physical, but the emotional kind of growing up, and not grown up yet? Do you think that Trayvon was going through any type of growing pains when he was in maybe the end of tenth and into the eleventh grade?"

I was once again feeling like my son was on trial instead of the man who killed him.

"Well, he was growing up, yes," I said. "He was transitioning from boyhood to manhood, so I'd guess he was, you know, maturing. So, yeah, I'm pretty sure he went through some different changes."

"And in your mind, was he having some trouble with some of those changes?" he asked.

I shook my head no. "I mean, looking back on it, I would say that maybe he had problems with it, but at the time, I just thought that he was a teenager," I said.

He drilled in on the tardiness, the suspensions, and the reasons for the latest one: being in an unauthorized area and finding jewelry in his backpack, as well as a screwdriver, which, O'Mara said, "they identified it as a weapon or something."

"Did they ever show you the stuff?"

I shook my head. "A lot of stuff is cloudy because it's been a long year, but I wanna say that he [the school administrator] had the jewelry there, because he asked if it was mine and . . . it was not mine, but I'm not remembering what the jewelry was," I said.

The attorney asked what concern the incident gave me "about what Trayvon was getting into."

I thought back to the afternoon I picked him up from school after being told about what had happened, and I told O'Mara that the ride home from school was "ugly."

"I asked him whose jewelry it was and where did he get the screw-driver, and of course he said his friend.

"He continued to say his friend, his friend," I went on. "And I asked him what friend this was, and he gave me a name. I don't re-member a name, but, you know, it was a mother–son conversation I had with him about that . . . because that was, to me, the first serious incident in school."

He finally asked, "Did that give you a concern that Trayvon was going down a path that you were worried about?"

"When the school calls, that's serious . . . and, yes, I was con-cerned," I said.

He moved on to a disagreement that Trayvon and I had had, and suggested that in November 2011 I demanded that Trayvon move out of our family house—which wasn't true, no matter how many times O'Mara asked it. He had read texts from Trayvon, which seemed to say that I had asked him to move out—or had kicked him out. "I don't know why he would say that," I said.

O'Mara finally came around to the time just two weeks before Trayvon's death, on February 13, 2012, when he was suspended from school.

"It had to have been close to Valentine's Day," I said. "And I always buy [my two sons] a gift for Valentine's Day, and I bought a gift for both my boys and, usually when I get home from work, Trayvon is there at the door. . . . And he walked me inside the house and I told him, because I was all excited, I told him, you know, I got gifts for them again for Valentine's Day and so I was pretty excited. But he told me that I wouldn't be happy with the information he had. . . . He said, 'It's about school.' And I asked him what happened. And so we sat down in the living room, and he told me that he had been suspended, and that the school found an empty bag in his book bag. And so I asked him, 'Where did you get it from?,' and he said that it was his friend's. And I was really disappointed with him, because with the last suspension he mentioned these friends, this friend. I was just really disappointed in him that he had been suspended again."

After more questions, O'Mara asked how I punished Trayvon for the suspension.

"He loved the outside, and he wasn't allowed to go outside. And play basketball or ride his bike or any of those things," I said. "He wasn't allowed to watch television. The only thing he had access to was his telephone."

Then, he asked about Tracy's fateful decision to take Trayvon to Sanford in the second week of his suspension.

At noon, after two and a half hours of questioning, we took an hour lunch break. In the afternoon session we returned to the subject of "street fighting." The killer's attorneys had texts of Trayvon's conversations with numerous friends, and O'Mara read extracts of them to me.

Was I aware of a text conversation Trayvon had on social media with one of my nephews before he went to Sanford "about getting a twenty-two handgun"? he asked.

"No," I said, and he asked me if I would have been surprised if such a conversation took place.

"Yes I would," I said. Because I had never heard this before, and I was certain that my son was not a thug, much less a criminal. Bernie de la Rionda cleared the air about Trayvon's problems in school—specifically the jewelry found in his backpack, which Trayvon insisted wasn't his—by producing a Miami-Dade school police department document. He had me read from it: ". . . no arrests in Miami-Dade" it read in part about that incident, which cleared up any intimation, or confusion, that my son was ever arrested for anything.

And I had never heard anything about him wanting to get a gun.

Anyway, the biggest question: why wasn't I being asked about the only gun that mattered in our case, the gun that was used to kill Trayvon?

Similar probing and repetitive questions would be asked of my son Jahvaris, then twenty-two, a fourth-semester information-technology student at Florida International University, starting a few minutes after my deposition was done, at 5:00 P.M. that same day.

"Were you aware that Trayvon was tardy often and sometimes would skip school altogether?" Jahvaris was asked by the attorney Don West.

"Tardy, yes," he said. "Skipping, I didn't know anything about that."

Was he aware that Trayvon was smoking marijuana? (No.) Was he aware of any fighting that his younger brother was involved in? (No.)

"Are you aware of any money being paid to anyone in your family for an appearance fee, separate from just the cost involved in making the appearance?"

"No," said Jahvaris.

"You do have a lot of time invested in these events," he was informed.

Yes, Jahvaris answered, but he had taken off from college since the day of his brother's death, on February 26, 2012, to support the movement.

Finally, after several hours of questioning, I was at last asked about the shooting of my son. I had done my best to keep my composure, but now, for the first time that day, I began to cry.

"Aside from the person not being arrested, I, particularly [as someone] who worked in a capacity of code enforcement for eleven years, did not think that it was proper for a neighborhood watch captain to do something other than watch and record or take down notes or something and wait for the police," I said. "I just thought that was strange that he wasn't arrested. I thought it was strange later finding out that they didn't have any procedures in place that said that they needed to do a drug and alcohol test on the person who shot and killed my unarmed son."

I paused.

"I just didn't think that the Sanford Police Department handled this properly, because he wasn't arrested and that he went home that day and my son did not . . ." I said, now crying. "I thought that it was inappropriate that they didn't provide enough information to us as the family, because Trayvon was a minor and we just felt like we needed more answers and . . ."

Later, O'Mara turned the questioning to our media appearances, specifically one on the *Today* show on April 12, 2012, when I misunderstood a question and used the word "accident" in regard to the meeting of Trayvon and George Zimmerman. The media—and now the attorney—incorrectly interpreted that as meaning that I thought the murder of my son was an accident, which was absolutely something I never believed.

"What did you mean on the *Today* show, when you said on TV that you thought that this event was sort of an accident that got out of control?" O'Mara asked.

"I meant that them actually meeting was the accident," I said. "I didn't ever say that I believed that the actual gunshot was an accident. So, that was something that I cleared up because I think people misunderstood what I meant, but I meant that them actually meeting was the accident, not that the accident was the gunshot."

They then moved on to the 911 tapes.

"So tell me what happened when the tape was played," the attorney said.

I said I heard "noises" at first, "people calling in." And then I said, "The tape that I heard was the tape that, um, actually had the gunshot on there, that actually had the yelling on there."

"Tell me what went through your mind," he asked.

"I recognized the voice that's on there," I said.

"What voice was that?" asked the attorney.

"It was Trayvon's voice," I said.

"What did you hear him say?" he asked.

"I heard him say 'help,'" I said. Now I heard his cries for help all over again in my mind, again and again and again. I started to cry.

"How many times did you listen to the tape before you were able to determine that that was Trayvon's voice?"

"I heard the tape once and that was it," I said.

"What did you say to anybody who was there?" he asked.

"I told them that was Trayvon," I said.

"Told who?"

"Everybody that was in the room," I said.

"The mayor, Tracy, Mr. Crump, Ms. Jackson," he said. "Is that true?"

I was crying harder now. "Yes," I said, pausing to wipe my eyes.

"Want to take a couple minutes?" the attorney asked.

I didn't want to take a couple minutes, because this was my life every day, twenty-four hours, and it wouldn't get better in a minute, an hour, or a lifetime.

"No," I said.

"Was it only played once?" he asked again of the tape.

"I only listened once," I said. "I don't know how many times they played it, but I heard it once and I left the office. That was enough for me."

He began hammering away on my dead son's voice. Did I have evidence—tapes, voicemails, et cetera—of Trayvon's voice? Did family members have audio samples of his voice?

"You are aware that we have subpoenas out to you and Tracy about trying to get some of that, correct?" he asked.

"To get some of what?" I asked.

"I'm sorry . . . to get recordings of Trayvon's voice," said the attorney. Finally, toward the end of the deposition, after several objections from Crump and de le Rionda, O'Mara said: "All right, if it gets to a point of a 1.310 violation 'cause I'm harassing her let me know and we can stop the deposition, but I'm just really trying to get through the last couple of questions." Then he returned to the subject of money, the trust for the Trayvon Martin Foundation: Was I responsible for the money that came in and out?

"Yes," I said.

He had been skipping all over the place with questions.

And then we were, mercifully, done—at least done with the questions from the defense attorney.

Now the prosecutor, de la Rionda, cross-examined me, asking me to clarify answers I had made, which, I assume he felt, the killer's attorney was using to make a point, which he—and surely I—felt wasn't correct.

"Ms. Fulton, I think we spent probably the first forty-five minutes of the questioning of, in this deposition of you regarding your finances, regarding the money that was gathered, either through the Trayvon Martin fund or the Miami Foundation or whatever, entities that are out there, whatever we call them," he said. "I'm going to flat-out ask you because the way the questions were asked it implied like you gathered all this money to steal it. Is, is that what, what you were trying to do?"

"No," I said.

"Did you take advantage of the fact that your son was murdered in order to make money?"

"No," I said.

"Is that why you've done this? To get money here . . . to gain from your son's death?" the prosecutor asked.

"No, I would much rather have my son back," I said.

"Did you wish that February 26 your son would've been murdered?"

"Absolutely not."

"Did you plan for your son to be murdered so that you could gain whatever amount of money has been obtained for the foundation here?" he asked.

Now O'Mara objected, but the prosecutor moved forward.

"Did you plan for your son to be murdered by somebody so that you could make you yourself or anybody in your family get this money?" he asked.

"No," I said.

"Have you had a hard time living in this world knowing that your son who you bore or brought into this world is no longer here?" asked the prosecutor. "Have you been able to live like you normally lived before his death?"

"No, nothing is normal anymore," I said, and that summed up everything that I felt that day, as a mother, and now as a witness heading into a trial.

During this same time, that strange bulge in my neck kept growing, sapping my strength, draining my energy, while also making my heart race so fast I was unable to sleep.

I thought it was part of the depression of losing my son, coupled with the constant traveling, interviewing, being forever on the go, and now this upcoming trial.

I returned to my doctor, and he examined my neck, specifically the bulge in it. As soon as he felt it, he immediately knew. "You have a thyroid disorder," he said, adding, "an extreme case. Most likely from the stress. Your heart is racing so fast I'm surprised you didn't have a heart attack."

Surgery was required to remove part or all of my thyroid, he said, as soon as possible. I told him I would have to wait until after the trial, for which I needed to appear strong, even though I was physically suffering.

On Monday, June 10, 2013, jury selection began. My sister was driving us to Sanford from Miami the Sunday before. The mood in the car was solemn but hopeful. We had some anxiety about what the trial would bring, what feelings and memories it would stir up, but we were ready to begin the process with full belief that justice would be done.

Suddenly, just outside Sanford, our car was flooded with lights and sound. Red and blue lights. And the screaming of a police siren. The Florida Highway Patrol was right on our tail. My sister pulled the car over to the shoulder of the road.

She rolled down her window when the stone-faced patrol officer approached.

"License and registration," he said.

She handed the documents over without question, and we waited while he ran her license back in his patrol car.

The minutes dragged on, until, finally, the officer returned, handed my sister back her license and papers and told us that we were free to go.

We drove the rest of the way under the speed limit, past Sanford and to the hotel in Lake Mary that would be our home for the next month. To me, every place seemed to be dreary, but it was very clean and well kept and the staff treated us kindly there.

We didn't know if the fact that we were pulled over just outside Sanford on our way to the first day of the trial was a strange coincidence or had been done intentionally. We knew there was a large contingent of law enforcement in Florida that didn't like us. Some supported what the killer had done. I guess they didn't understand because Trayvon wasn't their seventeen-year-old son. Others, even if they weren't sympathetic to the killer and even disagreed with the way the case was handled by the police, still didn't like their procedures being aired in a public courtroom. They didn't like the spotlight we brought to their internal processes.

Sanford is a relatively small town, and of course many people knew we would be heading into town that day. But I'd still like to think that being stopped was just a coincidence. Even as a coincidence, though, it shook us up. And the real drama of the trip hadn't even begun.

Jury selection began early the next morning. Parks picked us up from the hotel, and Tracy, my sister, my nephew, and I all climbed into his rental car. The courthouse had reserved a couple of parking spaces for us across the street, and every day there was a deputy waiting for us there to provide security as we entered and exited the courthouse. Everyone knew we were in town, so having security only at the courthouse seemed like a waste of time and money.

When we arrived at the courthouse for the first day of jury selection, I saw a mass of media tents and satellite trucks in what was called a "media village," which would be there for the duration of the trial. I hardly even noticed the media anymore, they'd become such a regular presence in our lives. The media showed up unannounced at my house, waiting for someone to come out, and sometimes knocking on the door and leaving letters or business cards on the door. My private life was over. My home was not a sanctuary anymore. But I couldn't be mad; the media had made all the difference in our case. The media—print, television, and social media—had been our ally from the beginning. Now the spotlight had become relentless, around us practically all the time.

When reporters saw us getting out of the car at the courthouse that first day, they quickly sprang into action, chasing us down, following us to the courthouse entrance, trying to get any reaction they could from us.

"How do you feel about your son being killed?" they yelled, as if the answer wasn't obvious and I hadn't answered it a hundred times before.

"How do you feel having to go through a trial?"

"How does it feel to sit in a courtroom with the man who killed your son?"

They were all yelling at once, a confrontation lit by the blindingly bright flashes from their cameras.

The simple act of walking into the courthouse could be overwhelming because of the increasingly expanding throng of lights, cameras, and reporters chasing after us, hurling questions about the case against our son's killer. Often when we got out of the car, there was such a large crowd waiting for us that we had to link arms and walk as closely together as possible to avoid being torn apart in different directions. I remember one time a reporter, running backward, shouting questions at us, fell over. Another time, when Tracy and I were flanked by Attorney Jasmine Rand on one side of us and Attorney Crump on the other, a reporter got so close to Crump that he stepped on his shoe and ripped the sole off. Attorney Rand tried to quickly grab the piece of Crump's shoe, but he told her to just leave it, and we hurried into the courthouse.

We eventually had to start coming into the courthouse through the back door. For lunch, at first we went to various restaurants just down the street from the courthouse. But as the trial ramped up, the media pressure became so intense it became impossible for us to leave the courthouse for lunch. Attorney Parks was able to get us a small witness room in the courthouse, where we could relax during breaks and eat lunch.

Once inside the courthouse and through security, we would have to wait a moment while an officer checked to make sure we weren't about to run into the killer or a member of his family since there was only one way in and out of the courtroom. Though this normally was successful, it didn't always work, and several times we would find ourselves face-to-face in really tight quarters with the killer's attorneys.

When the judge was almost ready for the day's proceedings to begin, a bailiff would knock on the door and say, "Five minutes." We never wanted to be late for the judge out of respect for her and the court. We would all rise without delay and hold hands, and either Crump or Parks, or a visiting pastor, led us in a short prayer.

On the first day of jury selection, my pastor, Arthur Jackson III, prayed for us. Many pastors from Miami traveled to the trial for support, including Bishop Victor Curry, Reverend Gaston E. Smith, Pastor Walter Richardson, and Reverend Gregory Williams.

"God, please continue to cover us in our quest for justice for Trayvon," Pastor Jackson prayed. "And keep us safe and strong, keep us out of hurt, harm, and danger's way. In your son Jesus's name. Amen."

"Amen," we all repeated. I opened my eyes and took a deep breath. Together we walked into the courtroom.

Our first shock was the seating arrangement. We were seated near the front, but between us we only had one row for me, Tracy, our attorneys, Tracy's family, and my family. I counted the seats: *six.* On some days, we would squeeze in seven. But that was it. There was no room for family or friends, who all had to watch the trial in our little side room on closed-captioned television. Meanwhile, the media always had at least twenty people in the courtroom and were given several rows of seats. We were never given an explanation for any of this, and were forced to rotate family members and friends who knew Trayvon personally and wanted to be there for us.

Throughout the trial, Tracy and I wrote notes on a scratch pad, which we passed between us. We went through so many notepads! It was the only way we could share our private thoughts in the middle of the trial's action because the cameras inside the courtroom, and those outside, were watching our every move.

So we confined our comments to the pad. We would read what the other had written and then scratch it out to keep it from prying eyes once we had read it. As we began passing that scratch pad back and forth with notes, suggestions, reflections, and, okay, more than a few curse words, I knew why the Lord had brought us together. We had been unlikely people from different corners of the world who had come together in marriage and then to raise two sons. We had been there for our children, during our marriage and after. We had stayed friends for a reason, and this was it: not only the tragedy that had befallen our son, but now this trial, for which we would look to each other for strength and support.

It began with jury selection, where our notes just summarized what we were thinking about the potential jurors, who sometimes defied whatever stereotypes we might have assumed about them just from their appearance, its own case against profiling. The story had already left its mark on a number of the potential jurors.

Juror B55: white female looked very young. . . . a student, I wrote on the scratch pad.

Juror B65: black female navy blue shirt. Lived in Sanford for 16 years and her pastor prayed for both sides. She had three kids, 21, 16 and 12. She had no cable and no Internet.

Juror E54: white tall male, blue shirt. Said he joined the protest about why Zimmerman wasn't arrested. Had a teenaged stepson 16 and 28. Said his sons wear hoodies.

Juror B35: black male, red shirt, pink hat, Crocs, 21-year-old son in Tallahassee. He said Rev. Sharpton and Rev. Jackson coming to Sanford interrupted traffic. He said Congressman Wilson said the person who shot and killed Trayvon hunted him and he didn't agree.

"I've never heard of the Trayvon Martin tragedy," one potential juror said.

What rock has she been hiding under? I wrote on the notepad and handed it to Tracy. A number of potential jurors who gave this answer were just too busy or didn't care about following the case. But we felt some of them, including a few who eventually made it onto the jury, were not telling the whole truth.

"Trayvon would be alive today if his father was involved in his life," another potential juror said. This really got to Tracy, who was as close to his son as a father could be. She didn't know us at all, and was already judging Trayvon based on her perceptions of us. I would soon learn that this type of thing wasn't uncommon.

Jury selection stretched past one week and into another. At the end of every day, we would climb back into Daryl Parks's rental car to return to the hotel, where we'd spend what was usually a sleepless night, and then return again the next morning, where we would start all over again: we went through the back door of the courthouse, bypassing the media village, and into the courtroom, where we squeezed into our allotted six seats, our every move scrutinized.

Once the jury was set, after nine days, I felt somewhat hopeful.

"We walk by Faith, not by sight. Second Corinthians 5:7," I tweeted. "Yes, the jury was selected yesterday and I still believe God has his arms around us. Be encouraged!"

In most states there are twelve people on a jury in felony trials; in Florida there are six (except for capital cases). The jury that would decide the fate of the man who killed our son was composed of six women: five middle-class white women and one Hispanic woman.

Tracy felt sure that at least three of these women would sympathize with us.

How did he know that? I asked.

"You can tell by the look," he told me.

I kept faith in the fact that five of them were mothers, and would surely have compassion as mothers. I prayed they could see the hurt and the pain I was dealing with, and that, as mothers, they could see Trayvon through my eyes, could see that an unarmed seventeen-year-old was no match for a twenty-eight-year-old man with a loaded gun. I also prayed that they would listen to the evidence and find the truth.

∼◦∼

The State of Florida v. George Zimmerman began on June 24, 2013, 485 days after our son was taken from us.

"The process begins," I posted on social media that morning. "I plead the blood of Jesus to cover my family. Amen."

Our road to justice had begun with media coverage. Media coverage had propelled it every step of the way. So it was fitting that before the court proceedings began, Crump had organized a press conference at the courthouse so we could address the mass of local, national, and even international media that had gathered.

"There are two important facts in this case," Crump told the reporters outside the courthouse, as our family stood behind him. "Number one, George Zimmerman was a grown man with a gun. And number two, Trayvon was a minor who had no blood on his hands, literally no blood on his hands. There was none of George Zimmerman's DNA found on Trayvon Martin's hands or under his fingernails. We believe the evidence is overwhelming to hold George Zimmerman accountable for killing Trayvon Martin. As these formal proceedings begin that Tracy and Sybrina have fought so hard over this past year and a half to get to, we understand that now it is time for the jury to do their duty and base the verdict and their decision on the evidence, the instructions of the court, and the law."

Tracy and I gave some very brief comments, ending with a request that our supporters pray for us, and with that, we headed into the courthouse, went through security, and met with the rest of our family members and attorneys. We gathered in a little circle, according to our tradition now, and joined hands to pray.

"Amen," we all said at the end of the prayer, and then each of us hugged one another, holding each other a little longer and tighter than usual. We then filed into the courtroom in a procession led by our attorneys.

The courtroom was filled to capacity, every seat taken, and even more people were watching from home, thanks to the ever-present, all-knowing eyes: the courtroom television cameras. In 1979, the Florida Supreme Court decided to allow cameras in the courtroom. For good or bad, those cameras would transmit every second of the trial—tears, rage, testimony, *everything*—to the world.

We felt confident. We knew that the defendant had killed our son. We knew that Trayvon was the victim. We believed we had a strong chance at a conviction.

We also knew it would still be a very tough battle. Our lawyers laid out the difficulties of turning what we knew to be true into a legal judgment. For the jury to convict on the charge of second-degree murder, the prosecution would not only have to prove that the killer didn't shoot Trayvon in self-defense—to get around Florida's Stand Your Ground law, which allows the use of deadly force by someone fearing for their life—they would also have to prove that he shot Trayvon in the grip of a "depraved mind," meaning he shot my son with hate and evil intent.

We thought the prosecution could prove the depraved-mind part of the charge. But we knew that the killer would also try to prove his claim of self-defense. That meant that he would not be the only one on trial.

Trayvon would be on trial, too.

Our family sat behind the prosecution's table on the right side of the courtroom, just behind State Attorney Angela Corey, who sat on the bench in front of us, taking notes and advising the prosecuting attorneys if they needed her for anything. The defense, led by Mark O'Mara and his fellow attorneys, sat on the left, with the killer at the table beside them—only he didn't look like the same killer we had seen at the bond hearing less than a year ago.

At the time he shot my son, the killer was a chunky 194 pounds; he had trained in kickboxing and mixed martial arts, which, it would be revealed, he practiced several times a week. Now he carried more than 300 pounds on his five-foot, eight-inch frame. His hair, shaved at the time of the shooting, had grown in, and he parted and slicked it down on the side. He was only twenty-nine, but the extra weight made him look at least forty.

O'Mara claimed the weight gain was due to stress and his client's inability to go out in public. But other media outlets wondered if the weight gain was a defense strategy. Would a heavyset defendant be more sympathetic to a jury? Would a heavyset, sluggish defendant seem more like a man that couldn't—or wouldn't—attack a seventeen-year-old?

Either way, all I saw when I looked at him was a killer. They could dress him up in a suit and tie, they could grow out his hair and put weight on his frame trying to make him look cuddly and innocent, but there has never been any doubt about who killed our son.

As the trial officially began, Judge Nelson, who we'd been told was a tough, firm judge, appointed to the bench by former governor Jeb Bush, ordered any witnesses in the courtroom to be sequestered from the proceedings. As the victim's family, Tracy and I were allowed to remain, but Jahvaris and Crump, who were on the witness list, were asked to leave. Later in the proceedings, O'Mara would argue that Tracy and I should be removed from the courtroom, since we were on the witness list and were expected to testify.

However, that request was overruled by the judge, and we were in the courtroom every single day. But we felt the absence of Crump and our son Jahvaris, who had been with us every step of the way.

There was another matter granted by the judge, which could be seen as yet another victory for the defense. Before opening arguments began, Judge Nelson ruled that the word "profiling" could be used in the opening statements, but not "*racial* profiling."

I thought back to the confusing questions about profiling at the bond hearing. The judge's decision not to bring racial profiling or any kind of discussion of race into our case, even while that was what much of our case was about, was the first important victory for the defense. We later found out that the defendant was looking for an African American burglar who had been breaking into houses at the Retreat. Racial profiling at its worst. A witness would be allowed to testify for the defense about being burglarized by two African American men as she and her infant hid in an upstairs bedroom—even though the only thing that Trayvon shared with the burglars was the color of his skin. So, even as our son was once again having his innocence undermined by implied racial associations, the prosecution couldn't talk explicitly about race, and especially not about the killer racially profiling Trayvon.

"But what other kind of profiling could possibly have been involved here?" wrote the attorney Lisa Bloom, summing up our feelings in a column for the *New York Times*. "Could jurors—and the public—seriously imagine that Mr. Zimmerman considered Mr. Martin a criminal solely because he was walking slowly in the rain as he chatted on the phone?"

We hoped that the jury would be able to see the racial aspects of the case through what the killer said on the 911 tapes. But we knew that the deck was stacked against that—and against us—from the beginning.

The jury was ushered in, and at last the trial was about to begin. The prosecution team had decided that John Guy—charismatic and tough—would give the opening statements for the state.

"Good morning," he said and then . . .

" 'Fucking punks. These assholes, they always get away,' " he began, dramatically quoting Zimmerman's crude comments to the 911 operator on the night of Trayvon's killing.

Two seconds in, and the trial was off with a bang.

"Those were the words in that grown man's mouth as he followed in the dark a seventeen-year-old boy who he didn't know," the prosecutor continued, turning to point at the killer, wagging his finger at him with every damning word. "And, excuse my language, but those were his words, not mine.

" 'Fucking punks,' " he continued. " 'These assholes, they always get away.'

"Those were the words in that man's chest when he got out of his car armed with a fully loaded semiautomatic pistol and two flashlights to follow, on foot, Trayvon Benjamin Martin, who was walking home from a 7-Eleven armed with twenty-three ounces of Arizona brand fruit juice and a small bag of Skittles candies."

The prosecutor paused for a moment to let that sink in, and then he said those words again.

"'Fucking punks. These assholes, they always get away.'

"Those were the words in that defendant's head just moments before he pressed that pistol into Trayvon Martin's chest and pulled the trigger. And then as the smoke and the smell of that fatal gunshot rose into a rainy Sunday Sanford night, Trayvon Martin, twenty-one days removed from his sixteenth year, was facedown in wet grass, laboring through his final breaths on this earth."

I looked over at the defendant. He sat stone-faced in his chair. No emotion, expression, or reaction. He didn't move his face or shuffle in his seat. He only sat there, staring back at John Guy.

"And that defendant, at that same time, was upright, walking around, preparing," John Guy continued. "Preparing to tell law enforcement why it was he had just profiled, followed, and murdered an unarmed teenager. Ladies and gentlemen, the truth about the murder of Trayvon Martin is going to come directly from his mouth. From those hate-filled words that he used to describe a perfect stranger and from the lies that he told to the police to try to justify his actions."

John Guy then began retracing the events of the night of February 26 in detail.

"The murder of Trayvon Martin was the product of two worlds colliding," he said. "In one world, a seventeen-year-old boy from Miami, Florida, a visitor to this town, who had gone to the store to get something to drink for himself and some candy for a twelve-year-old friend. But in the other world," Guy said as he turned around to face the defendant, "a twenty-eight-year-old grown man. Somebody who wanted to be a police officer. Somebody who had called the police numerous times about crime in his neighborhood. Someone who had become the neighborhood watch captain. And someone who believed, most importantly, that it was his right to rid his neighborhood of *anyone* that he believed didn't belong."

The prosecutor created a picture of our son for the jury: a teenager visiting his father and doing what young people do, watching TV and playing videogames. He was a kid out for a drink, picking up candy, and, "as teenagers are wont to do," talking with a girl "the entire way home" on his cellphone.

But there was another picture to be painted, he said, a picture of the defendant, an adult driving around his neighborhood with a loaded Kel-Tec 9mm semiautomatic pistol tucked inside the waistband of his pants, with a "live round in the chamber," said Guy. The defendant didn't see a "young man" out for snacks talking to a girl, Guy told the jury, he saw someone that was "real suspicious," "up to no good," a "fucking punk" that he didn't want to get away.

Get away with what? I often wondered. What was he doing besides walking while black?

Again, I looked over at the defendant. He remained stone-faced, unmoved by this extremely emotional retelling of the events.

Guy continued to list the defendant's fateful decisions on the night of February 26, 2012: ignoring the instructions of Sean Noffke, the Sanford Police Department dispatcher, who told him, "We don't need you to" follow Trayvon; deciding against meeting police at a bank of mailboxes as he had originally said he would. "Tell the officer to just call me and I'll tell him where I am," Guy quoted the shooter as saying. "Because George Zimmerman wasn't going back to the mailboxes, and he wasn't going back to his truck. He was going after Trayvon Martin." Guy picked up with Trayvon's call to Rachel Jeantel less than four minutes later, who heard Trayvon say to the killer, "What are you following me for?"

"And then Trayvon Martin's phone went dead," said the prosecutor, "and Trayvon Martin went dead."

He described the reactions of the first responders, who found Trayvon lying facedown in the grass, his hands clutching his chest, his phone beside his body . . . its earbuds near his head, with a bullet through his heart. He told the jury of the officer who quickly attempted CPR, pressing down on Trayvon's chest in an attempt to "push life into him," Guy said. And he mentioned the emergency medical technician who was unable to detect a heartbeat in Trayvon's body, and the officer who covered him with a yellow medical blanket.

Hearing the last moments of our son's life described in that level of detail broke my heart all over again. Every time I thought I'd heard it all and nothing could move me again, there was a new detail, a dramatic retelling, a tape, a document, a witness, that would bring me back to the moment. I put my head down and closed my eyes. I couldn't bear to watch or listen. Tracy was shaking. I saw him biting his lip, trying to clamp down on his emotions. But we both were crying.

"God is using me," I later tweeted. "Because how in the world am I able to listen to all this . . . by God's Grace."

John Guy continued. At the moment the EMT placed the blanket over Trayvon's dead body, the killer was full of life, talking and walking around. His injuries—a bloody swollen nose that was later proven not to be broken, and two cuts on the back of his head only a few centimeters long, neither requiring sutures—were minor enough that he refused medical attention. Guy recounted what he called the "tangled web of lies" that the killer told the police: about when the altercation occurred, his description of Trayvon's movements, why he got out of his truck, and how he said Trayvon attacked him, holding his hand over the defendant's mouth.

The prosecutor said the evidence would show there was no blood found on Trayvon's hands, and none of the killer's DNA was found on the cuffs or the sleeves of Trayvon's hooded sweatshirt.

I never believed it was a true fight.

He continued with what he called the lies the defendant told about what Trayvon said to him, never heard by witnesses. Lies about what the defendant said he did with Trayvon's body seconds after killing him, which would be disputed by photographs taken by a witness. Lies about Trayvon reaching for the defendant's gun that, when tested, showed no DNA evidence that anyone but the defendant had handled that gun that night. Lies about their verbal confrontation and where their physical struggle began.

Next, the prosecutor described the neighbors' 911 calls—the screams for help, and the gunshot that killed my son. "Listen carefully when the screaming stops," he told the jury. "It's right when the gunshot goes off. Trayvon Martin was silenced *immediately* when the bullet that the defendant fired passed through his heart."

Lastly, Guy turned to the defendant himself. He described him to the jury as a person who "wanted to be a police officer," a criminal justice major who took classes in the law of self-defense. He described his role as a self-appointed neighborhood watch "coordinator" who ignored his training "to see and report," "observe and call" the police, a man who instead became a vigilante who profiled Trayvon as a criminal in his neighborhood.

"That is just some of the evidence in this case," Guy concluded. "We are confident, that at the end of this trial, you will know, in your head, in your heart, in your stomach, that George Zimmerman did not shoot Trayvon Martin because he *had* to, he shot him for the worst of all reasons—because he *wanted* to."

It was so dramatic, exact, and, I believed, true, that I was almost unable to breathe.

John Guy thanked the jury and returned to his seat at the prosecution's desk. A short recess was called. Then the defense began their case, led by attorney Don West.

"This is a sad case, of course," he said. "As one of your fellow jurors commented during the jury selection process, 'A young man has lost his life. Another is fighting for his. There are no winners here.'" Then, a few minutes into his opening statement, West decided to tell . . . a joke. "Sometimes you have to laugh to keep from crying. So let me, at considerable risk, let me say I would like to tell you a little joke. I know how that may sound a bit weird in this context, under these circumstances. But I think you're the perfect audience for it, as long as you, if you don't like it or don't think it's funny, or inappropriate, that you don't hold it against Mr. Zimmerman. You can hold it against me if you want, but not Mr. Zimmerman. . . . Here's how it goes."

Then he said, "Knock, knock.

"Who's there?" he answered his own question.

"George Zimmerman.

"George Zimmerman who?" he asked.

"All right, good, you're on the jury!" he said.

The courtroom turned silent. The defense attorney's joke, at the start of a murder trial, had fallen flat.

"Nothing?" West asked. "That's funny."

Don West may have thought it was funny, but I didn't and neither did, I hoped, the six members of the jury. The joke felt like a slap of disrespect to the court, to us as a family, to Trayvon, to everyone who was in support of us. This was the most tragic, serious moment of our lives, and the defense attorney was trying to turn it into a joke. The joke was so unprofessional and inappropriate for a murder trial, with the victim's family sitting right there. I thought, *How heartless and unfeeling can you be?*

I looked over at the defendant at the defense table to see his reaction. Again, nothing.

West allowed the tension in the air to dissipate, then continued.

"George Zimmerman is not guilty of murder," he declared. "He shot Trayvon Martin in self-defense after being viciously attacked."

On a large projection screen on the wall opposite the jury, West displayed an aerial view of the Retreat at Twin Lakes. He described Zimmerman as an average citizen headed to the grocery store to buy food for his workweek, when on his way out of the housing development he saw Trayvon entering from an area where most residents do not enter.

"Little did George Zimmerman know at the time," West said, "that in less than ten minutes from his first seeing Trayvon Martin that he, George Zimmerman, would be sucker punched in the face, have his head pounded on concrete, and wind up shooting, and tragically killing, Trayvon Martin."

West also recounted the events of that evening and the defendant's role in the neighborhood watch program. He said reports that the defendant disobeyed police orders not to pursue Trayvon were untrue. He mentioned the defendant's call to the nonemergency line, Trayvon's calls with his friend Rachel Jeantel, and the 911 calls from neighbors, building a timeline and pointing out on his aerial view the neighborhood where each event happened as he prepared to play the tapes of the 911 calls for the jury. Then the courtroom sound system erupted with the sounds I dreaded.

The defendant sat quietly and listened to his own voice on the nonemergency call. Still, no expression.

His defense attorney continued to re-create the moments just before Trayvon's death, using the map and the defendant's nonemergency call to help the jurors listen to the call and visualize the scene. He played the moment in the 911 calls when the defendant got out of his truck. We could hear the tones indicating the door open, and the quickening of the defendant's breath as he pursued my son.

When the dispatcher told the defendant that he didn't need for him to follow Trayvon, the defendant said, "Okay." He gave the dispatcher his name, phone number, and address, immediately regretting giving his address because he had lost Trayvon and didn't want anyone else to overhear where he lived. The dispatcher promised to have a police officer call the defendant to let him know his whereabouts. And the defendant hung up the phone.

Trayvon meanwhile, West said, was still on his phone with Rachel Jeantel.

"Second-degree murder requires an act reckless, indifferent to human life," West said. "A depraved-mind act, ill-will, hatred, spite."

He paused for a breath. "What Rachel Jeantel will tell you in her conversation with Trayvon Martin at the moment that this actually became physical was that Trayvon Martin, I'll use my words, that Trayvon Martin decided to *confront* George Zimmerman."

West claimed that instead of going home, Trayvon hid and then turned on his pursuer, out of the darkness, and said, "Why are you following me?"

I tried to write some suitable insult on the notepad, which had become my trial diary, but I was too upset. I couldn't write. I knew what was coming next: the 911 call from the neighbor Jenna Lauer, which included the sound of the gunshot that killed Trayvon. I didn't want to hear it again, not in public with so many reporters' cameras bearing down on me. I rose from my seat. Leaving on live television was better than breaking down, I figured, so I left the courtroom, which, surely, the cameras captured. Almost immediately my mom, watching from home, texted me, "Are you okay? I just saw you walk out of the courtroom." I told her that wasn't true; I'd just gone to the restroom, but I didn't feel so well. She wrote me back: "You'll be fine."

Tracy told me what came next. West said Jenna Lauer and her husband heard a verbal exchange, then a shuffling in the grass followed by screams for help. That was when she decided to call the police. The court heard the phone call, which recorded the struggle and the screams, and then the loud *bang* that went through Trayvon's heart and ended his life.

At the sound of the shot, the defendant still remained stone-faced.

"All of the witnesses," West continued, "whether they agree to anything else, they all agree those are the screams of someone in a life-threatening situation, someone screaming repeatedly, over and over and over, for help."

By the time I got back into the courtroom, West was going through a list of every witness from the Retreat at Twin Lakes. They were divided into two parts: those who believed the defendant's story, like John Good, who said he saw Trayvon "mounted" on top of the neighborhood watchman. And those who didn't believe him, like Jayne Surdyka, who said she thought the cries for help were Trayvon's.

The attorney weaved the story of a vulnerable defendant screaming for help, pleading with anyone who could hear his cries to stop Trayvon's supposed attack—"the most traumatic event in his life," West said.

And I thought, *Who yells for help with a loaded gun? That just doesn't make sense to me.*

Soon after, the judge called a lunch recess.

. . .

When we returned to the courtroom after lunch, Don West told the court:

"No more bad jokes, I promise that," he said, apologizing to the jury if he offended any of them, but never apologizing to us. "I'm convinced it was the delivery, though. I really thought that was funny. I'm sorry if I offended anyone."

West proceeded to prop up neighbor John Good's claim that Trayvon was on top of the defendant. He said that the forensic evidence showed the hole in Trayvon's hoodie was made when the gun was pressed up against it, but the hole in his body was consistent with a shot made at a distance. This meant, West claimed, that Trayvon's hoodie was pulled away from his body the moment he died. Which meant that Trayvon could only be on top of the defendant, leaning forward.

West told the jury the fact that Trayvon had no blood on his hands—his pursuer's or his own—didn't matter, because the police at the scene never bagged his hands to preserve the evidence. And the lack of DNA evidence on the gun and on Trayvon's hoodie proved nothing, he said. Because Trayvon's clothing was wet from the rain and police officers failed to store the evidence properly, using a sealed plastic bag instead of a paper one, which caused the clothes to mold and destroyed any DNA evidence that may have been on the clothing.

I'm no detective, but I've watched enough criminal trials on television and shows like *Law & Order* to know that rain can't totally wash all the DNA away.

He brought up the scream on the 911 call, saying that the defendant insisted to police it was *him* yelling for help and that we couldn't prove anything through science or voice-recognition experts. Because there wasn't enough of a voice sample to come to a definitive conclusion.

All these technicalities made me feel like leaving the courtroom again.

Then West brought me into his opening arguments.

"On the other hand, as one might expect, there will be witnesses to say, 'I've also listened to the recording, and I think that's Trayvon Martin's voice,'" he said. "I would expect his mother to say that. She certainly *wants* it to be his voice."

I didn't *want* it to be Trayvon's voice. I *knew* it was Trayvon's voice.

West claimed we didn't know what we were talking about. "They have not involved themselves in understanding the evidence of the case, though," he said, which raised an objection that was sustained. At this point I wanted to scream: *"But we did!* The evidence shows that George Zimmerman killed our son!" But with the reporters and court television cameras on me, as well as surely every eye in the court, I struggled to keep still—and quiet.

West continued bringing up evidence, refuting evidence, discrediting my son, and discrediting the prosecution's version of events.

"If I've heard it once, I've heard it a thousand times," he said, finally concluding his opening. "That Trayvon Martin was unarmed. What the evidence will show you, is that's not true. Trayvon Martin armed himself with the concrete sidewalk and used it to smash George Zimmerman's head. No different than if he picked up a brick or bashed a head against a wall. That is a deadly weapon."

Tracy and I both startled at this claim and looked at each other in disbelief. *A concrete sidewalk is a deadly weapon?*

The first witness the state called was Chad Joseph, now fifteen, the son of Brandy Green, Tracy's girlfriend, and Trayvon's young friend in Sanford. When Trayvon said he was going to the 7-Eleven store on the day he was shot, it was Chad who asked him to buy him a bag of Skittles.

Chad was a seventh grader on the night of February 26, 2012. At the time of the trial, he wasn't yet in high school. When the judge swore him in, he stood there, a smart, skinny kid in a neat white polo shirt, now in the middle of a murder trial. He held his thin right hand up in the air, unsure of what to do next.

"Do I repeat that?" he asked after an awkward moment.

"You have to say yes," the judge explained.

Chad said a nervous "Yes," and took the stand, where prosecutor John Guy questioned him briefly. Chad explained that he and Trayvon were home on the Sunday night of the killing, playing video-games and waiting for the All-Star game to begin. When Trayvon left for the 7-Eleven store, Chad said, he stayed behind to continue play-ing videogames in his room on the second floor of his mother's house.

At some point, Chad called his cellphone to see where he was.

"Did Trayvon Martin answer his cellphone when you called him?" Guy asked.

"Yes," said Chad.

"Did he tell you what he was doing?"

"Yes."

"And what was that?"

"He said he was on his way back," Chad answered.

"Did he tell you anything about the weather conditions outside?"

"That it was raining."

That was the last time he would speak to Trayvon. He learned Trayvon had been killed when he returned home from school on Monday.

I thought defense attorney O'Mara stumbled in his cross-examination. Chad had a hard time understanding O'Mara, and couldn't remember some of the details from that evening. Like: Was Trayvon talking to anyone else on the phone while they were playing videogames? And how long had they been playing videogames that day? He didn't know how long it would take to walk the distance from his house to the spot where Trayvon was killed. He said he knew he could throw a football that far, but was unsure about a soft-ball.

We felt the state attorneys would ask Chad more questions to es-tablish Trayvon's character—a feeling that would continue to haunt us throughout the trial.

Next up was Andrew Gaugh, the cashier who helped Trayvon at

the 7-Eleven. When Guy asked if Trayvon looked or did anything suspicious, Gaugh said no. But when O'Mara questioned him, he asked if he remembered *anything* about Trayvon coming into the store that night—or if he was just recalling him from the video—and the cashier said he didn't remember him at all. He was face-to-face with Trayvon and he didn't seem to think he looked suspicious.

Next up, the 911 operator Sean Noffke. He described the defendant's call to the dispatcher, at least before shooting Trayvon, as standard. The state played the nonemergency call again, and the defendant's words that Trayvon looked "suspicious . . . like he's on drugs or something" resounded through the courtroom. And then, once again: "These assholes, they always get away."

Noffke testified he could tell when the defendant had gotten out of his vehicle and begun following Trayvon, because he heard the car door's chime when it opened and the wind created static on the phone. He said it was against policy to give any commands to callers. Never would he tell them to chase a suspect, but neither would his suggestion that the killer stop following Trayvon bear any resemblance to a command.

I thought back to what he said: "Are you following him?" And after the defendant said, "Yes," he said, "Okay, we don't need you to do that."

Which sounded like a command to me.

On cross-examination, the dispatcher testified that there was no hate or malice in the voice of the defendant, despite what I thought were very hateful words. I felt sure that O'Mara was trying to show that his client was calm and collected.

They played the tape again.

"These assholes, they always get away."

"Was there any anger in that comment that you heard?" O'Mara asked.

"It sounded calm to me," Noffke said.

Again the cross-examination was brief and unsettling, and soon the first day had ended. We returned to our hotel for another sleepless night—I didn't know what to make of this testimony yet, but we were anxious about what was coming next. Later that night, back in the hotel, as coverage of our trial dominated the evening news, I wrote a note to myself: *June 24: I don't know what I expected the evidence to show. The opening statements were very sad for me.*

My family drove up to Sanford from Miami to support us in court in shifts. One set of relatives would leave as soon as another arrived. My sister Stephanie, who stayed for most of the time, slept in a hotel room adjacent to mine, and I stayed with my cousin Penny. In the beginning, she would turn on the news, which covered the trial nonstop. It was trending at or near the top of every social media platform, an inescapable topic of discussion that had galvanized the nation.

Guilty or not guilty.

A shooting by "a depraved mind" full of spite and hate—or a case of self-defense?

This had become my life, and after spending all day in court, I'd frankly had enough of the topic. So I decided not to watch news or commentary about the case after court. Instead, we'd have dinner with our family members and attorneys, where, of course, they would discuss the case, and then I would find escape in watching old television comedies: *Sanford and Son, Good Times, The Golden Girls,* whatever could bring a moment of escape.

Because in the morning, I knew, it would start all over again.

Up early after a sleepless night, we once again rode from our hotel in Lake Mary to the courthouse in Sanford in Parks's rental car. So that we could escape the media village, Parks dropped us off in the back, where we once again went through security and into our little room, then into the hallway, to join hands together and pray.

The state called Wendy Dorival, the volunteer program coordinator at the Sanford Police Department who had helped the defendant establish the neighborhood watch program and given the presentation on crime prevention, home safety, and community engagement at the defendant's request. Part of her instructions, of course, were to tell volunteers to call the Sanford Police Department's nonemergency line if they saw something suspicious.

"Do you tell them to do anything else at that point?" John Guy asked.

"No. They're the eyes and ears," Dorival said.

"What do you tell volunteers about following someone they believe might be involved in criminal behavior?"

"We tell them they don't do that. That's the job of law enforcement."

"And what do you tell neighborhood watch participants about confronting someone that might be involved in criminal behavior?"

"Not to confront . . . let the police department do their job."

Again, I wanted to scream, "But Trayvon was not involved in any criminal behavior!" I was worried that the prosecution—our side—was allowing the defense and its witnesses to eat away at the innocence of Trayvon.

Guy then put up a slide that was a part of Dorival's presentation for introducing residents to the neighborhood watch program. At the top, in big, bold letters, it read: "Neighborhood Watch is . . . NOT the Vigilante Police."

"What did you explain to the defendant and other attendees about that slide?" Guy asked.

"Basically that they are the eyes and ears of law enforcement . . . that they're not supposed to take matters into their own hands . . . and to let law enforcement take the risk of approaching a suspect," Dorival said.

Dorival was the second witness from the Sanford Police Department, and she, like the dispatcher, seemed to us to be biased in favor of the killer, as well as most Sanford police personnel seemed to be. It appeared to us that the people who were supposed to enforce the law and aid in administering justice were now seemingly taking the killer's side.

.   .   .

There *were* people who supported us, but were afraid to show their support. When I would go to the restroom, people would come up and say, "We're with you." Some of them were from the police department. Maybe they were parents, too, and could imagine what it must be like to lose a child who wasn't committing a crime. But they wouldn't say that, or show their support, in public. There were the issues of job security, promotions, and more. So they remained silent when others could hear them. Even so, their support was a boost of confidence, especially coming from Seminole County.

Often, throughout the trial, my cellphone would vibrate and I would look down and find a text from my pastor, Arthur Jackson III. He would send me inspirational lines from scripture, text messages of support, prayer, and praise:

> Romans 8:28: We know all things work together for the good of those that love the Lord, to those who are called according to his purpose.

> Psalm 30:5: For his anger lasts only a moment, but his favor lasts a lifetime; weeping may stay for the night, but rejoicing comes in the morning.

> Psalm 23: The Lord is my shepherd; I shall not want . . .

> Psalm 121: I will lift up mine eyes unto the hills, from whence cometh my help. My help cometh from the Lord, which made heaven and earth. He will not suffer.

Sometimes his text just read, "Hey, I'm thinking about you and praying for you, be encouraged."

Several times during the trial, I would turn around to find pastors sitting in the row behind me, giving me the ministry of presence. They didn't have to say anything; they gave me strength just by being there.

I would need that support today. Because they were going to show the crime-scene pictures of my son's dead body.

The prosecution called a high-ranking officer who arrived at the crime scene after Trayvon was shot: Anthony Raimondo, a sergeant with the Sanford Police Department and a former marine with more than fifteen years of law enforcement experience. He didn't seem like he could sugarcoat the cold, hard facts if he wanted to—it seemed like his temperament was to go straight into it, no matter how unpleasant. He took the stand in his police uniform, his head and face neatly shaven to testify about finding Trayvon dead on the ground.

By the time Raimondo arrived at the scene of the shooting, two other officers were already there. One had the defendant in handcuffs; Sergeant Raimondo instructed the officer to put the defendant in a patrol car. Another officer was standing over Trayvon's body, which was facedown on the ground with his hands beneath his body. The photo was shown.

I caught only a glimpse of it, and it broke my heart, never to be healed again. It hurt so badly. My God, please give me strength. I quickly turned away. Tracy must have looked longer than I did, because it was so traumatic for him that he stood up and left the courtroom. I looked over at the killer: he showed no emotion whatsoever.

Raimondo described how he tried to find a pulse, and when he was unable to find one he rolled Trayvon over on his back. When he still couldn't find a pulse, he attempted CPR, putting his mouth on my son's mouth and trying to breathe for him.

Later, another photograph was displayed showing Trayvon lying faceup, with his head, stripped of its hoodie, cocked back, and his mouth and his eyes open, staring toward the sky.

He didn't look like a thug who attacked a stranger in the night.

He looked like a kid.

At this point, I kept my head down and began to silently pray: "Lord, please help me remain calm. Please help me to stay strong for Trayvon."

Later I tweeted, "The love I have for my son exceeds the death of my son. I love you Trayvon forever!!!!!" And I prayed, *My God, please give me strength.*

Raimondo continued, describing how another officer attempted to help him give Trayvon CPR, compressing his chest as Raimondo breathed into his mouth.

"Did you hear anything when you were performing CPR on Trayvon Martin?" Guy asked.

"Yes, sir," Raimondo said.

"What was that?"

"Bubbling sounds, sir."

"What did those bubbling sounds indicate to you?"

"It meant that air was either getting into or escaping from the chest in a manner it was not supposed to, sir."

"And what did you do upon hearing those bubbling sounds from Trayvon Martin's chest?"

"I called out to the crowd that was gathering nearby, and I asked for Saran Wrap and Vaseline, sir."

"What would be the purpose of Saran Wrap and Vaseline?"

"I was going to try to seal the chest wound, sir."

Raimondo described the last attempts to revive my son.

A neighbor rushed out and gave him a plastic grocery bag, with which he attempted to seal the bullet's exit wound. He lifted Trayvon to a seated position with one hand on Trayvon's stomach and another behind his head. He felt the cold can of the fruit juice in the front pocket of Trayvon's hoodie, but he couldn't find the bullet hole in his back. At this point, an ambulance arrived, and the EMTs hooked Trayvon up to an EKG machine. Unable to revive him, the sergeant testified, they pronounced him dead at the scene.

"I put an emergency blanket over Mr. Martin's body, sir," said Raimondo.

"What was the purpose of that?"

"Well, one, it was respect for the deceased," he said. "Two is to mitigate trauma that witnesses or family members may be exposed to if they arrived on scene, and then three was to preserve any physical evidence on the body, sir."

I still couldn't bring myself to look as Guy showed more pictures of Trayvon's body at the scene: one from every angle, one with the blanket on, another with the blanket off. All I could do was try not to look and continue to pray.

Back in our hotel in the suburb of Lake Mary, I typed notes on my cellphone. On this night, I wrote many things, including: *Sanford Crime Scene Unit said Trayvon had $40.15, a red lighter, a cellphone, head phones, Skittles, Arizona fruit punch, his watch and khaki pants.*

I was shattered, filled with grief and pain from all I'd seen and heard throughout the day. My body was showing the strain: I was still losing weight at a rapid rate, which I knew was due to my thyroid disorder. The weight was coming off me so fast that my clothes began to hang on me. I looked in the mirror and could see myself disappearing, pound by pound. I couldn't show weakness. Not now. Not when we had come this far. So where my body seemed to be wasting away, I'd put on more clothes so no one would notice. I called it "layering up"; I'd put on thermal undergarments, which bulked up the clothing on top of it. I wanted to look like myself. But I was disappearing.

No amount of layering could disguise the enlarging bulge in my neck. But I couldn't tend to that now. I had to keep moving forward, afraid that if I stopped, I would never move again.

I laid out my clothes for the next day in court: the suit the public would see and the layers to bulk it up beneath, which nobody would know about but me.

Somehow, when I drifted off to sleep in the hotel room bed that night, I felt hopeful. Because I knew that the next morning would bring the prosecution's star witness, the last person who spoke with Trayvon on his ever-present cellphone, only minutes before he was killed: Witness #8, the twelfth witness to testify at the trial thus far, Rachel Jeantel.

· · ·

According to the attorney Lisa Bloom's book about our case, *Suspicion Nation,* Rachel Jeantel spent the two days before she was called to testify alone in a small room in the courthouse and was told by the prosecution to review her grueling video depositions, which surely brought up bad memories. She had driven five hours from her home in Miami Gardens to Jacksonville to give her deposition, only to be kept waiting for so long that she finally escaped back home, and only came back a month later under court order.

She was nineteen now and frankly scared about the murder trial that lay ahead. The prosecution had only spent twenty minutes preparing her, we'd later find out. "Just tell your story, who you are, how you knew Trayvon. Stay calm, be respectful. . . . Your testimony should last an hour," Bloom wrote that de la Rionda told Rachel before she took the witness stand. Two women from her church had helped her with her clothes, and a Miami attorney, Rod Vereen, tried his best to help coach Rachel after being contacted by friends who knew her, who, according to one newspaper, told him, "There's a [young lady] who is going to testify. She has no idea what she is in for."

Finally, Rachel Jeantel entered the courtroom. The door opened like a curtain on a theater stage, and here she came: a young black woman, swinging her arms back and forth, and wearing black from head to toe. Her hair was in a bun with bangs, and she wore large hoop earrings and high-heeled shoes.

When she was sworn in she affirmed the oath in a low, flat monotone, so faint that I strained to hear her. I wondered if she had even said it. Being the last person to speak with Trayvon, Rachel could shed light on exactly what happened that night—that's what we were hoping for; that was what a lot of the prosecution's strategy hinged on. But things wouldn't go as hoped or planned.

She took the stand, and I could see she was more than a little nervous; she was terrified. But I could also see a glint of steely determination. I hung on to that glimpse of something hard inside her.

Bernie de la Rionda began his examination, establishing that Rachel and Trayvon had met in elementary school, and they had been talking and texting on and off on the phone throughout the entire day and into the night of February 26, 2012. And when Trayvon walked to the 7-Eleven, Rachel was on the phone with him.

De la Rionda then moved on to when Trayvon returned to the Retreat at Twin Lakes.

"Did he describe when he was at the complex something happening?" de la Rionda asked.

"Yes," Jeantel said.

"Tell us if you can what he described happening."

"A man was watching him," she said.

"When he told you that a man was watching him, did you say anything to him?"

"No. I didn't think . . ." and then she trailed off.

The court reporter stopped and asked her to repeat herself.

"No. I didn't think it was a big [deal]," Jeantel repeated, but it was still difficult for anyone to hear what she said.

"You're doing fine," the prosecutor reassured her. "You have to get close to the microphone so everybody can hear you."

This kind of exchange became common during her two days of testimony. She was misunderstood either because she spoke too softly or because she used slang that the lawyers and the jury just didn't understand—sometimes I didn't understand her words, either. The defense would try to use this against her character, but it was just who she was, a shy teenager speaking the way she always did.

"Did he then say something was happening?" de la Rionda asked.

"Yes. He said a man kept watching him," Rachel answered.

"Did you say anything back to him . . . ?"

"Yes, I had asked him how the man looked like. He just told me . . . the man looked creepy . . . excuse my language, 'cracker.' "

A commotion rose up in the courtroom, but it was unclear if this was because people just couldn't hear her or they were shocked by her use of the word "cracker."

"They're having trouble hearing you," de la Rionda said. "So take your time."

" 'Creepy-ass cracker,' " Jeantel repeated, and then was made by the judge and de la Rionda to repeat it so the jury and court reporter could type what she was saying into the record. De la Rionda didn't ask her to clarify that "cracker" in a situation like this wasn't meant as a strong racial slur—it was just like saying "creepy-ass dude." Instead, he just asked her to repeat it again. "I had asked him how the man looked like. He looked like a creepy-ass cracker."

"Does that mean to you like a white individual?"

"Yes . . ."

"What did you say to him or what did he say to you after that?"

"He kept telling me the man was looking at him. So I had to think it might be a rapist."

Again the court reporter complained that she couldn't hear her answer, and Rachel was asked to repeat it. Only minutes into the testimony and her body language was already suggesting she was fed up. She rolled her eyes and took a deep, annoyed breath.

"What did you say to him or what did he say to you?" he asked.

"He said, 'Stop playing with him like that.' "

Again she was asked to repeat herself.

"He said, 'Stop playing with him like that,' " she said.

"Did Mr. Martin say the guy kept looking at him?"

"Yeah. And then he just told me he just wanted to try to lose him. By starting walking back home, back home because the rain calm a little bit."

She began describing how Trayvon said he was going to start walking home, but the man kept following him. Again, she had to stop after being asked to repeat herself. By now, everyone in the courtroom—judge, lawyers, jury, and, especially, Rachel Jeantel—was visibly upset over her first twelve minutes on the witness stand.

"Give us your answer as slowly, and clearly, and loudly as you can," Judge Nelson said.

As Trayvon began walking home, she said, they started talking about the NBA All-Star game that was coming on television that night.

"And then what happened?" de la Rionda asked, referring to their conversation as Trayvon tried to make his way home.

"He said, 'That nigga is still following me around.'"

The judge again asked her to repeat her words.

"'That nigga [is] still following me around,'" she said.

"Pardon my language," de la Rionda said. "But did he use the word 'nigger' to describe the man now?"

"Yes. That's slang."

"That's slang?"

A juror raised her hand and again asked Rachel to repeat herself. The introduction of the N-word was unsettling, but, again, I knew that if Trayvon said it, there was nothing racial about it. The killer clearly isn't black. I knew that Trayvon, Rachel, and other teenagers use words like "nigga" and "cracker" and "dude" interchangeably, which would be impossible if they were racially specific slurs. But the defense tried to interpret this as meaning that Trayvon, not his pursuer, was a racist, and used this intentional misunderstanding to sway the jury's emotions, even though if anyone interjected race into what happened on February 26, 2012, it was the defendant.

Rachel continued her testimony through a number of objections by the defense. Soon, she was forced to repeat herself after nearly every statement. The judge ordered someone to move the microphones closer to Rachel. But it did little to help. Through it all Rachel managed to explain that she told Trayvon to *run*, but he said he didn't need to run, because he was almost back to Brandy's townhouse. But then Rachel testified that he said the killer was suddenly right next to him. She heard a sound, and the phone hung up. She called back and Trayvon answered, saying he had run away from his pursuer.

"I asked him where he at, and he told me he at the back of his daddy's fiancé house," she testified. "I said, 'You better keep running.' He said, 'Nah.' He lost him."

"What happened after that?"

"A second later, Trayvon said, 'Oh, shit! . . . The nigga behind me.' . . . I told him, 'You better run!'"

But again Trayvon assured Rachel that he was almost back to Brandy's townhouse.

She then described hearing Trayvon say to his pursuer, " 'Why are you following me for?' And I heard a hard breathing man say, 'What you doing around here?' "

She started screaming, "Trayvon! Trayvon! What's going on?" But before he could answer she heard a *bump* from his cellphone's headset. She heard what she described as the sound of "wet grass," and she kept calling my son's name.

"Trayvon! Trayvon!" she testified as saying.

She said she heard Trayvon yelling, "Get off. Get off." That was the last she would hear. Because his phone cut off at 7:16 P.M., and Trayvon was dead about a minute and a half later. Not much time for a fight. She tried calling him back, but no answer. She didn't know for certain that Trayvon was dead until the following Tuesday when she got a text at school with a link to a news article about the shooting, she testified.

De la Rionda ended his examination asking Rachel why she didn't go to Trayvon's wake, although she had originally said she had.

"I didn't want to see the body," she said, reaching for a tissue and beginning to cry.

Why did she lie to Tracy about why she didn't go to the funeral or the wake, saying she was in the hospital? she was asked.

"I felt guilty. . . . I was the last person that talked to his son."

After asking her about whose voice she believed was crying for help on the 911 tape—"Trayvon," she said. "Sounds like Trayvon's."— the prosecution rested after only thirty minutes of questioning.

West's cross-examination for the defense was highly charged.

"Good afternoon, Ms. Jeantel," he said.

"Good afternoon, *Mr. Don*," she said, rising up in her chair.

West began by establishing how long she'd known Trayvon, how they had reconnected on February 1, her birthday, and the nature of their friendship. Then he continued with questions about what she heard on the phone between Trayvon and his pursuer that night.

He introduced Defense Exhibit 16, the records of the cellphone calls between Rachel and Trayvon from February 26, which he handed to Rachel and asked her to confirm each of the calls, from 5:09 P.M. leading up to the last call between 7:12 and 7:15 P.M. Next came an exhausting series of questions about the calls, questions about what she knew of Trayvon's movements while she was on the phone with him that night.

"I'm confused," she said at one point.

"After he told you that he saw the man again," West said later, "the next thing you heard him say was, 'Why you following me?'"

"Next thing I heard? . . . I heard [Trayvon say,] 'Why you following me?'" Rachel said.

There was a brief moment of silence in the courtroom as the defense lawyer paused to consider his next question. Rachel must have felt that the sudden silence was odd.

"You can go," she told West, encouraging him to keep going with his questioning. "*You can go!*"

"I'm sorry," said West with a small smile. "It takes me a little bit of time sometimes to come up with the next question."

"You can go!" she said again.

"Okay," said West. More questions followed. I was nervous and hoping that the cross-examination of Rachel would close out soon—she was shaky on the stand, and I was worried about her, but even more worried about what the jury was making of her testimony. West continued to drill into Rachel's story even more.

"After the event on February 26," West continued, "then a day or two later you realized that Trayvon Martin had died [and] you realized that you were the last person to have talked with him and you didn't report that to anyone."

"They said they had got the person who shot Trayvon," she said, meaning she believed the killer had been arrested that night.

"But you did not report it to law enforcement?"

"No. I thought they were supposed to call you. Call the person. Like, track the number down, see who the last person [he talked to] was if somebody got shot."

"You thought they were supposed to call you?"

"Yeah . . . They already had the person that shot Trayvon."

"You thought, 'Case closed'?"

"Yeah," she said. "Do you watch *First 48*?"

"I'm sorry, *First 48*?" asked Don West.

"A show," Rachel said. "*First 48*. When a victim dies, they call the number that the victim called before. And they hadn't called my number, so, and they had already gotten the person. So, case closed, I thought."

I started to wonder if this nineteen-year-old young lady was smarter than anyone thought—like, was she making the attorney look foolish? Had she turned the tables? She was asking him flippant questions in her flat monotone, antagonizing West the same way he had seemingly tried to antagonize her. I didn't really know how to read the situation—it was a strange interaction, a kind of battle of opposites. But my nerves were on edge.

"I told you I do not watch news!" she exclaimed at one point as West repeatedly asked her if she'd seen the news reports of Trayvon's death on television. "I do not watch news!"

West then walked her through "the sequence" of the events that happened immediately after the shooting and up to her first being contacted by Tracy on Saturday, March 17. She explained how she didn't want to meet with us at first, how she felt guilty about being the last person to speak with Trayvon before he died, and how she didn't want to meet with us "because of the situation."

With the courtroom television cameras catching her every pause, stumble, and expression, and the defense using the lies she told out of guilt and fear to whittle away at her credibility, Rachel told the convoluted story of how she asked her mother for permission to meet with me and tell me "what happened that night when her son died."

"You didn't really want to?" West asked.

"I'm not the kind of person who want to see people crying . . . emotional . . . her son *dead* . . . and I was the last one to even talk to her son."

He asked her about our first meeting, and she told him about the letter she gave me and how "Trayvon was being followed that night."

"Is that partly why you didn't go to the memorial service?" West eventually asked. "Because you didn't want people there to know you were the last person and that you didn't want to talk to Ms. Fulton about that?"

"The funeral?" she asked. "Why I didn't go? . . . I didn't want to see the body. You got to understand. You got to understand! *You're the last person to talk to the person, and he died on the phone after he talked to you. You've got to understand what I'm trying to tell you. I'm the last person . . .* You don't know how I felt."

Her voice began to crack. She looked like she was close to crying again.

"You think I really want to go see the body after I just talked to him?" she continued.

"I understand what you're saying, but—" West said.

"I didn't even know he was out!" Rachel said of the killer.

"And then what you did, in order to explain that . . . under oath . . . was that you created a lie, and said that you'd gone to the hospital?"

"Yes," she said.

West seemed to be attacking her credibility, pushing her hard about why she lied about her age, and about being in the hospital as an excuse for not going to Trayvon's memorial. Eventually, he asked her about the recorded phone interview she did with Crump, which would be broadcast on ABC News, pointing out various discrepancies.

"I can explain the Crump interview," she said. "I really did not want to do the interview with Crump, so I hurried up on [the] Crump interview. Because I really didn't want to be on the phone talking about a situation, a deadly situation. I don't talk about death . . . I had told you from when we met I rushed. I told the state. I rushed the Crump interview. Crump interview . . . don't mean nothing to me."

"You didn't take it seriously?"

"Nope."

"You were at your home, right?"

"In a closet! You think I want to be in a closet that long?"

West approached the witness stand and showed Rachel her transcripts of both the interview with Crump on ABC News and her deposition. He was getting ready to point out the discrepancies between the two. As he walked back to his spot in the courtroom, Rachel gave him a sideways look. Her patience, I knew, was growing thin.

"I had told you and it said on the depo paper that you have right now that I had rushed on the interview between me and Crump," she said.

He showed her the transcript of her deposition again and asked her what she had said she heard the killer say "in the deposition, under oath" after Trayvon said "Why you following me?"

The defense attorney said she had previously said the killer responded, "What [are] you talking about?"

"No," Rachel said, tapping her fingernails for emphasis on the desk, trying to clarify what she heard: that Trayvon was the victim, the one who had been pursued. But she couldn't get the right words out. "I had told you. You listening? I had told you what happened to me and Crump interview I had rushed on it. Are you listening?"

"Are you saying you rushed through it and you didn't think about it carefully enough to be sure you told it accurately?" West asked.

"Yes," said Rachel.

West let her answer just marinate for a second. He wanted a moment to let the discrepancies in her testimony really sink in with jurors. I felt my nerves fraying again. He then moved on to question her consistency in identifying Trayvon's voice on the "911 call with the screams for help."

It was getting late in the day, Bernie de la Rionda objected, saying that the lines West was referencing in her deposition, which he asked Rachel on the witness stand, didn't include Rachel's full response to the question.

"Take as much time as you want," West told Rachel over de la Rionda's objection. "Or maybe we could take a break until the morning if that's what you would like—"

"*No!*" Rachel exploded forcefully before West could finish his statement. "I'm done today," she said. "I'm leaving today. *Nope.*"

"Are you refusing to come back tomorrow?" West asked.

"To you?" Rachel asked.

We braced ourselves for Rachel's response. But the judge was quick to interrupt.

"We need to keep this a question-and-answer about her testimony," the judge said. "Any other matters dealing with scheduling, I will make that decision. So if you'll continue to keep reading, please."

Rachel sat back in her seat and continued to read her deposition.

"Do you admit then that you were asked, 'Who was screaming for help?' and you answered, 'It *could* be Trayvon,' " Don West asked Rachel.

After some back-and-forth, she said, "I told you it sounded like Trayvon, because Trayvon has kind of a baby voice."

They continued like this for a while.

West then asked to recess for the day.

"How much more time do you think that you need to finish your cross," Judge Nelson asked West.

"I don't know for sure," he said. "I would think we should plan on at least a couple of hours."

I looked over at Rachel, who let out a frustrated "*What?!*" and dropped her head into her hands, shaking her head. Her personal nightmare wasn't over. She would have to testify for another day.

Rachel entered the courtroom on the fourth day of the trial a different young woman. The high heels she wore the day before had been replaced with flat shoes, making her at least comfortable. She wore a ruffled bronze-colored blouse under a black blazer. She sat erect in the witness chair. Her speech had slowed and she spoke more deliberately. She began answering questions with a simple yes or no, followed by the word "sir"—without the ad-libs and slang flourishes that heated so much of her testimony on the day before.

"Are you okay this morning?" West asked Rachel a half hour into her second day of testimony. "You seem so different than yesterday.

Just checking. Did someone talk with you last night about your demeanor in court yesterday?"

I knew she had spent the night in a hotel room with no television or radio. "No," she responded. "I went to sleep."

West began Rachel's second day on the stand by questioning her about the letter she wrote to me shortly after Trayvon's death.

The defense had learned about the letter Rachel gave to me in her March 19 deposition. She had not mentioned it in any of her previous statements, because she felt it was a personal letter to me and didn't understand the relevance it might have on the case.

West approached the witness stand and gave Rachel a copy of the letter to read to the court.

"I want to object to this witness, and the letter," Bernie de la Rionda said, standing.

Lawyers from both sides met at the judge's bench and discussed the objection in private. But I couldn't figure out why; West was allowed to continue.

"Ms. Jeantel," he began, asking Rachel to take a close look at the copy of the letter, "do you recognize that letter as being one that you said earlier was prepared to be given to Ms. Fulton?"

She said yes.

"And that letter was prepared with the assistance of a friend of yours?"

"Yes," she repeated. She told her friend what she wanted to say in the letter. Her friend then wrote the letter by hand because Rachel was worried that if she wrote it, she said, it wouldn't be legible. The contents of the letter were entirely Rachel's, but it was written in her friend's handwriting—and her friend wrote it in a cursive script.

Don West knew what was coming next, and he must have known it would be dramatic, something that could devastate the jury's perception of Rachel. I again worried for the young lady on the stand.

West had asked Rachel about the letter during her deposition, saying, "I'd like to hand it to you and have you take a look," he had said back then, handing her the letter.

"I have one problem about this," Rachel told West during her deposition.

"Sure, that's what I'd like to know," said West.

"I don't read cursive," she said. "I don't know how to read cursive."

"Do you have enough difficulties reading that you wouldn't be able to proofread it to see if it is accurate?" he asked.

"I already told you, I don't know how to read cursive," she said.

Now, in court, West was asking her the question again.

"Are you able to read that copy well enough that you can tell us if it's in fact the same letter?" West asked.

"No," said Rachel, characteristically quiet to the point of shyness.

"Are you unable to read that at all?"

"Some of them, I do not—"

"Can you read *any* of the words on it?" West said.

"I don't understand, um, cursive," Rachel said, even more quietly now. "I don't read cursive."

The weight of the world would come down on that line—"I don't read cursive"—and unfairly cast Rachel as being illiterate, which wasn't true. I wanted to read it for her. I kept thinking that this is someone's daughter, who has to go through this at such a young age.

"Are you claiming in any way that you don't understand English?" West would later ask.

"I don't understand you," Rachel would reply. "I do understand English."

"My question is when someone speaks to you in English, do you believe that you have any difficulty understanding it because it wasn't your first language?"

"I understand English really well," she would say. It was only reading cursive that was difficult.

"I'll read the letter then," said West. "*I was on the phone when Trayvon decided to go to the corner store. It started to rain, so he decided to walk through another complex because it was raining too hard. He started walking then noticed someone was following him.*"

He paused at one point, as if struggling to read the letter himself.

"*Then he decided to find a shortcut because the man wouldn't follow him. Then he said the man didn't follow him again. Then he looked back and saw the man again. The man started getting closer. Then Trayvon turned around and said, 'Why are you following me?' Then I heard him fall, then the phone hung up. I called back and text, no response. In my mind I thought it was just a fight. Then I found out this tragic story. Thank you, Diamond Eugene.*"

"Is that the letter that you and [your friend] prepared to give to Sybrina Fulton?"

"Yes," she said.

"And contrary to what you said at the deposition," West continued, "this letter does not, in fact, contain any response that the person gave to Trayvon Martin when he said, 'Why are you following me?'"

"Yes," she replied.

"Further, you say that you thought this was just a fight?"

"Yes," she said.

Soon West decided to pull out the word that had gone mostly unspoken until now. He asked if she had heard about the national conversation on race that Trayvon's death had triggered on the news—or if someone else had informed her about it. Again, Rachel told West she didn't watch the news, and that no one had told her how the case had grown into a national story about what West called a "racially charged event."

"What did you base your answer [on] that you thought it was a 'racial thing'?" West asked.

"Because [of] how the situation happened," she said.

Unbelievably, it seemed the defense was trying to turn the question of racism against us. Because if they could show that the event was racially motivated—and that it was Trayvon who was the racist, calling Zimmerman "a creepy-ass cracker"—then perhaps they could lead the jury into believing that Trayvon would attack the neighborhood watch volunteer.

"Tell me, what is it about this event specifically that convinced you it was racially based?" West asked.

"Trayvon was being followed," Rachel responded. "And it was

around seven, and it's not that late. And it's in the rain. Like, come on now."

"Everything that you've told us is based upon whatever Trayvon Martin *told* you that you could remember and then what you interpreted it to mean," said West. "So when you say it's a 'racial event,' what did he tell you that made you think it was a racial event?"

"Somebody was watching him, and then he described the person that was watching him and following him," said Rachel. "And that was kind of strange that a person [kept] watching you and following you. Like he's being stalked."

"What makes that racial?" asked West.

"Describing the person," she said of Trayvon's description of his pursuer.

"Describing the person is what made you think it was racial?"

"Yes," she replied.

"And that's because he described him as a 'creepy-ass cracker'?"

"Yes," said Rachel.

"So it was racial, but it was because Trayvon Martin put race in this?"

"No," said Rachel.

"You don't think that 'creepy-ass cracker' is a racial comment?"

"No," she replied.

Rachel was supposed to be the prosecution's star witness. But the prosecutors had only questioned her briefly. Now being pressured by West's cross-examination, she was on the defensive. Under intense questioning, Rachel began answering questions with a single "Yes, sir" or "No, sir."

"When Mr. de la Rionda was asking questions about what happened and who said what," West continued, "you were making it sound different than it actually was to keep from hurting Ms. Fulton's feelings?"

"Yes, sir," Rachel said, and West asked her if the only thing she said that wasn't accurate was the language Trayvon used to describe his pursuer.

West asked her again about the interviews she did with Crump and the letter she gave me, and why she never mentioned that she heard Trayvon saying "Get off! Get off!" until she mentioned it in her deposition. She answered that no one else but prosecutor de la Rionda had asked her about it, and that she was anxious to get off the phone during the telephone interview with Crump.

"I was not being asked for that part," she said.

"So you made the decision then not to tell Mr. Crump that you'd actually heard Trayvon Martin say 'Get off! Get off!' because you were in a hurry?"

Rachel had clearly had enough. "First of all," she said, "Crump is not law enforcement. He's not an officer. I knew that he was not an officer. So, like I told the mother from the beginning, if an officer wants to talk to me and know the exact story, everything about what happened that night, they will reach me at my number. *You got it?*"

It was good to see her get her spirit back—and it made us happy to see Rachel testing West. She was sassy, and giving him a taste of his own medicine, something we couldn't do.

West began questioning Rachel about the moments before her phone call with Trayvon cut off: the bump on his phone and Trayvon breathing heavily from running away from the killer.

"When you talked to Mr. de la Rionda on April 2nd down at Sybrina Fulton's home," he said, "at one point in the interview he said to you, 'So the last thing you heard was some kind of noise, like something hitting somebody?'"

"Trayvon got hit," said Rachel. "Trayvon got hit."

"You don't know that, do you?" West said, his voice rising, verbally confrontational. (Rachel said, "No, sir.") "You don't know that Trayvon got hit. You don't know that Trayvon didn't at that moment take his fists and drive them into George Zimmerman's face."

"Please, lower your voice," Judge Nelson said, interrupting.

"Do you?" West asked.

"No, sir," said Rachel.

"That's when the phone cut off?" ("Yes, sir," she answered.) "That's what you wrote in the letter?"

"Yes, sir."

Rachel's sassiness seemed to now be fading. She appeared sad, like the guilt she had carried the past year had found her again and was suddenly dragging her down.

Still, she was far from giving up.

At one point, West began questioning the truthfulness of what Trayvon was communicating to her about his actions and the actions of the killer, and Rachel kept answering questions with variations of "That's what Trayvon told me, sir."

"Of course you don't know if he was telling you the truth or not," West said, a smile flashing across his face.

"Why he need to lie about that, sir?" asked Rachel.

"Maybe if he decided to assault George Zimmerman he didn't want you to know about it."

"That's real retarded, sir," she said. "Trayvon did not know him."

We knew what Rachel meant and that she was right. She was telling the truth about what she knew, even if it was slang that was sometimes hard to understand.

"At the point, though, that all of that happened, you are saying now that you knew something had taken place," said West. "But the reason you didn't do anything about it, telling anybody what you had heard, come forward to the police, is because in your mind it was just a fight, correct?" ("Yes, sir," Rachel answered.) "And in fact it was just a fight Trayvon Martin started. That's why you weren't worried, that's why you didn't do anything. *It was because Trayvon Martin started the fight* and you knew that."

I eagerly waited for Rachel to unleash some classic line. But before she could, Bernie de la Rionda immediately stood up from the prosecution table and objected. West was badgering the witness, he said. But he was overruled.

"No, sir!" said Rachel defiantly. "I had told you before I did not know this man was out of jail. I don't know what you're talking about."

West kept trying to make Trayvon the approacher and aggressor, but Rachel defiantly stuck to her story. At every question she said,

"No, sir." She would answer insisting that George Zimmerman, not Trayvon, was the aggressor.

At one point the attorney told her, "I thought, in fact, that you said that it could have been, for all you know, Trayvon Martin smashing George Zimmerman in the face is what you actually heard . . ."

"What?" she asked.

"Yes, just earlier today," said West.

"By who?" she asked.

"By you," she was told.

"You ain't get that from me," said Rachel.

West soon rested his cross-examination after two or more hours, and after a short redirect by de la Rionda, Rachel's time on the witness stand was finally over. It had been an emotional roller coaster. I was intensely relieved that it was over. We returned to our hotel for the night.

That night, television news and the Internet erupted with comments about Rachel, including vicious insults about her appearance, intelligence, and speech. She had lost a friend. She stood up for him in court. And she paid a price for it, which she didn't deserve.

I had been worried for Rachel, who I knew was a nice young lady and a loyal friend who had bonded with our son. She was a very important witness, the last person to speak to Trayvon. But I didn't believe she was prepared enough for the witness stand.

As for the defense, they turned her testimony into what seemed like a referendum on Rachel, just as they had done with Trayvon, attempting to turn both of them into caricatures of what some people think about young black people.

Tracy told me later it felt like time-of-possession in a football game: the numbers told the story. The prosecution questioned Rachel for a little over thirty minutes, the defense for almost seven hours over two days. I felt she had done her best given the circumstances, but I worried the prosecution had done irreparable damage, not only to our star witness, but to our entire case.

CHAPTER 12

Tracy

ᨆ

June 28, 2013–July 10, 2013

I knew the justice system wasn't color-blind. There's one set of rules for us and a different set for other groups—different races, ethnicities, religions, ethnic groups. The rules for us—for African Americans—had been in place for a long time in this country. And the rules were not going to help us. So from the beginning, I was worried about the jurors that had been selected for the trial.

Could they see this tragedy through the eyes of black parents?

I got my answer when I heard a potential white woman juror say, "Trayvon wouldn't have been suspended had his father been involved in his life." She didn't know me from a can of paint. But she assumed that I wasn't involved in my child's life. My heart sank a little when I heard that—we have a long way to go. Little did she know that I was always a part of my son's life.

By June 28, 2013, the fifth day of the trial, most people in Sanford and the outlying areas knew who we were. We knew that some people in the Sanford area, and beyond, didn't like us. But we didn't care. We also met many people who supported us—from the desk clerks at

our hotel in Lake Mary to the McDonald's on the road to the courthouse where we would stop every morning for breakfast—people
knew our names and why we were there.

"Good luck," many of them would say.

Because most of them were people like us: hardworking, family-
oriented, struggling to get through the day.

At the McDonald's, we would pick up our breakfast from the
drive-thru. Some days, we would have three cars or vans of lawyers
and family going through.

"Six egg-and-cheese McMuffins," we would say. "Coffee, orange
juice, hash browns . . ."

"Good luck, Tracy," the clerk would say while giving us our food.
"Good luck, Sybrina."

Then we would drive to the courthouse in Sanford. By the time
the trial had gotten under way, we had become a little paranoid—and
not only from threats on our lives and the lives of our families that we
were routinely receiving online, by phone, and in the mail. We also
thought we were possibly being followed. Bringing thousands of protesters into a town with a population of fifty thousand does change
things. Our case created a mood that the local citizens weren't used
to, especially when national civil rights leaders began streaming into
town. Again, I wouldn't say that the overall community was against
us. But we definitely were foreigners in a foreign place.

Our attorney Daryl Parks would drive us, taking a different route
from the hotel to the courthouse every day. A sheriff's department
deputy would meet us in his squad car a mile from the courthouse.
He was a nice guy, big and burly, and we would follow his car closely
as he led us into town. Driving behind the deputy, snaking down side
streets, evading the steadily growing mass of media, Parks would
drop us off at the back entrance of the courthouse every morning
before eight.

Once we were dropped off, our attorneys would park in our spaces
in front of the courthouse. Then our attorneys would usually address
the media, every representative and every network and news outlet

trying somehow to get a new way to talk about the case they had covered so much already. Once the trial began, our attorneys had started doing interviews for us—we were getting too many requests to deal with. We were under such a constant media siege that we soon began staying inside the courthouse throughout the entire day.

Passing through the metal detector, we would remove our shoes, belts, and any metal objects, and then proceed into the hallway beside the elevators to wait for the sheriff's personnel who would bring us through the hallway and into the courtoom. We had to face the killer and his family every day in court. We had to walk through the same doors as they did, and down the same hallway. And of course we had to sit in the courtroom very close to where they sat.

We all had security badges. They gave the killer and his family the same thing—the same badges, same parking spaces, same number of seats in the courtroom. Where does it say that the defendant in a murder case gets the same rights as the victim? I'm not sure about the answer to that question. And I'm sure there are good reasons to be fair. But I just had a strong feeling that if the defendant was black and the victim a white child, it might have gone a different way.

The prosecutors rarely came to the small witness room that we'd been given for lunch and breaks and never asked us for input. They met with us prior to the trial, but the strategy was all theirs, for better or for worse.

Trial day number five would bring the testimony of an important observer to the actual event: witness number six, the 911 caller Jonathan Good. He worked in "finance," he would tell the court, and was a resident at the Retreat at Twin Lakes on the night of Trayvon's killing. He was one of the very few eyewitnesses who claimed to have actually seen the struggle between Trayvon and his killer, if for only a few seconds.

He entered the courtroom, a young man in a white dress shirt and candy-striped necktie. He sat down, and under questions from de la Rionda he told his story. He said he was at home with his wife in the living room watching TV when he heard a "faint" noise coming from an area near the back of his house, followed a few minutes later by more noise.

"The same noise," Good said. "Just louder. It seemed like it was getting closer."

He stepped halfway out his sliding glass door, keeping one foot inside.

"It looked like a tussle," he said, and he thought it might be an attack involving a dog.

"What's going on?" he yelled into the darkness. "Stop it!"

Then, he testified, he began to make out the shapes of two people on the ground, one on top of the other. He couldn't see their faces, only the color of their clothing.

"The color of clothing on top," de la Rionda said. "What could you see?"

"It was dark," said Good, which would lead the jury to believe it was Trayvon, in his dark gray hoodie, on top.

"How about the color of clothing on the bottom?"

"I believe it was a light white or red," he said, which was the color of the jacket the killer was wearing that night. Although he only saw "ten seconds max," he also claimed the person on the bottom was lighter-skinned.

He said that as the struggle moved "up to the concrete," the person on top was "straddling" the other who was faceup below him. Good said it "looked like there were strikes being thrown, or punches being thrown," but because of the lack of lighting he was unsure if what he saw were punches or the person on top holding the other down. What he was sure of was that he saw the arms of the person on top moving downward.

If it was a fight, however, it must have been a short one. Rachel's call with Tray got dropped at 7:15; the screams on the 911 call came a minute later.

He heard someone yell "Help," but couldn't say "one hundred percent" whether it was the man on the top or the man on the bottom. He called 911. The prosecution played Good's 911 call for the court.

"Police, I just heard a shot right behind my house," he said on the call. "They're wrestling right in the back of my porch. . . . The guy's yelling help, and I'm not going outside . . . I'm pretty sure the guy's dead out here. Holy shit!"

Good had compared the "straddling" position of the person on top to a move made in mixed martial arts, saying, "It just looked like something I'd seen on TV before."

"Did you ever see the person on top pick up the person from the bottom and actually slam them into the concrete?"

"No," he said.

"Did you ever see the person on top slamming the person on bottom's head on the concrete over and over and over?"

"No," he repeated.

"Did you see at any time the person on top grab the person on the bottom's head and actually slam it into the concrete?"

"No," he said again.

Of course not, as this was a claim made by the killer, which we believed never happened.

So much for the defense's opening statement about the concrete being used as a "weapon," I thought.

After showing exhibits of the crime scene, de la Rionda asked Good when he heard the gunshot in relation to making the 911 call. Good said that after stepping outside and hearing one or two cries for help, he returned inside to pick up his phone. As he was waiting for the dispatcher to pick up, he heard the gunshot.

What de la Rionda said next after about forty minutes of questioning stunned us: "Thank you, I have no further questions at this time." This was a witness saying that Trayvon was on top of his killer, attacking him, and the prosecution didn't question how he could be so sure about the color of the people's clothing on that dark and rainy night? I was beginning to feel like the prosecution was overconfident that the jury would connect the few clues they gave them, but I didn't think they'd given them nearly enough to convict—they were making it harder to convict than it needed to be.

That feeling deepened when O'Mara then began his cross-examination. Good admitted to O'Mara that he was reluctant to get involved in the case, and he had requested to remain anonymous. And he *had* remained anonymous to everyone except the police, prosecutors, and defense attorneys until now, with one exception: he had spoken to the media.

"What you saw was the person on top in an MMA-style straddle position, correct?" O'Mara said.

"Correct," said Good.

"That was further described, was it not, as being a 'ground and pound?'"

"Correct," answered Good.

"What is 'ground and pound' as you define it?"

"The person on top being able to punch the person on bottom, but the person on bottom also has the chance to get out or punch the person on top. It's back and forth," said Good.

Was this what he saw—or was he merely describing what "ground and pound" is?

"The person who you now know to be Trayvon Martin was on top, correct?"

"Correct," said Good.

"And he was the one who was raining blows down on the person on the bottom, George Zimmerman, right?" O'Mara continued.

"That's what it looked like," Good said.

"You couldn't actually see fist hit face, right?"

"No," he replied, and a discussion of where he was and what he saw continued.

"Do you think that it was the person on the bottom who was screaming for help?" O'Mara asked.

"I mean, rationally thinking, I would think so," Good said.

Rationally thinking? Wouldn't it be more rational to think the un-armed person on the wrong end of a gun would be the one screaming—regardless of who was on top and who was on the bottom?

Bernie de la Rionda questioned him in redirect. Using a pair of water bottles to represent the two men, he demonstrated the body positions of the killer and Trayvon as Good described them. He asked Good to reiterate that he didn't hear any sounds that would be made by punches or slaps, and Good admitted that he used the term "ground and pound" simply to give a better description of what he saw. But what he saw was only a downward movement of arms and he couldn't say there were actual blows inflicted on the person on the ground. But de la Rionda stopped there, and never brought up the important point: if Trayvon was beating the shooter so badly, straddling him in a "ground and pound" position, with blows to the head so fierce it would lead the bigger, older man to become disoriented and begin screaming for his life, how could he suddenly see Trayvon reaching for his gun and then be able to retrieve his gun and fire? And if the killer was on his back, as Good claimed, how could Trayvon even have seen the gun holstered behind him as he lay on the ground, let alone been able to reach for it?

Things just didn't add up. It could not have possibly happened the way the killer told the story.

The prosecutors told us they were going to question Good about that, but the questions were never asked. De la Rionda returned to the prosecution table without attempting to address these issues. Not once did this line of questioning come into the trial. Why? Along with this, why didn't they try to "humanize" Trayvon, as the attorney Lisa Bloom would write, to show him as we knew him? I didn't understand what was going on.

After Good's testimony, we left the courthouse and headed back to our hotel, where the television was filled with news and commentary about our case.

"If he was raining blows, MMA-style, you think there would be some physical evidence of that on his fists," Reverend Sharpton said on one of the never-ending news shows. "Second, it was testified that Zimmerman had MMA training. If Zimmerman had MMA training and there was an MMA attack going on, why didn't he use his MMA training to defend himself?"

It was a Friday night after a long day, and a long first week, in court. Every weekday night after a day in court, we would have dinner with our attorneys and family. And if it was a Friday, we would drive back to Miami.

I spent a lot of time alone at the trial, which was something I was accustomed to doing. As a truck driver, I spend my days mostly alone, a one-man band, driving between restaurants and hotels, making deliveries. Sometimes my girlfriend, Brandy, would come up to support me during the trial. Usually, members of my family were there. But most evenings, I had nothing to occupy me but the case. I would find myself alone and praying.

"Continue to show us favor, Lord," I would pray. "Continue to cover us."

I prayed for Trayvon, for Sybrina, for Jahvaris, for myself. But I also prayed for justice. It was still early, but I already had the feeling it wasn't going our way. It just seemed so bizarre. A phrase kept coming to me: *My son had been intensely alive!* My son had been a life force, a teenager who had hopes and dreams and so much love. But in death, he became a figure we could only see through the dark mirror of evidence and testimony, a cursed single night when our son and all that life inside him was reduced to a stranger, a black kid in a hoodie, a young man in the shadows. A suspect. The prosecution hadn't yet personalized Trayvon for the jury and had allowed the defense to characterize him in a way that I didn't recognize.

If the defense was going to put Trayvon on trial, couldn't the prosecution call Trayvon's grandmothers, aunt, uncles, classmates? All I had heard about Trayvon in this trial was what the defense was saying about him. And if I was feeling that way, I'm sure the jury was, too. I knew these six women didn't—and couldn't—feel close to Trayvon. Not that the prosecution didn't use nice adjectives when talking about him, but I didn't think they were asking the right questions of the witnesses, or even calling the right kind of witnesses, the kind that would help build a fuller picture of him. So while the killer sat in the court, day after day, in his suit and tie and blank expression, the victim was absent, unaccounted for, and yet, somehow, put on trial.

I would approach prosecutors de la Rionda and Guy about my concerns.

"Where are the character witnesses for Trayvon?" I would ask.

"Why would Trayvon approach a man he didn't know?"

All I would get from them was "We'll see." The prosecution seemed content with a passive approach. But I didn't feel they were proving the truth beyond a reasonable doubt—that George Zimmerman killed my son—and I was worried we were losing the momentum we had built over all the time we'd spent on the road in our march to justice over the past year and four months.

I still kept faith in the jury. I was comfortable with six women, but I was concerned that there were no people of color on the jury, except for one Hispanic woman, who would later tell author Lisa Bloom that the others trivialized and mocked her. They were technically sequestered at the Marriott in Lake Mary but they were seen in public, and there were even reports that they went bowling and on other excursions.

But I continued to pray that even though none of them were black, they would have the compassion and insight to realize that race shouldn't be a divisive issue in this case. We believed, now and then, that the death of a child is the same for white parents as it is for Latino parents as it is for Asian parents as it is for black parents, and that our case, as Sybrina had said, was not about black and white, but right and wrong. As long as the women on the jury could understand that, I believed we still had a chance. But I think our hopes might have been misplaced. Race was an issue, bubbling under the surface of everything.

Another one of our best chances for justice appeared on Monday, July 1, when de la Rionda called Chris Serino, the lead detective in the shooting of my son, to the stand.

The square-jawed detective wore a black suit, black tie, and dark, closely cut hair. Serino led the investigation for the Sanford Police

Department from its first night to meeting with me on two mornings after the shooting, all the way up to consulting with Chief Bill Lee and even members of the state attorney's office. A career police officer, Serino had nearly twenty years of experience in law enforcement, including time as a federal officer with the Department of Defense. I knew he would tell the truth and help our case—if he was asked the right questions.

He shrugged his broad shoulders as he settled into his chair and introduced himself in the kind of gruff, gravelly voice you might expect from a career cop.

He gave some details about the night of February 26, 2012. When he arrived at the Retreat at approximately eight P.M., Trayvon was dead on the ground and the killer had already been taken into custody by the police department. He said he tried to identify Trayvon through a fingerprint scan, but he wasn't in the system. Around midnight, Serino headed back to the police station, where he met the killer for the first time. Another investigator, Officer Doris Singleton, had already interviewed him, but Serino decided to interview him again.

De la Rionda played a portion of Serino's interview tape for the court, leading up to the killer's claim that Trayvon mounted him and began punching him in the face and the head. When Trayvon began pounding his head against the concrete, the killer said, he started yelling for help but Trayvon smothered his mouth and nose. The killer tried to slide out from underneath Trayvon, but realized his shirt had come up and felt Trayvon reaching toward his right side where his gun was holstered, it would turn out, behind his back, which "the prosecution had failed to raise this point at trial," wrote the attorney and author Lisa Bloom in her book about the case.

"You're gonna die, motherfucker," we could hear Zimmerman saying on the interview tape, quoting what he said Trayvon had told him.

But the killer, in his version of the story, was quicker and grabbed the gun first.

"What happened then?" Serino asked.

"I shot him," the killer said.

Trayvon immediately sat up after the shot went through him. "You got me," the killer said Trayvon told him before dying.

He said "somehow I got out from under." Trayvon as he died. He thought Trayvon was armed with something in his hands, so he spread my son's arms apart and climbed on top of him until, Serino asked, the police "arrived and you surrendered?" to which the killer agreed.

That was pretty much the extent of Serino's first interview, and for the most part Serino took him at his word. They scheduled a time to meet the next day for a walk-through of the events at the Retreat, and Serino instructed the killer to go home and get some rest.

Go home and get some rest.

I'd heard this story a dozen times now, but it was always like a punch to my stomach.

De la Rionda then played the video of the walk-through at the Retreat. By now Sybrina couldn't bear to look at the video screen hanging on the courtroom's far wall. They had shown Trayvon's lifeless body too many times on it, and she couldn't stand to see it again. She left the courtroom before the lights were dimmed and the video screen showed George Zimmerman on the day after the killing.

In the video, he took Serino and two other investigators through his version of the events. He showed them where he was when he first saw Trayvon. He showed them where he parked and where my son died. He gave his version of what happened, saying that Trayvon confronted then attacked him.

De la Rionda had one more video to show the jury, this one from a few days after the shooting. In this video, Serino interviewed the killer in an interrogation room at the Sanford police station. Officer Doris Singleton joined Serino, and the three of them sat around a table in a small room with a two-way mirror on one wall. The killer repeated his version of the events from that night, but this time Serino and Singleton had some tougher questions for him. They drilled him about why he didn't identify himself as neighborhood watch as well as the details of their fatal encounter.

"I can't pinpoint where you were smothered, that's the problem I'm having . . ." Serino said, once they moved to his desk to play the 911 tape.

"And when we're listening to the screaming, doesn't sound like there is a hesitation in the screaming," said Officer Singleton. "It sounds like it's continuous, and if someone's being hurt [imitates scream being muffled] it's gonna stop. But we don't hear the, we don't hear it stop."

Again, thoughts raged through my mind: *Because his mouth was never covered up! And he wasn't the one yelling.*

Sure enough, when Serino played the tape for the killer, he had said, upon hearing the voice screaming for help, "That doesn't even sound like me."

After this was mentioned again, I looked over at the jury, expecting some reaction. There wasn't much. Did this register with them? Didn't they just hear the killer admit that he *didn't* recognize his own voice calling for help?

After a recess, then a few follow-up questions by de la Rionda, the prosecution rested. *No more questions.* Again, I couldn't believe it. The defense would spend hours questioning witnesses, tearing down their stories, and here, with the lead investigator on the stand, the prosecution rested after less than two hours.

The prosecutors never gave the detective the chance to paint a true picture. Never asked, "Detective, did you believe the killer's story?"

And I thought, *Oh, no.*

At the very least I thought de la Rionda should have asked Serino about his recommendation on his report that Trayvon's killer be arrested and charged with manslaughter. A career police officer thinking there is enough evidence to charge the killer with manslaughter is something I believe that the prosecution should have drilled into the minds of each juror: not only had the public demanded the arrest of the killer, but the person who best knew the facts within the Sanford Police Department—Chris Serino—had recommended charging him with manslaughter when he wrote his police report on the incident.

I kept repeating in my mind: *Ask him about his recommending the charge of manslaughter!*

But the question was never asked.

Serino also wrote in his report that the killer "failed" to identify himself in any way to Trayvon and acted in ways "inconsistent with those of a person who has stated he was in fear of another subject," and had missed chances to "defuse the circumstances surrounding their encounter."

It seemed to me from Serino's expression that he was also surprised that his testimony for the prosecution was so brief. He clearly had more to say, but more wasn't being asked of him. Of course, we knew that prosecutors don't like to be combative with police officers. Technically, they're on the same team, both paid by the city, county, or state, and Serino had met and been cooperative with prosecutors during the investigation, so surely neither wanted to be openly confrontational with the other. The fact remained that a lot was left on the table by the prosecution.

But confrontation was at the core of the defense.

When O'Mara rose to begin his cross-examination, he listed Serino's responsibilities as chief detective and then commented, it seemed, on the lack of questioning from the prosecution.

"You haven't testified to virtually any of that yet, though, have you?" he asked.

"As to the methodology of the case?" Serino said. "No, I haven't."

"Basically, the only thing you've testified so far is the statements from my client?"

"Correct, yes."

O'Mara then had Serino walk the jury through the steps he took that night. He spoke with the killer a few minutes after midnight, nearly six hours after the shooting. By then he had also spoken with other witnesses, like John Good, and had reviewed all the information gathered up to that point, including an interview with the killer conducted by Officer Doris Singleton. Initially, working with "a lot of information," compared to what was originally available, O'Mara suggested the killer's version of events, told to both Singleton and Serino, appeared to line up.

"Did you notice any significant differences that caused you concern based upon your years of experience as an investigator?" O'Mara asked.

"Not immediately. No, sir," Serino said.

"Did he seem to be cagey in his answering to you?" O'Mara asked. "Did he seem to be sidestepping your [questions] in any form or way to get around answering your questions?"

"No, sir," Serino said. "He was being straightforward, in my opinion."

He agreed with O'Mara's term that the killer did seem to have a "flat affect about everything that had happened to him that night," which meant he was strangely calm. Serino would suggest to the killer that he get some kind of psychological "help" to deal with it.

"Did it come across to you, though, that he was just uncaring . . . ?" O'Mara asked. "Or was it truly your thought that he was reacting to the trauma?"

"I didn't know him prior to this . . . ," Serino said. "That was one of the concerns, that may have been that he was uncaring or other things were going on."

"Would you expect that there were going to be some differences [in his story]?" O'Mara asked.

"Absolutely."

"And why is that?"

"Because we're not robots as people," he said.

"As a matter of fact, if someone were to come to you and have the exact same story down fact for fact, and word for word, sentence for sentence each time you talked to them, what would you think about that person's honesty or veracity?" O'Mara asked.

"Either they're being completely honest, or completely false to the extreme," Serino said.

After some back-and-forth, the attorney asked, "Because at this point you had fairly specific evidence that Mr. Zimmerman was acting in self-defense that night, correct?"

"I had information that would have supported that."

Wait! I thought. *Why would he suggest on his report that Zimmerman be charged with manslaughter if he thought it was a case of self-defense?* Again, things just didn't add up.

O'Mara moved on to the third interview Serino did with the killer. Serino talked about the other evidence he'd gotten and how he realized the only living person who knew how the incident began was the man on trial. Of course, there were the 911 calls and statements from John Good, but only the killer knew how the confrontation started.

"I had nothing of substance to basically toss it in to confront him with as far as the interview went," Serino said, "other than a suspicious lack of remembering the streets, how many streets he had in his neighborhood and other oddities."

"So then what you decided to take on," O'Mara said, "is what's called a 'challenge interview,' correct?"

"At this point, I wasn't ready for one, but yes."

"You were also under quite a deal of pressure to get this case moved forward, correct?" (Serino answered, "Yes.") "And had to move even quicker than you would have otherwise have moved on this case because of some of the external pressures that we now know existed in this case?" asked O'Mara. ("Yes, sir.") "And it was for that reason that you may have moved a little bit quicker than you otherwise would have liked to interview Mr. Zimmerman in this sort of aggressive context, correct?"

Serino said yes. As a result, he had little to challenge Zimmerman with and described this third interview as "mild." Serino also noted that this case was particularly difficult because it was possible, at least from a detective's perspective, that "in this particular case, I mean he could have been considered a victim, also."

O'Mara then asked Serino about the defendant's profiling of Trayvon and his reasons for questioning him about his intentions and thought process.

"You sort of hit him with that pretty straight out of the box, right, hoping for maybe a response that would give you an insight as to whether or not he was profiling Trayvon because Trayvon was black?" O'Mara said. "So you asked him, 'If he would have been white, would you have reacted the same way?' "

Serino answered, "Yes, sir."

We all knew that if Trayvon would have been white, the killer probably wouldn't have reacted in such a manner.

Serino said it didn't matter, and to him he seemed straightforward in his response. "There were external concerns about that . . . and I needed to get that clarified," Serino said.

"You also had a concern that you evidenced to him or challenged him on because you had an issue as to whether or not his rendition of getting hit dozens of times were supported by the forensic evidence, correct?"

"In my view, yes, they were lacking."

The killer had told investigators he had been hit nearly *thirty* times, but Serino felt the injuries he sustained were not severe enough for that much pounding. The detective added that people often panic during an altercation and exaggerate the facts, so while this concerned him, he didn't feel it indicated an outright lie.

In my book, when you exaggerate the facts, that is a lie. There is no way Trayvon hit him thirty times.

O'Mara asked Serino again about his bluff that Trayvon may have filmed the incident on his phone, to which the killer responded that he hoped someone had. Serino again said this meant to him that, "Either he was telling the truth or was a complete pathological liar."

He knew that Trayvon wasn't filming anything, because he was trying to get away from his killer!

"So if we were to take pathological liar off the table as a possibility, just for the purposes of this next question, you think he was telling the truth?" O'Mara asked.

"Yes," Serino replied.

But he'd given me the impression that he hadn't believed the killer's story!

With that, the court then recessed for the evening.

O'Mara played Serino like a piano. And Serino, who had seemed so skeptical of the killer when we first talked, and who recommended in his report that the killer be charged, seemed to be walking all that back. Once again, we felt that law enforcement, whose testimony is almost always helpful to the prosecution, was working *against* us. Why? When we returned the next day, and before the jury entered, de la Rionda led off with an objection.

He argued that the end of Serino's testimony from the previous day should be stricken from the record because he was giving his opinion, which, coming from a police officer, might bias the jury.

After briefly reading over some of the case law, Judge Nelson agreed that Serino's opinions should be stricken. The jury was then brought in and given that instruction, as if that alone would cause them to forget everything flying in Serino's testimony the day before.

Why hadn't the objection been made before Serino finished giving his testimony? Before the jury had a night to sleep on it?

It wasn't much of a victory for the prosecution.

O'Mara trudged forward, playing a portion of the recording of Serino's third interview with Zimmerman, in which he played for the defendant the 911 tapes and asked his client if he recognized the voice screaming for help.

"In the transcript," O'Mara said, "there was a suggestion yesterday that Mr. Zimmerman said, 'It doesn't even sound like me.' Do you remember that?"

Serino said yes.

"Did that change the direction of your interrogation of him at all?"

It didn't, he said. When asked if the killer's comment about the voice on the 911 tape—"That doesn't even sound like me"—caused any concern, he said, "No, it did not."

On his redirect, de la Rionda, thankfully, had more questions for Serino.

He replayed the killer's words from the nonemergency-line call that became the first words of this trial, "These assholes, they always get away."

"Is that something you would use in reference to somebody you're going to invite over for dinner?" de la Rionda asked. "Would you call them 'these assholes'?"

"No, sir, I would not," he said.

De la Rionda played more of the nonemergency call.

"Is the word, pardon my language, 'fucking punks' something that you would refer to, something good about people when you would reference them?" he asked.

"No, sir, it's not," Serino said.

"Does that statement not indicate ill-will, hatred, and spite against somebody else, sir? . . . Calling somebody and referencing them as 'fucking punks'?"

"That is ill-will and spite, correct," Serino said. De la Rionda was finally trying to link the killer's words to the kind of mindset—"a deranged mind" was the legal definition—that could lead to a conviction.

"Did the defendant ever indicate that he was happy that there were burglaries being committed at Twin Lakes?"

"No, he did not."

"In fact, didn't he actually say this?" And then de la Rionda played another portion of the killer's interview with Officer Doris Singleton, in which the killer references his wife becoming scared after the burglaries that took place in the neighborhood and said that was the reason for starting the neighborhood watch program. In describing his role as the neighborhood watch coordinator, the killer said he often calls the nonemergency line when he sees something suspicious, but "these guys always get away."

"Didn't he say that to the nonemergency operator also, but he used more colorful language, pardon my language, 'These assholes always get away,' correct?"

The detective agreed that he had.

"If somebody were to believe that another person is a criminal, could that be a form of profiling?" de la Rionda continued.

"It could be construed as such," Serino said, after O'Mara objected.

"Was there any indication that Trayvon Benjamin Martin, the young man . . . just turned seventeen, was committing a crime that evening, sir?"

Of course, he said, there wasn't.

De la Rionda's pace was now quickening, and we were glad for that. He moved on to the killer's claim that he left his truck and followed Trayvon down a path between the townhomes because he needed an address to give to the police and couldn't remember the name of the street he was on.

"Right there on that corner," de la Rionda said, pausing the video walk-through on a frame with a townhome facing the spot where the killer said he parked, "lived Ms. Lauer.

"I want to show you a photograph in front of Ms. Lauer's residence," he said. "Isn't there a numerical address right there in front of her house?"

There was, and de la Rionda zoomed in on the frame to show the numbers: 1211, which Serino confirmed as the correct address.

"The defendant in that reenactment, when he's pointing at all the back of all these houses where he's claiming he doesn't have an address," de la Rionda said, his arms now outstretched in the air, "[but] there's an address right there staring at him, isn't that true, sir?"

"Yes, there is," Serino said.

De la Rionda then showed an aerial photograph of Twin Lakes. He highlighted a portion of Zimmerman's interview in which the killer stated he couldn't remember the name of the street he was on when he left his truck. But in the photograph, de la Rionda pointed out that there are only *three* streets in the Retreat, and the street the killer was on, Twin Tree Lane, was the same street that led to the main entrance of the neighborhood. With only three streets in the complex, how could you not know what street you were on?

Which meant the killer knew where he was, knew the terrain. It was clear that he exited his truck for one reason: to follow Trayvon and make sure he did not get away.

Finally, de la Rionda pointed out one more major hole in the killer's story.

The killer had claimed that after he shot Trayvon he had spread his arms apart until the police arrived, in fear that Trayvon might have a weapon. But the first pictures taken at the scene by police officers showed Trayvon's body lying facedown, not with his hands outstretched, but underneath his body.

"Could someone say that that was inconsistent with the defendant's statement that his hands were straight out, that he had put his hands out?" de la Rionda asked.

"That positioning as seen there, yes it is," Serino said.

After de la Rionda rested his redirect, O'Mara began questioning Serino again, now more forcefully than ever.

Regarding his client's use of the term "assholes," O'Mara suggested to Detective Serino that the killer could have been "generalizing," and not explicitly meaning Trayvon. "Because you know from your investigation that he was a bit frustrated that his neighborhood was being assailed by burglars, right?"

Serino said yes.

O'Mara mentioned his client's admission that he had been following Trayvon.

But wait: during one of the killer's renditions he said he was not following Trayvon, but was just walking in the same direction.

"Anything wrong with following somebody like that?" he asked.

An objection caused the question to be rephrased: "Do you think there was anything wrong with him following him to see where he was going?"

"Legally speaking, no," Serino said.

But if you are in fear of your life, why would you get out of your vehicle to follow someone?

"Another challenge that you made to Mr. Zimmerman concerned this question about the hands over the face," O'Mara continued after a series of other questions. "And yet in the screaming on the 911 [recording] there wasn't a great deal of muffling, would you agree?"

"No, sir, there was not, yes," Serino said.

"May it also be that you perceive getting smothered even when somebody has a hand on your broken nose?" ("Possibly, yes," said Serino.)

Again, this was not consistent with the evidence. There was none of Zimmerman's blood at all on Trayvon's hands.

"Would you agree that there may have been some screams muffled enough so they simply didn't show up on the tape?"

"There could have been, possibly."

After O'Mara returned to the defense table, de la Rionda cross-examined Serino briefly, before saying "No further questions," and Judge Nelson excused Chris Serino from the witness stand.

Watching the detective depart, I couldn't help but feel as though I was watching our great hope go up in smoke. We had suffered yet another major defeat in the case. The detective had all of the right answers. But he was never asked the right questions.

Six days later Serino was called back to testify again. O'Mara asked Serino about playing the 911 call for me for the first time. I had lost my son the day before, and, through a cloud of unfathomable grief and confusion, I said I wasn't sure about whose voice was screaming for help on the tape. That would be misinterpreted by the police—and surely now by the defense—as meaning that I felt it wasn't Trayvon, but his killer, yelling for help, which was one hundred percent false.

"Did there come a time that you met with Tracy Martin and his girlfriend, Brandy Green, in your office?" O'Mara asked.

"Yes, sir, there was," Serino replied.

O'Mara then asked detailed questions about our meeting, even down to how we were seated when Serino played us the 911 calls. When asked if I'd thought it was Trayvon screaming on the recordings, the detective testified that I'd looked away and said "No" under my breath.

. . .

On Wednesday, July 3, Trayvon's hoodie made an appearance, in one of the most dramatic moments of the trial.

During the testimony of Amy Siewert, a crime laboratory analyst in the firearms division of the Florida Department of Law Enforcement, prosecutor John Guy brought out the actual hoodie Trayvon was wearing the night he was killed. The article of clothing that I had seen him wear so many times was now mounted behind glass in a frame with the arms stretched out and the hood pulled up. The bullet hole was clearly visible over the heart, surrounded by dried blood.

By this time, hoodies had become a symbol of our movement for justice. But now it was an exhibit in the trial, and the first time people in court—and watching on television—had seen the actual hoodie that Trayvon was wearing on the night of his death. Amy Siewert explained that she had examined the hoodie as part of the initial investigation and had also done "distance testing" to calculate the distance of the gun from Trayvon's chest when the fatal shot was fired.

Prosecutor Guy lifted the framed hoodie in front of the jury so that Siewert could better illustrate the steps she took in the investigation, and I could see the courtroom reflected in the glass. Everyone's faces—black, white, young and old, my face and Sybrina's face and our family members' faces—all staring back from the reflection within the shape of the hoodie.

It was a powerful moment. This hoodie that had first made the killer suspicious of Trayvon, the hoodie that had sparked the chase and the fatal gunshot, the hoodie that would later be transformed into a symbol of our struggle for justice, was now front and center in the courtroom, another visual representation of how powerful our movement for justice—not just for Trayvon but for all of the young men and women who would follow him in death from senseless violence—had become.

We could all see ourselves in that hoodie, but what we saw was uncertain. Could the jury see the case from our eyes, from Trayvon's eyes? Or did the jury see the case from the eyes of the killer and the defense?

First Guy, and then O'Mara on redirect, questioned the witness about the hole in the hoodie in detail, complete with close-ups of the bloody hoodie and bloodier sweatshirt underneath with the bullet hole just beneath the Nike logo. The witness talked about gunpowder, things called "sooting," trigger pulls and gun rates, all of the complicated science of ballistics. My mind reeled with the science and statistics, and what did it all prove?

"The clothing displayed residues and physical effects consistent with a contact shot," she said.

"Meaning the muzzle or the end of the barrel of the gun was up against the sweatshirt when it was fired?" Guy asked the witness.

"Correct," she said.

All of which meant that my son was shot through the heart at point-blank range. That same day, the prosecution called Florida Department of Law Enforcement DNA analyst Anthony Gorgone. He testified that none of the killer's DNA was found under Trayvon's fingernails and none of Trayvon's DNA was found on the killer's gun—which we felt put to rest the notion that Trayvon grabbed the gun.

July 4, 2013, fell on a Thursday, and the court recessed with the trial set to resume the next day, a Friday. We spent that Fourth of July in our hotel in Lake Mary, and we didn't go anywhere to watch the fireworks. We couldn't go out in public like that. Still, that Fourth of July was very significant for us. I was increasingly sure that the trial wasn't going our way, that our side of the story wasn't being fully told in court. But I also reflected on how far we'd come from those cold, lonely moments when I first found out about Trayvon's death. The story didn't die, because we had a free press and some reporters who were willing to fight with us in public forums, even when officials wouldn't. Our pleas for justice went all the way to the White House, to the country's democratically elected president, Barack Obama. And even if the prosecution of the case felt insufficient, we were having our day in court. We were ordinary people—the most ordinary, if that even makes sense. And on that Independence Day we felt blessed to be living in a country where voices like ours could be heard and justice could be given a chance to prevail.

But I knew that our country's history was more complicated than any Fourth of July story would tell. In fact, the America of 2013, an America that was tuning in every night to watch highlights from the trial and debates over the case, was very different in some ways from the one in which I write this book in 2016, when a tragic series of other young black men have died from senseless violence, many by police bullets, and where cities like Ferguson, Missouri, have gone up in flames. Our son wasn't nearly the first young black person to be killed, but the larger movement around it marked the beginning of a new response to the violence.

At that time, we saw Trayvon's case as an isolated event, a senseless killing calling out for justice. That was before the wave of killings, before we met parents like Ron Davis, whose seventeen-year-old African American son Jordan Davis was shot dead by a forty-five-year-old white software developer who fired ten bullets at Davis and his friends in their SUV outside a Jacksonville convenience store, mainly because he felt they were playing their music too loud. It was before Ron Davis told us about what he called "the injustice of the justice system," where white officials choose white jurors, where less than ten percent of judges are African Americans, where defendants or their supporters pay for the best possible defense attorneys, leaving victims' families and prosecutors outmatched by defense attorneys using the soon-to-become-familiar strategy of blaming the victim for their own death. "He was no angel," these defense attorneys would say over the dead bodies of young black men. It was perverse.

"They don't want you here," Ron Davis would tell us of the court system.

But that understanding would come later. There on that Fourth of July, we believed our case stood alone, and were hopeful that it would never happen to another parent's child. We also felt grateful to even be heard in a court in Florida, and have a judge and jury consider our case. Even getting the case to trial was a major victory, and so we followed what Crump told us to do: handle ourselves with dignity and composure, and let the anger pass when we felt it, even though at times I felt like it would consume me.

But on that July 4, 2013, we also felt gratitude, as Americans with a right to a fair trial, even if we had to fight through the gloom of our own grief and waken the nation's conscience to achieve that right.

When we returned to court after the holiday, the prosecution called Sybrina to the stand. Many would say that it was insensitive to force a grieving mother to testify, and later, in his closing arguments, de la Rionda would defend his decision to call Sybrina, saying, "Ms. Fulton—people asked why you even questioned her. How dare you question the mom of a passed-away seventeen-year-old?" he said.

"Doctors cut people sometimes when they do their work," he would continue. "That was something I had to present to you . . . about the way it happened and how it happened. And, you know, the impact and just how moms think about these things, both sides. Because I know that both moms believe with their heart, with their soul that that was their son's cry for help. You have to. You want to, and it's just the way you get through it."

She walked into the courtroom that day in a dark suit, her jacket worn over a beige blouse. She wore glasses and a pearl necklace with matching earrings. Her hair was up in her familiar bun. And while it had been many years since we had been husband and wife, we were forever in this fight together for the love of our kids. It was tough for me to watch her endure the agony of the trial.

The courtroom was small, and the man who killed my son sat at the defense table not far from the witness stand where Sybrina was now sitting. I could feel the tension in the room. I glanced over at the killer. Sybrina, staring back at him, was steady and strong. The woman who was once so filled with grief that she couldn't get out of her bedroom had found the inner resolve to be a warrior when she needed to.

She stated her name, and de la Rionda began his questioning.

"Are you married, ma'am?" he asked.

"I'm divorced," Sybrina answered.

"Do you have any children?"

"Yes, I do."

"Can you tell us who they are and their names?"

"My youngest son is Trayvon Benjamin Martin. He's in heaven," she said.

I looked over at the jury. I couldn't tell anything from their blank expressions.

"And my oldest son is Jahvaris Lamar Fulton," said Sybrina.

After asking Sybrina to state the basic facts of her life, de la Rionda said, "Was Trayvon Martin right- or left-handed?"

"Trayvon was right-handed," she said.

This was an important detail since the gun the killer claimed Trayvon was reaching for was holstered behind his right side, which would have required Trayvon to reach for it with his less dominant hand.

"Prior to your son's death, had you heard him crying or yelling?"

She had, of course. But de la Rionda was getting ready to once again play the tape of the 911 call with Trayvon's bloodcurdling screams for help and the fatal gunshot. Sybrina remained stoic as she heard the last of our son's screams again. There was a brief silence in the courtroom after the tape, then de la Rionda asked his next question.

"Ma'am," he said, breaking the silence, "that screaming or yelling, do you recognize that?"

"Yes," she said.

"And who do you recognize that to be?"

"Trayvon Benjamin Martin," she said without hesitation.

The prosecutor, without asking a single question about Trayvon's background or character, had no further questions at that time.

O'Mara stood up and attempted to apologize for our loss, but de la Rionda was quick with an objection, saying O'Mara's conduct was improper since he was not asking a question. The judge sustained the objection, and O'Mara began his cross-examination.

"Will you tell us the first time that you listened to that tape?" O'Mara asked. "Where were you?"

"I was here in Sanford," Sybrina said. "I believe it was in the mayor's office."

"That was pursuant to a request made by your lawyers to have that tape released, correct?"

It was.

"I imagine that it was probably one of the worst things that you went through to listen to that tape, correct?" O'Mara asked.

"Absolutely."

"And that if it was your son in fact screaming, as you've testified, that would suggest that it was Mr. Zimmerman's fault that led to his death, correct?"

She agreed.

"And if it was not your son screaming," O'Mara continued, "if it was in fact George Zimmerman, then you would have to accept the probability that it was Trayvon Martin who caused his own death, correct?"

"I don't understand your question," Sybrina said, remaining composed.

"If you were to listen to that tape and not hear your son's voice, that would mean that it would have been George Zimmerman's voice, correct?"

"And not hear my son screaming? Is that what you're asking?" Sybrina said.

"Yes, ma'am."

"I heard my son screaming," she said definitively.

"I understand," O'Mara said. "The alternative, the only alternative, would you agree, would be that if it was not your son screaming that it would be George Zimmerman, correct?"

De la Rionda objected due to speculation, and Judge Nelson again sustained.

"You certainly had to *hope* that was your son screaming even before you heard it, correct?" O'Mara said.

"I didn't *hope* for anything," she said. "I just simply listened to the tape."

"And in your mind, as his mother, there is no doubt whatsoever that it was him screaming, correct?"

"Absolutely . . ."

He mentioned the other people who listened to the tape in the mayor's office.

"Every one of them then told you that they agreed with your opinion that it was Trayvon Martin's voice, correct?"

"They didn't tell me anything."

O'Mara asked Sybrina if anyone had prepared Sybrina before the tape was played, telling her "that you would soon be listening to screams from the event that led to your son's death."

No one had told her anything about the tape before she heard it, she said. Not the mayor. None of our attorneys or family members present, and how could they? They hadn't heard the tape yet, either, and I had only heard portions of it.

"The question is, whether or not anyone told you to prepare yourself for the event, for the trauma of having to listen to somebody scream moments before your son was shot?"

The answer was still no.

"You just needed to listen to it one time, correct?"

"That's it."

O'Mara said he was finished with questions, subject to recalling Sybrina as a witness if needed, and de la Rionda had a few questions on redirect.

"You were asked by defense counsel about hope," he said. "Were you still hoping that he would still be alive?"

Of course she was.

"I don't know how else to ask this, but I'm going to ask it," de la Rionda continued. "Did you enjoy listening to that recording?"

"Absolutely not," Sybrina said.

De la Rionda was finished, but again O'Mara stood up from the defense table.

"At the risk of another objection," he said, "I don't mean to put you through this any more than necessary, than we need to, but you certainly would hope that your son Trayvon Martin did nothing that could have led to his own death?"

"What was your question again?" she asked.

"You certainly hope, as a mom, you certainly hope that your son Trayvon Martin would not have done anything that would have led to his own death."

"What I hope for," she said, "is that this would have never happened and he would still be here. That's my hope."

"And now dealing with the reality that he is no longer here, it is certainly your hope as a mom, hold out hope as long as you can, that Trayvon Martin was in no way responsible for his own death, correct?"

"I don't believe he was," she said.

O'Mara rested, returning to the defense table.

Sybrina's testimony was over in less than thirty minutes.

The prosecution moved on, calling my son Jahvaris to the stand next, with John Guy leading the questioning.

Jahvaris, then twenty-two, was both an honor student and an extremely respectable young man. He stood by us every inch of the way in taking his brother's death to the nation, taking time off from his studies at Florida International University from the moment we found out that Trayvon had been killed. Jahvaris had never enjoyed being in the public eye. He had to first endure depositions and now testify at the trial of his brother's killer—but he did it all without hesitation.

We went out to dinner one night, Sybrina, Jahvaris, our attorneys, and me. We had tried to keep the gory details of his brother's shooting away from Jahvaris. But on this night, we got into a conversation about where the bullet went through Trayvon's body, and Jahvaris asked us to explain.

"Trayvon was shot through the heart," I said.

I didn't realize Jahvaris didn't already know.

Jahvaris's body suddenly seemed to give out from under him. We had to pick him up and take him outside. Jahvaris was clearly holding a lot of pain inside him, but rarely let it slip out.

Jahvaris is a strong young man of impeccable values, intelligence, and courage, and from the moment he entered the courtroom, in his dark suit, white shirt, and red 5000 Role Models tie with a design of large black hands touching smaller black hands, I knew he would conduct himself as he always has: with intelligence, poise, and complete control.

"That's my brother," he said early on in his testimony of Trayvon, adding, after a series of questions about their age difference and other things, "We were very close."

Under questioning by prosecutor Guy, Jahvaris said that even though he was four and a half years older than Trayvon, they still did all the things that brothers do together.

"Since your brother's death," Guy said, "have you had an opportunity to hear a tape that contains screaming and a gunshot?"

"Yes," he said. "Anywhere between ten and fifteen times."

"And how have you heard it? Have you heard it on a computer, on TV, on the Internet, or what?"

He had heard the tape first on a computer that day in the mayor's office and later on television.

"Do you recognize any voices on that tape?" Guy asked.

"Yes," Jahvaris said. "My brother."

"What parts do you recognize as your brother's voice?"

"The yelling and the screaming."

Jahvaris said he had heard Trayvon yell a number of times before, but never like that.

Guy finished his questioning—again, quickly—and O'Mara began to cross-examine, again, in detail.

O'Mara said that Jahvaris wasn't as certain that the screams were Trayvon's when he spoke to a reporter from CBS Miami about the tapes, and the defense attorney quoted what Jahvaris had said at the time: "You said, 'Honestly, . . . really haven't listened to it. I've heard it. I would think it was my brother, but I'm not completely positive,' correct?" O'Mara asked.

Jahvaris agreed, and confirmed O'Mara's questions about listening to the tape with the family in the mayor's office.

"From having listened to it," O'Mara continued, "it was your thought that it *might* be Trayvon, correct?"

"When we heard it in the mayor's office I guess I didn't want to believe that it was him," Jahvaris said, pausing. "So that's why during that interview I said I wasn't sure. . . . Listening to it was clouded by shock and denial and sadness. I didn't really want to believe that it was him."

That same day, July 5, brought the prosecution's last witness, the medical examiner Shiping Bao, who performed Trayvon's autopsy. "His heart was beating until there was no blood left," said the medical examiner, estimating that Trayvon could have remained alive for between one and ten minutes after the shooting. It chilled me to know that his last minutes of life were spent alone with his killer.

When the screen before the jury displayed a picture of Trayvon's body as it arrived at the medical examiner's office, Sybrina left the courtroom.

At the end of the medical examiner's testimony, after nine days and thirty-eight witnesses, the prosecution rested, allowing the defense to begin presenting its case.

I was the eleventh witness for the defense. I was disappointed that the prosecution hadn't called me—so the jury could hear and hopefully feel the heartbreak of the father of the victim—and that I was instead being called by the defense.

The defense attorneys were bulldogs, and they did their job, making the jury see the side of the killer they wanted them to see. The prosecution's job was to show that this was a child who had been killed, a kid who was walking in peace from the 7-Eleven and was pursued by a stranger.

The defense called character witnesses for the person who killed our son. But other than Sybrina and Jahvaris the prosecution did not. Why? They could have called more character witnesses for Trayvon: parents, grandparents, teachers, counselors, friends, all of whom could have shown that he was a person, not a caricature. But they called none. For the life of me, I couldn't figure out why they didn't call more people who knew Trayvon best, to show who he really was.

Now, with the trial nearing an end, I had begun pressing the prosecutors every day on their strategy—"Why didn't you call a certain witness? Why didn't you follow a certain line of questions? Didn't you see that opportunity?" They tried to assure me that they were listening but had it under control. I still had questions.

For instance, they called Sybrina and Jahvaris to testify. But they didn't call me. I was the last parent to see him alive. I was the first parent to know he died. Why didn't the state call me? Although I didn't understand why the state didn't call me, I did know why the defense did: they were going to try to get me to admit that I had originally said that it wasn't Trayvon's voice screaming for help on the 911 tape, which I had endlessly said, in interviews and depositions, was not what I had said.

The *New York Times* called me the defense's "key witness," in their attempt to convince the jury that it was the killer, not my son, screaming for help on the 911 tape.

That morning, I prepared myself for what I knew would be a battle ahead, dressing in a dark blue suit and matching tie. I was ready to tell my story, eager to clarify what I knew to be true. I was ready to defend my son, who, as the victim, shouldn't have needed defending. But here we were.

"You've been here for testimony throughout the trial, correct?" Mark O'Mara began. "Including today when we had a couple officers testify about an event where you had gone to meet with investigator Chris Serino at [the] Sanford Police Department. Do you remember that [meeting]?"

"Yes," I said. Both Brandy and I met with Serino less than two days after Trayvon's death, to make sure he had verified that Trayvon had been identified.

"My understanding," O'Mara continued, "was that you listened to a number of tapes, one of which was the tape that we're identifying as the Lauer 911 call, correct?"

"Yes," I said.

"I understand that it was difficult to listen to. It included the shot that ended your son's life," O'Mara said. "At the end of that tape, do you recall Officer Serino asking you whether or not you can identify your son's voice?"

"Not those exact words," I said. "But something to that nature, yes."

What had actually happened, and what I said on the witness stand, was that after Serino had played the tape he asked me, "Do you recognize the voice?"

I remembered the day vividly, even in all my disorientation and devastation. And when Serino played the tape for me that morning, without giving me any context as to what I would hear, and the sound of the gunshot came echoing through the room, the last thing on my mind was to analyze it.

"I didn't tell him, 'No. That wasn't Trayvon,'" I said. "I kind of . . . I think the chair had wheels . . . and I kind of pushed away . . . from the table and kind of shook my head and said, 'I can't tell.'"

"So your words were 'I can't tell'?"

"Something to that effect. But I never said, 'No. That wasn't my son's voice.'"

Like Jahvaris had testified, "shock and denial and suffering" had clouded my thoughts, and I desperately wanted to believe that this was all a mistake and Trayvon was still alive.

"You heard Officer Serino testify that you said 'No,' correct?" O'Mara said. "And you heard Officer Singleton also testify that she was about eight or ten feet [away] and she heard you say 'No,' or an indication that you acknowledged that was not Trayvon's voice, is that correct?"

"I had no idea that she [Officer Singleton] was even in the vicinity," I said. "The first I had heard Officer Singleton was within earshot of my meeting with Serino was in her testimony in court, when she said about hearing the tape, 'I was choked up myself.'"

"Did you ever ask to hear the tape a second time?"

"Not at that moment, no."

"Did you ever tell anybody that you had listened to a cleaned-up version of the tape and were then able to identify the voice on it?"

"What do you mean 'cleaned-up version'?"

"I'm asking you, sir."

"To my knowledge, the tape that I listened to was the same tape that's circulating," I said. "That's the only tape I know about . . ."

"Did you ever tell Sybrina Fulton, your ex-wife, that you had listened to the tape at Officer Serino's desk?"

"There was a lot of stuff going on," I said. "We had just buried our son, a lot of emotions. And you know you just don't think of every little detail that you've been through. Obviously it was a tragic, and still is, a tragic time for us, and so just to answer your question, 'Did I tell Ms. Fulton I listened to the tape?' No, I didn't."

The tape, the tape, the tape. The tapes we begged to be released, the tapes that gutted us to listen to, the tapes that we were sure would make the truth clear to everyone. And now, the trial was turning out to be about that tape, but in a way I never would've predicted. The tape of my son dying, after what I knew could only be his own high-pitched screams for help, followed by the fatal gunshot. *Why would the man with a gun be the one screaming for help?* The tape was the evidence the defense tried so hard to use to prove that Trayvon's last moments on Earth were spent in attack instead of trying to ward off his attacker. But I wasn't budging on what I knew to be true. It was Trayvon's voice.

By now the 911 tape had become a he-said-she-said kind of thing: we knew it was Trayvon's voice, while the killer's camp said it was the defendant's voice. Even the voice experts who were called in, by both the media and the lawyers on both sides, couldn't verify the voice a hundred percent, which only fed the debate.

I felt that Detective Serino's interview after the shooting said it all.

"Hear that voice in the background? That's you?" he asked.

And the killer replied, "That doesn't even sound like me."

"After listening to the tape maybe twenty times," I testified about the day in the mayor's office when we were allowed to listen to it as many times as we wanted, "I said that I *knew* that it was Trayvon's voice. I didn't direct that toward any family members. Matter of fact, I think the family members had started leaving out of the room. It was too much for them. They couldn't take it. And I just decided to sit there and listen to it."

De la Rionda soon began his cross-examination.

"Mr. Martin," de la Rionda began, "even at this time is it hard for you to believe your son is no longer living?"

"It's very difficult to believe that Trayvon is not living," I said. "As I said over and over, that was my best friend in life, and to have him gone is tragic."

"Now in terms of being sure we understand the context," he said, "your son was killed late evening Sunday, February twenty-sixth, and you would have gone over to the Sanford Police Department the morning . . . I believe it was the twenty-eighth, do you recall that?" (I answered, "Yes.") "And I believe also you only found out your son was dead at some point, actually the twenty-seventh. Is that true, that Monday?"

"Correct. Yes."

"Was it still hard for you to believe your son was dead?"

"It's still hard to this day that he's dead," I said.

De la Rionda tried to describe this event, asking if officers had come to the townhouse and showed me a picture of "a body there on the ground?" Before I could answer, O'Mara objected and the attorneys approached the bench.

"I was asking you about the twenty-seventh," de la Rionda said when the trial resumed. "Investigator Serino had come and shown you a photograph, is that correct? And you identified it as being your son, correct?"

"Correct," I said.

De la Rionda moved on to the next day, Tuesday, listing the various 911 calls and their contents, asking if I had heard all of the tapes on the day I went to the Sanford Police Department.

"I don't think Detective Serino played each call in its entirety," I said. "He played some of each call leading up to the last call with the fatal shot."

"Am I safe to assume that you were still, at that time, were in denial in the sense of not wanting to believe that your son was dead?" de la Rionda asked.

"Correct."

"This was an emotional time for you. Would that be fair to say?"

"Very emotional."

De la Rionda restated what happened after I heard for the first time the gunshot that killed my son. "You pulled your chair back in disbelief," he said. "You realized that was the shot—"

"That killed my son, yes," I said.

"Did you really know what to do at that point?"

"From that point until today, my world has just been turned upside down."

"Then after you heard the cries for help . . . and then also the shot," de la Rionda said, "*right there,* Investigator Serino asked you about the recording, if you could recognize the voice, correct?" (I answered, "Correct.") "And I'm assuming that was difficult for you to even contemplate, identifying or not identifying the voice, is that correct?"

I tried to answer Serino as best I could, I said:

"There was a lot of commotion in that recording, wasn't there?" de la Rionda said. "The yells for help, the person calling, and then most importantly the shot, too. In terms of your mind, what was going through your mind. Can you describe for the jury what was going through your mind when you were listening to that?"

"Basically," I said, "I was listening to my son's last cry for help. I was listening to his life being taken. And I was trying to come to grips that Trayvon was here no more. It was just tough."

De la Rionda asked if, during our meeting in the mayor's office, we were played all of the 911 tapes or just the Jenna Lauer tape that recorded the gunshot in the background. I told him I couldn't remember if it was all the tapes or just one, but I did recall taking control of the mayor's computer and replaying Trayvon's screams over and over and over again.

"Why?" de la Rionda asked. "Were you trying to deal with this? Why were you doing that?"

"It wasn't as much I was trying to deal with it," I said. "I was just trying to figure out the night of February 26, 2012, why did the defendant get out of his vehicle and chase my son?"

This was a chance for the state to bounce back—to get back to the story of that night. But they didn't. And just like that, I was done.

No further questions were asked of me by the prosecution and I felt another opportunity slip away.

On the morning of July 9, the defense called another expert witness, Dr. Vincent Di Maio, a nationally renowned forensic pathologist and medical examiner from San Antonio, Texas, with more than forty years of experience.

The doctor took his seat at the witness stand in a suit and yellow tie.

As Dr. Di Maio testified, photographs from the autopsy, including a close-up of the bullet's entry wound in Trayvon's chest, were projected on the far wall of the courtroom.

I looked over at Sybrina, knowing this wouldn't be easy for her. I could feel the effort she was making to keep herself composed, but she never looked at the photograph.

The defense was arguing that, based on the bullet wound, Trayvon must have been on top of Zimmerman at the time of his death. We didn't doubt that there had been a struggle, a fight, somebody on top and somebody on bottom, and maybe Trayvon and Zimmerman both at one point had the dominant position. We didn't doubt that Trayvon was fighting for his life. Whatever the conflict was, it began the moment the neighborhood watch captain decided to follow Trayvon.

Dr. Di Maio went on to describe Trayvon's wound in detail. The bullet entered his chest an inch to the left of center between the fifth and sixth ribs; it passed through the right ventricle of his heart and became lodged in his right lung.

In his description, Dr. Di Maio kept referencing the photo of the wound, which had been up on the wall now for several agonizing minutes. I stared at the photo for what seemed to be hours, while Sybrina diverted her eyes and looked down.

The defense lawyer moved away from the wound itself and on to the effects the wound would have had on Trayvon as he breathed his last breaths. How long was he alive? How long was he conscious? And what would he have been physically able to do after being shot?

"The ability to move," Dr. Di Maio said, describing the last moments of my son's life in a cold, analytical manner, "is determined by the amount of oxygen in your brain, for which you have a reserve of ten to fifteen seconds . . . that's minimum."

The amount of blood in the brain "depends on blood pressure and how severe your wounds [are]," he said. A moment later, he added, "Now, how long can your heart beat?

"In this case," he continued, "you have a through-and-through hole of the right ventricle [of the heart], and then you have at least one hole, if not two, into the right lung. So you're losing blood, and every time the heart contracts it pumps blood out of the two holes in the ventricle and at least one hole in the lung."

He said in Trayvon's case, his heart would have been pumping faster than usual, more than a hundred times per minute, due to the physical nature of the struggle and the fact that he had been shot, each pump pushing blood out of the holes in the heart and the lung.

After two minutes, Trayvon would have lost half of his blood supply. The blood he had left would not have been able to reach his brain, making death imminent.

"So assuming these conditions," Dr. Di Maio said, "he's going to be dead within one to three minutes after being shot."

In terms of being conscious, the doctor said Trayvon would have been aware for less time as oxygen levels in the brain dropped.

No parent wants their child to suffer; even a few seconds is far too much. My eyes were red with tears. I could feel Sybrina's leg shaking. Then she rose and exited the courtroom.

"From what I understand you to say then," West continued, "for at least ten to fifteen seconds after Mr. Martin sustained the shot, he would have been capable of talking and of voluntary movement?"

"He could," Dr. Di Maio said. "Some people just lose consciousness immediately. It's psychological, it's not physical, but he has the potential for ten to fifteen seconds minimum."

"Could that include moving his arms from an outreached position to underneath his body during that ten to fifteen seconds?"

"Yes," Di Maio said. But once consciousness is lost there is no more voluntary movement and, gratefully, no more pain.

On July 10, Dennis Root, a "use of force" expert witness, was called by the defense. A retired twenty-two-year veteran Florida policeman, he was certified as an instructor in hand-to-hand combat, defensive tactics, and impact weapons.

He taught classes in open-hand combat techniques like blocking, choke holds, and takedowns, and the use of pepper spray. Late in his career, he had become an instructor in firearms, licensed by the state as well as the NRA, and focused much of his teaching on justifiable uses of force in various situations.

Root followed the case as it dominated the media, and he soon began, with the defense, reviewing evidence, including the 911 calls, witness statements, police and medical reports, and crime-scene photos.

O'Mara led Root through a series of questions: about Root's background, his interpretation of the events of the night of February 26, 2012, and if it would have been appropriate to use force, and even a gun, in a self-defense situation.

Then, John Guy began his cross-examination.

"The defendant told you that his head was repeatedly slammed into concrete?" the prosecutor eventually asked.

"His words were, his 'head was slammed into the concrete,'" Root said.

"You didn't ask him how many times?"

"No, not how many times it happened."

"And you didn't ask him *how* his head was slammed, right? Whether Trayvon Martin grabbed his ears, or grabbed his face, or grabbed his jacket?"

"No, I didn't ask him specifically how his head was being impacted into the concrete," he said. "I, again, generalize statements from Mr. Zimmerman himself. . . . But his perception was that the downward blows, his head hitting the concrete, his head was being slammed into the concrete . . ."

"I think you said you reviewed some medical records," Guy said. "Did you review the medical record where the woman measured the longest laceration on the back of his head was two centimeters?"

"They weren't that large, if that's what you're asking?" Root said.

Guy pointed out that two centimeters is less than an inch, and the other cut on the killer's head was less than one centimeter, which a medical examiner from Jacksonville had previously testified was "insignificant" and "not life-threatening."

"You would agree with me, that of all the people you heard from, either talked to or had written statements or audio statements, the person with the best vantage point would have been the defendant, right?" Guy asked.

"Of course," Root said.

"The defendant told you in his statement that Trayvon Martin was straddling him," Guy said. "And you understood from the context of your conversation, that Trayvon Martin was over the defendant's belly button, right?"

"Over his waist area," Root said.

What Guy did next surprised us: he brought out a life-size foam dummy and laid it faceup on the floor in front of the witness stand. The lawyers at the defense table must have been surprised, too. They all stood with curious looks to try to get a better view.

Where is he going with this? I thought.

"So as the defendant described it to you," Guy said as he got down on his knees with the dummy between his legs, his hips above the dummy's abdomen, "is this the way he described it? In the area of his belly button?"

"What's really important right now, sir," Root said, "number one, you've got your knees up pretty high on his waist. If you want to slide down just a little bit more."

Guy shuffled back and forth in order to move back in the direction of the dummy's feet.

"There you go," Root said, confirming that the prosecutor was now in the right position.

"By the way," Guy said, "did you have the defendant do this?"

He had not.

"If this person, this mannequin," Guy continued, "were carrying a firearm on their waist, where would the gun be right now in relation to me?"

"It would be at your left inner thigh," Root said.

Guy pointed to his thigh to illustrate to the jury the location Root was describing and added, "Underneath my leg, right?"

Root agreed, on the condition that the defendant was right-handed.

"Were you aware," Guy continued, "that the defendant described to his best friend that when he slid down, the defendant slid down, that Trayvon Martin was up around his armpits?" And he moved his knees up directly underneath the dummy's shoulders to illustrate his point.

"No," Root said, "I've not heard that."

"Where would the gun be now?"

"Now the gun would be behind your left leg."

Root said that the killer was slipping down between Trayvon's legs during the altercation, and that was what the killer claimed exposed the gun to Trayvon's view. Guy asked if Root had asked the killer *how* he reached for the gun. He said he hadn't. But what was more important than how he reached for his gun was the location on his hip where the gun was holstered.

During the walk-through video, the killer indicated that the gun was in his waistband, *behind* him. So how could Trayvon see the gun if it was behind his back under his jacket, if Trayvon was on top of him?

De la Rionda would eventually mention the location of the killer's gun in passing during closing arguments—"It wasn't right here in the front; it was toward the back, and it was hidden"—and John Guy would say in his closing arguments, "If Trayvon Martin had been mounted on the defendant as the defendant claims when [he] went to get his gun, he never could have got it. I don't have to pull out the mannequin again and sit on it. You remember . . . if he was up on his waist, his waist is covered by Trayvon Martin's legs. He couldn't have got the gun. . . . It's a physical impossibility." But I didn't feel the jury realized the importance of this—which is that it would be almost literally impossible for Trayvon to have *seen* and reached for the gun. The killer's story seemed to be a not-very-well-thought-out fantasy. And it was transparent. De la Rionda just had to hammer in on this simple fact for the jury. But he didn't.

O'Mara asked to borrow Guy's "doll," and laid the dummy on the floor in the same position Guy had placed it earlier. From a straddling position, he questioned Root about he killer's injuries and if they could also be consistent with slamming the back and sides of his client's head to the concrete while resisting an attack. Root said they *could* be.

O'Mara then brought up the fact that the gun had been discharged against Trayvon's hoodie, but with a distance from his chest, to which Root suggested that the only way that could have happened was if Trayvon was leaning over his killer, and that if he had been trying to get away, the weight from the can of iced tea would have caused Trayvon's hoodie to fall against his own chest.

O'Mara went through different positions above the dummy, sliding up and down its chest, at each position pointing to where he claimed his client's gun was holstered and asking if the gun would have been "available." Each time Root said it was.

"How much thrashing or movement was happening in that dynamic event between these two men at that point?" O'Mara asked.

"I would have to say a lot," Root said. How could this be true? From the time Trayvon's phone got disconnected until the time of his death was only a minute and a half. As O'Mara picked up the dummy and placed it back behind the prosecution table, and I wondered, *Was the dummy a dumb thing to introduce, and had it just backfired on the prosecution?*

The defense would call a total of eighteen witnesses, everyone from the killer's trainer, who called him "physically soft," to a neighbor at the Retreat, who testified about burglaries committed by young black men, and the prosecution would call thirty-eight witnesses. But what everyone remembered from those final days was Dennis Root and John Guy's dummy. "Who was the winner in the use of a dummy to demonstrate the fights between Zimmerman and Trayvon Martin?" wrote Hal Boedeker in the *Orlando Sentinel* in a story titled "Mount-Your-Dummy Day." "Not the state, most analysts said."

The trial was taking its toll on all of us: long hours, endless witnesses, and constant replaying of that terrifying tape and gruesome photographs of our son's last hours on earth. We were all mentally and physically exhausted, as was the defense. "We're not physically able to keep up this pace much longer," Don West complained to Judge Nelson at the end of a thirteen-hour day of testimony. "We've had full days every day. Weekends. Depositions at night."

Judge Nelson didn't show sympathy and instead demanded to know if the defendant planned to testify on his own behalf.

"I object to the court inquiring of Mr. Zimmerman as to his decision about whether or not to testify," said Don West.

"Your objection is overruled," said Judge Nelson.

The killer would not testify, and why should he? His lawyers had done their work, challenging though it was, and as far as the state was concerned, the prosecutors and police, well, it was already clear that he was getting better treatment than my son.

And with that, on July 10, the defense rested, after four days, half the time taken by the prosecution.

But I couldn't rest. Ever again. That night in the hotel room that had become my second home, I thought of the long and almost impossible road that had taken us to this point. We had come so far, from not knowing how our son had died to knowing almost everything; from being alone in our struggle to being supported by many parts of our nation and maybe even the world. Now the trial was coming to a close. Once it was over, would Trayvon rest in peace and be forgotten? Could something larger come out of this trial, this death, this loss—something bigger than a verdict against a single individual? Could change actually come, if we continued to honor our son, both in his life and in his death? If we continued saying his name, would his name continue to stand for something?

Something deeper than his death. Something bigger than his unfinished life. Something that could last longer than this trial. Something that would turn his passing into power.

CHAPTER 13

Sybrina

⌒

July 12, 2013

I closed my eyes and prayed in the courtroom as closing arguments began on the morning of Thursday, July 11, 2013. It had been eighteen days since the trial began, and now it would come down to final arguments from both sides. The prosecution went first with Bernie de la Rionda delivering a two-hour presentation.

"A teenager is dead," de la Rionda said as he stepped up to the podium to face the jury that early afternoon. "He is dead through no fault of his own. He is dead because another man made assumptions. . . . He is dead not just because the man made those assumptions, because he acted upon those assumptions, and unfortunately . . . because his assumptions were wrong Trayvon Benjamin Martin no longer walks on this Earth. . . .

"Unfortunately, this is one of the last photos that will ever be taken of Trayvon Martin," he said, holding up the picture of Trayvon's body lying dead in the grass at Twin Lakes. "That is true because of the actions of one individual, the man before you, the defendant. . . .

"A man who after shooting Trayvon Martin claims to not have

realized he was dead," he continued. "What did he do? . . . Did he render or attempt to render the same aid that the heroic officers from the Sanford Police Department did? Who didn't wear the mask they normally would wear, but gave mouth-to-mouth, performed CPR, in an attempt to bring life back into that young boy?"

He referred to the neighbor, Jonathan Manalo, one of the first to arrive at the scene, who testified that the defendant told him he had shot our son in self-defense. "Recall what he told Mr. Manalo: 'Please call my wife,' and then apparently Mr. Manalo was taking too long or something and he said 'Just tell her I killed him.' Just kind of matter-of-fact. Those acts, those actions, speak volumes of what occurred that evening, Sunday evening. . . .

"He profiled him as a criminal. He assumed certain things, that Trayvon Martin was up to no good. That is what led to his death. Trayvon Martin . . . He was there legally. He hadn't broken in or sneaked in or trespassed.

"He followed him, he tracked him. Because in his mind, in the defendant's mind, this was a criminal, and he was tired of criminals committing crimes out there. Again, that's not a bad thing. It's good that citizens get involved. But he went over the line. He assumed things that weren't true. And instead of waiting for the police, instead of waiting for the police to come and do their job, he did not. Because he, the defendant, wanted to make sure that Trayvon Martin didn't get out of the neighborhood. . . . That night, he decided he was going to be what he wanted to be: a police officer."

The prosecutor was building up to essentially this question: Who was more afraid in the moments before the confrontation, the seventeen-year-old minding his own business? Or the grown man with a loaded gun?

Once again, he talked about the tape where the killer says to the dispatcher, "These assholes, they always get away," saying that this indicated the hatred, ill-will, or spite needed to convict.

"Hold the defendant responsible for his actions," de la Rionda said. "Hold him accountable for what he did. Because if the defendant hadn't assumed that—Trayvon Martin would have watched the basketball game and George Zimmerman, I'm assuming, would have gone to Target or done whatever he does on Sunday evenings, and we wouldn't be here."

De la Rionda asked jurors to think back to the defendant's claim that he saw Trayvon circling his vehicle. Assuming that's true, he said, "He says he's [Trayvon] got something in his hands. Why does this defendant get out of the truck if he thinks that Trayvon Martin is a threat to him? Why? Why? Because he's got a gun. He's got the equalizer. He's going to take care of it. He's a wannabe cop. He's gonna take care of it. He's got a gun . . . and he's not going to put up with it. And if the police are taking too long to respond . . .

"[Trayvon's] body speaks to you, even in death. It proves to you that this defendant is lying about what happened," de la Rionda said at one point.

"See, because what's important is the defendant, in an attempt to convince the police that he was really shooting this man, this boy, in self-defense, he had to exaggerate what happened," he said. "That's why he had to at some point say, 'Oh, he was threatening me.' It was almost like the levels of fear escalated."

He outlined the escalation that the killer claimed: from Trayvon hitting him and getting him on the ground to the struggle, in which "he got the upper hand," to Trayvon threatening to kill him and putting his hand over his mouth, suffocating him and pinching his nose. "And then he went for the gun . . . See how he's exaggerating everything?"

He was more than a wannabe cop, said de la Rionda; he "studied the law" and knew the "bullet points in terms of what's required" for self-defense.

He reviewed the testimony from Rachel Jeantel and her telephone call timeline, and the witnesses who made 911 calls.

He also reviewed the physical evidence, including Trayvon's hands, which, in death, were underneath him, clenching his chest, which raised the question: why, as life was leaving him, would Trayvon somehow lift himself up and place his hands back under his chest? He showed the Kel-Tec PF-9 9mm gun to the jury, and asked, "Look at the gun, look at the size of this gun—how did the victim see that in the darkness?"

He played a video, in which the killer, when asked if Trayvon seemed afraid on the night of their encounter on a television interview with Sean Hannity, suggested that maybe Trayvon wasn't actually running. "It was like skipping, going away quickly. But he wasn't running out of fear," he said. Which de la Rionda demonstrated as ludicrous by skipping in a carefree manner across the courtroom.

It was ridiculous: How often have you seen a teenaged boy skip down the street?

"How many arms did Trayvon Martin need for punching, moving to the sidewalk, grabbing the head, smothering the mouth and nose, grabbing for the gun all at the same time?" he asked.

In his two-hour closing argument, de la Rionda noted the inconsistencies: the killer's claim of being hit twenty-five times, which the physical evidence—the cuts on the back of his head and his supposedly broken nose—didn't prove; the absence of Trayvon's DNA or fingerprint evidence on the gun; the killer's claim that he was scared of Trayvon while still getting out of his truck to follow him, all of which meant that his actions and the physical evidence didn't meet his self-defense claim.

He closed with this: "Some of the people you heard from were the parents of both the victim and the defendant. Unfortunately, the only photographs left of Trayvon Martin are those M.E. photographs. . . . They can't take any more photos and that's true because of the actions of one person . . . the man before you . . . the man who is guilty of second-degree murder."

De la Rionda's dramatic closing reviewed the evidence clearly, strongly, and presented the jury with all the right questions, but we returned to our hotel that night with more questions than answers. The next day the defense would present its closing arguments, led by Mark O'Mara.

. . .

O'Mara also mentioned the defendant's desire to be a police officer, a "wannabe cop," which, he said, contrary to the prosecution's portrayal, was a good thing, a man wanting to help his community, a place ravaged by crime and suspicion.

He spoke for around three hours.

He put on a pair of sunglasses, loosened his tie, and put on a pinkie ring, to warn the jurors against making rash judgments against his client based on first impressions.

And he said of the prosecution, "They are supposed to use words like 'certainty' and 'definite,' and 'without question,' 'beyond a reasonable doubt.' . . . What aren't good words of good prosecutors are 'maybe,' 'what if,' 'I hope so,' 'you figure it out.'"

He exhibited a "Self-Defense Burden of Proof" chart. "The state carries a burden, without question, of proving to you beyond a reasonable doubt that George Zimmerman did not properly act in self-defense . . . ," he said. "George Zimmerman is not guilty if you have just a reasonable doubt that he acted in self-defense."

He talked about the shooter's injuries. "No injuries are necessary to respond with deadly force. Not a cut on a finger. The statute is clear—a reasonable fear of bodily harm. . . . So the injuries, icing on the cake of self-defense."

He had also introduced life-size cutouts to show the jury the heights of Trayvon and the shooter.

Then, he walked to the far side of the courtroom and picked up a jagged chunk of concrete more than two feet long and four inches thick. I've never seen a piece of concrete that thick, and the attorney appeared to struggle under its weight as he carried the rock across the courtroom and prepared to lay it on the floor in front of the jury. "How many times was it said, that Trayvon Martin was unarmed?"

The concrete chunk landed with a thud on the floor. "That's cement," O'Mara said, then dramatically brushed his hands together and wiped them on his suit pants before he continued.

"That is a sidewalk," he said. "And that is not an unarmed teenager with nothing but Skittles trying to get home. That was somebody who used the availability of dangerous items, from his fist to the concrete, to cause great bodily injury. . . . And the suggestion by the state that that's not a weapon, that that can't hurt somebody, that that can't cause great bodily injury . . . is disgusting."

My mother wrote out the words, "This is so fake!" on her notepad and passed it to me.

I agreed with my mom. He presented this horrible hunk of concrete as if Trayvon were walking around with it in his hands, threatening people. It was the sidewalk! Between the concrete and the cutouts and the rest, it was almost too much to believe and, we felt, wasn't based on the facts.

In closing, he said, "The state never, ever loses their responsibility to take away reasonable doubt from you. Don't let them do it with innuendo . . . sympathy . . . yelling. . . . Don't let them do it with screeching. Because none of that matters. Because we have a definition of reasonable doubt, and now you do. You look at that definition. You go back to that room and say, 'Let's talk first about self-defense. If I think George may have acted in self-defense, we are done.'"

I looked over at the jury: the six women were expressionless, but I could sense that the closing remarks had affected them. O'Mara thanked the jury for their time and attention. Before he rested the defense's case he had one more request of the jury. "I want you to really, really, look at those instructions, apply them, and just say he acted in self-defense, find him not guilty. Let him go back and get back to his life," he said.

"The human heart, it has a great many functions," began John Guy after a short recess in an emotional one-hour rebuttal. "It moves us, it motivates us, it inspires us, it leads us, and it guides us. Our hearts. In big things, like what we choose to do for a living, and in little things, like what we do every day at any moment in the day. So if we really want to know what happened out there behind those homes on that dark rainy night, should we not look into the heart of the grown man and the heart of that child?"

Guy put up a slide of the words the shooter used to describe Trayvon, and asked if the words "fucking punk" were casual references to a perfect stranger, or did they reveal what was in the shooter's heart moments before he pursued and then killed Trayvon?

"What was in Trayvon Martin's heart?" Guy asked the jury. "Was it not fear that Ms. Jeantel told you about? The witness who didn't want to be here, the witness who didn't want to be involved. But the witness, the human being, that was on the phone with the real victim in this case, Trayvon Martin, right up until the time of his death." Guy asked, "isn't that every child's worst nightmare, to be followed on the way home in the dark by a stranger? Isn't that every child's worst fear? That was Trayvon Martin's last emotion.

"As a man speaks, so is he," he said in a reference to a Bible verse, which he called "an old saying but a good one."

He showed a slide with the last words Rachel heard Trayvon say: "What are you following me for?"

"If ever there was a window into a man's soul," Guy said, "it was the words from that defendant's mouth on that phone call. And if ever there was a question about who initiated the contact between that grown man and that child, it was again those defendant's words when he told Sean Noffke [the 911 operator], 'Just have the officer call me on my cellphone and I'll tell him where I am.' George Zimmerman was not going back to the car . . . or the mailboxes. And if there was ever any doubt about what happened, really happened, was it not completely removed by what the defendant said afterward, all of the lies he told. All of them. What does that tell you?

"There's only two people on this earth who know what really happened," Guy said. "And one of them can't testify, and the other one lied . . . about the things that really, truly matter, and not one lie, over and over and over again. . . . Why did he have to lie if he had done nothing wrong? . . . If that defendant had done only what he was supposed to do—see and call—none of us would be here.

"The defendant didn't shoot Trayvon Martin because he had to," Guy said. "He shot him because he wanted to. That's the bottom line."

At various points in his closing, he showed slides and said:

"HE LIED," read one. "About Trayvon Martin covering his nose and mouth . . . About his head being slammed over and over."

"HE CHANGED," read another. "About what Trayvon Martin said to him . . . About whether Trayvon Martin touched his gun."

Guy challenged the notion proposed by the defense that there was no evidence the shooter followed Trayvon after the nonemergency-line dispatcher asked him not to and he responded with "Okay."

"The common sense that tells you if Trayvon Martin was the one on the hunt, would he still have been on his cellphone?" he asked. "Would the earbuds still have been in his ears if he was getting ready to attack somebody? Really?"

"Yet, he told the police—not just the police, his best friend. Remember his best friend in the world? That Trayvon Martin was squeezing his nose," Guy said. "Do you really think if that were true there wouldn't be George Zimmerman's blood on these sticks that they pried under his [Trayvon's] fingernails? . . .

"Let me suggest to you, in the end this case is not about standing your ground," he said at one point. "It's about staying in your car, like he was taught to do, like he was supposed to do."

The prosecutor reminded the jury of the requirements for the justifiable use of deadly force: "A person is justified in using deadly force if he reasonably believes that such force is necessary to prevent imminent death or great bodily harm to himself." He showed photographs of the shooter's head with a few minor scrapes and a swollen nose.

"Ask yourself, 'Who lost the fight?'" he said to the jury, repeating that twice. "Who lost the fight? Who lost the fight? . . .

"Let me address one more thing with you before I close. . . . It was brought up by the defense in their summation this morning and it was brought up by the defense in the trial . . . RACE," he said. "This case is not about race, it's about right and wrong. It's that simple. And let me suggest to you how you know that for sure: Ask yourselves, all things being equal, if the roles were reversed and it was twenty-eight-year-old George Zimmerman walking home in the rain with a hoodie on to protect himself from the rain, walking through that neighborhood and a seventeen-year-old driving around in a car who called the police, who had hate in their heart, hate in their mouth, hate in their actions. And if it was Trayvon Martin who had shot and killed George Zimmerman, what would your verdict be? That's how you know it's not about race.

"To the living we owe respect, but to the dead we owe the truth," he said, showing the jury the photograph of our son. "What do we owe Trayvon Martin? [Seventeen] years and twenty-one days, forever. He was a son. He was a brother. He was a friend. And the last thing he did on this earth was try to get home.

"This is the dead," he said.

"The self-serving statements, the lies, from his own mouth," he added, pointing to the defendant. "And the hate in his heart, words that they can't now take back. The physical evidence, which refutes his lies, and the law that her honor is about to read to you, the law that applies [to] all of us . . . This is the truth. Thank you for your time."

The case was now held in the hands of the jury, while I felt there were still so many unanswered questions.

How could the trial end and Trayvon's side of the story never be told?

Following closing arguments, Judge Debra Nelson read the jury their instructions and the law that applied to the case. By now, she had granted the prosecution's request to allow the jury to consider the charge of manslaughter, as well as second-degree murder. We all stood, and I watched the jurors—all female, five white, one Hispanic—exit. And an undeniable and very definite feeling overcame me, something so strong I couldn't deny it.

Leave.

I just didn't want to be there. Somehow, I knew: this isn't going to turn out well. Whether the verdict was guilty or not guilty, I just did not want to be there. It was just a feeling that I got, a voice screaming inside me: *I have to leave this place, this area, these surroundings. I needed to go home.*

Our attorneys were suggesting and recommending that we stay just in case the jury had any additional questions. But what questions could they have that we would need to answer? Any questions would have been directed to the state or the attorneys.

So why did I need to stay? So the media could see my reaction once the verdict was read? I didn't want to put myself, or my family, friends, and supporters, through that publicly, and I thought it would be a grave injustice to my fallen son.

I wasn't going to give the killer the satisfaction of watching me cry if things went his way. So I was very aggressive with my decision to leave.

"I'm leaving," I told Tracy and my family in the conference room at the courthouse.

"What?" said Tracy. "We have to stay for the verdict."

Tracy was still holding out faith in the jury. They were, after all, a group of mothers, and he hoped they would see Trayvon as their son as much as ours. But the cultures were too different. I had a sinking feeling that they wouldn't see things like that. After sitting through the trial, I just didn't believe they would come back with a guilty verdict. Because I honestly didn't think the state had proven its case beyond a reasonable doubt.

"No, no, no, you've got to stay, you've got to stay here, they may have questions," the attorneys told me.

"I'm just not getting a good feeling, and I want to go home," I told them, ready to leave and get back to the safe haven of home.

"We have to stay here for the verdict," Tracy repeated.

"Parks and Crump said you guys need to stay here," echoed my mom.

The lawyers told me I needed to stay to address the media once a decision had been made. They sounded hopeful. They had based their careers on a belief that our justice system worked, that the bad guys with the guns pay for their crimes, sooner or later—in civil court, on appeal, but eventually they would be held accountable.

But I had already made up my mind; I had seen the system fall short on its promise of justice for black Americans too many times. I had done my best to remain strong throughout the trial, the endless replaying of the 911 tapes and the horrible photographs of my son's corpse sprawled on the ground. I wasn't going to allow the cameras, the press, and the public to see me break down now.

"I'm just uncomfortable," I said. "I'm starting to get sick."

Which was true. My stomach hurt and I had a headache and a terrible feeling. I turned to my family members in the room.

"I cannot stay here," I said. "If you want to stay, fine. I'll go get on a plane, I'll go rent a car, I'll walk home if I have to. But I'm going home."

Finally, Tracy said, "Well, if you leave, I'm leaving, too."

"We're all leaving," said my family.

So we did.

I called Daryl Parks and just said, "We're leaving."

But we couldn't just walk out of the courthouse.

The sheriff's department had to escort us out, and that wasn't easy, with the world's media and a growing crowd outside awaiting the verdict, and awaiting our reactions to the verdict. That morning, we had driven our own cars to a place a safe distance away from the courthouse, from which point Daryl Parks had driven us to the courthouse as he always did. Now that we were leaving, the sheriff's department came up with a plan for our exit: they drove a van up to the loading dock at the back of the courthouse, and we all climbed in and drove away. They dropped us off at our cars, and several sheriff's department squad cards escorted us to the Florida Turnpike, where we were safe to drive, anonymously, back home.

I rode with Tracy in his truck, down the same roads, highways, and turnpike that we had taken so often since Trayvon's death a year and a half before. It was a familiar ride, but on this day it was different.

It was about to be over.

On the drive home, we talked about the trial and all that we had been through. We talked about how, only about seventeen months before, our lives were shattered by this tragedy. Trayvon was preparing to finish high school; Jahvaris was heading off to college. We talked about the media's constant presence in our lives.

We talked about how nobody who hasn't been through it knows how it feels to have lost a child. Even the jury. We didn't believe they understood why Trayvon was wearing a hoodie: that it was a fashion statement worn by all races and nationalities, and not a sign of criminality. And we didn't think they understood that our peaceful protests were not—as one of the jurors stated—"riots."

We didn't understand why the judge had ruled against the use of the phrase "racial profiling."

It was a Friday evening when we turned into my driveway. I told Tracy good night and went inside, showered, and went straight to bed, praying before I turned the lights out, praying our thanks, praying for Trayvon, praying for justice.

Almost everyone else—the media, the attorneys, the protesters—stayed in Sanford.

Back home in Miami, I didn't watch television. I had barely watched it during the trial, and I wasn't going to begin now. But people told me what was happening, about the endless legal analysis and commentators speculating on the case and what the jury might think or do, and the action on the streets of Sanford.

Outside the courthouse during the jury deliberations, crowds still gathered. Sanford had split into two factions, just as the country had. Trayvon supporters made up the majority, we believed, but there was a small, loud, aggressive group supporting the killer.

Many of Trayvon's supporters simply wanted their voices to be heard, frustrated by what they saw as an ongoing legacy of injustice.

It was reported that one young woman lay in the grass outside the courthouse, a hoodie pulled over her head, with a bag of Skittles and a can of iced tea lying next to her. Like Trayvon, her arms were spread wide and her legs were crossed, headphones still in her ears. "Let's Not Lose Any More Children to Gun Violence. Justice for Trayvon," read a sign beside her.

There were shouting matches between our supporters and those of the killer. Protesters gathered near the Goldsboro Welcome Center and outside the courthouse. People carried signs with Trayvon's image calling for justice and chanted, "We want guilty! We want guilty!" Others wore black T-shirts with President Obama's words: "If I had a son, he'd look like Trayvon."

The next morning, Saturday, July 13, I went over to my sister's house, where family and friends gathered to wait. We weren't expecting the verdict that day. We just wanted to be together, for support, as we waited for the decision, which we thought might take several days.

We were all sitting around chatting about TV shows and things. Day turned to night, and eventually everyone was getting ready to go home. It was after nine P.M. when our attorneys got the call: after a little more than sixteen hours of deliberation, the jury had reached a verdict. Our attorneys Crump, Parks, Rand, and Jackson entered the courtroom to listen, at last, to the jury's decision.

This time I did watch. I huddled around the television with everyone else in my sister's family room, hoping for the best but fearing the worst. All of us held our breath.

The ever-present courtroom cameras brought us the event live. We could see everyone in the courtroom stand as the jury entered. The six women looked exhausted and grim, their faces seemed upset, even though they had deliberated for such a short time.

"Members of the jury, have you reached a verdict?" Judge Nelson asked.

The jury foreperson handed the verdict form over to the deputy, who delivered it to Judge Nelson. The judge read the verdict silently, without expression, before handing it over to the clerk, who read the verdict aloud.

"In the circuit court of the Eighteenth Judicial Circuit and for Seminole County, Florida, *The State of Florida versus George Zimmerman,*" she said. "Verdict: we the jury find George Zimmerman not guilty, so say we all."

And just like that, it was over.

After a year and a half of searching for answers and demanding justice in the killing of our son, the man who admitted to shooting Trayvon was found not guilty of second-degree murder. Not guilty of manslaughter. Not guilty of anything. Those two words felt burned into my brain—Not Guilty—and forever pierced my heart.

Judge Nelson released Zimmerman's bond and informed him that his GPS tracking device would be removed.

And he was free to go.

"You have no further business with the court," said the judge.

The killer only blinked. Then, as the news sunk in, he flashed a big grin. Hugs and handshakes from his defense team encircled him.

While our side said nothing.

The television station cut to a scene in front of the courthouse.

"No! No!" screamed the protesters as news of the verdict circulated. Many hung their heads and cried.

I don't remember anyone saying anything in my sister's family room that evening. I don't even remember us talking about it. I know I didn't say anything. I was just numb. The verdict didn't make me happy or sad. It just confirmed the fact that I felt that the justice system was not equal and the justice system does not work for African Americans. It also sent a message that you can shoot and kill someone that is unarmed and just trying to get home. And you can get away with it.

Tracy and I tweeted messages to our supporters.

"Lord during my darkest hour I lean on you," I wrote. "You are all that I have. At the end of the day, GOD is still in control. Thank you all for your prayers and support. I will love you forever Trayvon!!! In the name of Jesus!!!"

"Even though I am broken hearted my faith is unshattered," Tracy tweeted. "I WILL ALWAYS LOVE MY BABY TRAY."

While those outside the courthouse tried to make sense of the verdict, both the defense and the prosecution held press conferences.

Flanked on both sides by her prosecutors, Guy and de la Rionda, Corey spoke first, repeating her promise to seek the truth, to get both sides of the story and present the facts in court. "As Mr. Guy told the jury yesterday, 'To the living we owe respect, to the dead we owe the truth,'" she said. "We have been respectful to the living. We have done our best to ensure due process to all involved, and we believe that we brought out the truth on behalf of Trayvon Martin."

She thanked the media and her team of lawyers and assistants, and she gave her sympathies to us as a family before turning over the lectern to de la Rionda.

"I am disappointed, as we all are, with the verdict, but we accept it," he said matter-of-factly. "We live in a great country that has a great criminal justice system," he said. "It is not perfect, but it's the best in the world, and we respect the jury's verdict."

Guy was more emotional. He didn't have much to say, but what he did say was delivered in the same passionate style he had used in the courtroom. "We have from the beginning just prayed for the truth to come out and for peace to be the result, and that continues to be our prayers and we believe they have been answered."

Richard Mantei, who played a smaller role in the trial, focused his comments on our family, thanking us for how we handled ourselves throughout the case. "They've been dignified, they've showed class," he said. "They have kept their pain in check when they needed to and they have grieved when they needed to. . . . It can't have been easy and it won't be easy. I know you all have a job to do, but when you approach all that, keep them in mind, too."

Our attorneys held a press conference of their own that night, although they were all still numb and reeling from the rendering of the not-guilty verdict. The next morning I called Crump and told him that a not-guilty verdict was not the end of our fight for justice, if not for Trayvon, then for other people's children; it was only another beginning. Our attorneys became our voice after the verdict. They were swamped with media requests from around the world, and we all had a responsibility to use that moment to send a positive message, to bring a message of hope for a better future for the Trayvons yet to be born. We had an international audience interested in knowing what happened to my son, and what would happen next, after the not-guilty verdict. Attorneys Crump, Parks, Jackson, and Rand all did dozens of interviews for three days straight—Parks said he did thirteen interviews on the Sunday after the verdict alone, saying, show after show, that the jury couldn't see Trayvon as their child, and that the defense put Trayvon on trial but the prosecution didn't put the killer on trial. The killer was portrayed as the good guy, the helpful, friendly neighbor to people in the community, while Trayvon was incorrectly portrayed as a thug.

They were on every major American network—including CNN, MSNBC, and FOX—and on international networks, too, reaching audiences as far away as Australia and Japan. Jasmine Rand speaks Spanish, so she also did appearances updating the Spanish-speaking world on Telemundo and other stations that broadcast in Central and South America. Our attorneys continued to be our voice, telling the world that a not-guilty verdict did not mean George Zimmerman was innocent and that the verdict was a report card on the status of racial equality in our nation. While we had failed to deliver the equality promised in our Constitution, under no circumstance would we give up fighting for justice and equality for the other Trayvon Martins in the world. The defense put Trayvon on trial, and now our nation had been put on trial by a global community that, like our family, was not willing to accept that an adult man could shoot an unarmed seventeen-year-old walking home from a convenience store in a hoodie and walk away free.

Outrage over the verdict spread worldwide, in living rooms, on streets, and even stages.

The singer Beyoncé took a moment of silence for Trayvon at a concert in Nashville, and then sang the chorus of "I Will Always Love You," a Dolly Parton song made popular by Whitney Houston.

Stevie Wonder announced he would not play another concert in Florida until the state government repealed its Stand Your Ground law. (Florida still hasn't repealed the law.)

In Limerick, Ireland, Bruce Springsteen dedicated his song "American Skin (41 Shots)," the song inspired by the twenty-two-year-old unarmed Bronx man who died after four plainclothes police officers fired forty-one shots at him, to Trayvon, saying, "I want to send this one out as a letter back home for justice for Trayvon Martin." I looked up the song, and the lyrics stopped me cold—they reminded me of what my mother taught me, what I taught Trayvon, and the unfair burden put on some Americans because of the presumption of guilt that follows them:

If an officer stops you, promise me you'll always be polite

Even President Obama issued a brief statement shortly after the verdict, asking for "calm reflection" and to "ask ourselves if we're doing all we can to widen the circle of compassion and understanding in our own communities."

I went to sleep that night feeling hopeless, feeling angry, hurt, and more than a little disgusted, and, most of all, wondering what to do next.

In the following days, so many people would come to our side, lending their voices, their support, their anger, and their rage. Beyoncé and Jay Z joined a "Justice for Trayvon" vigil in New York City. Jay Z and Justin Timberlake dedicated a rendition of the song "Forever Young" to Trayvon in a concert at Yankee Stadium.

Six days after the verdict, at 1:33 P.M., President Obama addressed the press, and the nation, about Trayvon's case and the issue of race. It was a seventeen-minute monologue that spoke volumes and will, to my mind, go down in history as one of the most eloquent statements about race in America.

"When Trayvon Martin was first shot, I said that this could have been my son," he began. "Another way of saying that is, Trayvon Martin could have been me thirty-five years ago. . . .

"There are very few African American men in this country who haven't had the experience of being followed when they were shopping in a department store. That includes me. There are very few African American men who haven't had the experience of walking across the street and hearing the locks click on the doors of cars. That happens to me—at least before I was a senator. There are very few African Americans who haven't had the experience of getting on an elevator and a woman clutching her purse nervously and holding her breath until she had a chance to get off. That happens often. And I don't want to exaggerate this, but those sets of experiences inform how the African American community interprets what happened one night in Florida. And it's inescapable for people to bring those experiences to bear.

"How do we learn some lessons from this and move in a positive direction?" the president asked, urging protesters to take a nonviolent path. "If I see any violence, then I will remind folks that that dishonors what happened to Trayvon Martin and his family," he said. "But beyond protests or vigils, the question is, Are there some concrete things that we might be able to do? . . .

"Number one, precisely because law enforcement is often

determined at the state and local level, I think it would be productive for the Justice Department, governors, mayors to work with law enforcement about training at the state and local levels in order to reduce the kind of mistrust in the system that sometimes currently exists."

This would include "training police departments across the state on how to think about potential racial bias and ways to further professionalize what they were doing," he said.

"Along the same lines, I think it would be useful for us to examine some state and local laws to see if it—if they are designed in such a way that they may encourage the kinds of altercations and confrontations and tragedies that we saw in the Florida case, rather than defuse potential altercations."

As for the Stand Your Ground law, the president asked what kind of message is being sent if "someone who is armed potentially has the right to use those firearms even if there's a way for them to exit from a situation, is that really going to be contributing to the kind of peace and security and order that we'd like to see?

"And for those who resist the idea that we should think about something like these Stand Your Ground laws, I'd just ask people to consider, if Trayvon Martin was of age and armed, could he have stood his ground on that sidewalk? And do we actually think that he would have been justified in shooting Mr. Zimmerman, who had followed him in a car because he felt threatened? And if the answer to that question is at least ambiguous, then it seems to me that we might want to examine those kinds of laws.

"Number three—and this is a long-term project—we need to spend some time in thinking about how we bolster and reinforce our African American boys. And this is something that Michelle and I talk a lot about. There are a lot of kids out there who need help who are getting a lot of negative reinforcement. And is there more that we can do to give them the sense that their country cares about them and values them and is willing to invest in them? . . .

"And then, finally, I think it's going to be important for all of us to do some soul-searching. There has been talk about [whether we should] convene a conversation on race. I haven't seen that be particularly productive when politicians try to organize conversations. They end up being stilted and politicized, and folks are locked in to the positions they already have. On the other hand, in families and churches and workplaces, there's the possibility that people are a little bit more honest, and at least you ask yourself your own questions about: Am I wringing as much bias out of myself as I can? Am I judging people as much as I can, based on not the color of their skin but the content of their character? That would, I think, be an appropriate exercise in the wake of this tragedy."

I had to take a breath. It was all too surreal, that our son's death had motivated an American president to finally speak about race issues that had so long been festering beneath the surface of life in this country.

"And let me just leave you with a final thought," he continued, "that, as difficult and challenging as this whole episode has been for a lot of people, I don't want us to lose sight that things are getting better. Each successive generation seems to be making progress in changing attitudes when it comes to race. It doesn't mean we're in a post-racial society. It doesn't mean that racism is eliminated. But when I talk to Malia and Sasha, and I listen to their friends and I see them interact, they're better than we are—they're better than we were—on these issues. And that's true in every community that I've visited all across the country.

"And so we have to be vigilant and we have to work on these issues," he said. "And those of us in authority should be doing everything we can to encourage the better angels of our nature, as opposed to using these episodes to heighten divisions. But we should also have confidence that kids these days, I think, have more sense than we did back then, and certainly more than our parents did or our grandparents did; and that along this long, difficult journey, we're becoming a more perfect union—not a perfect union, but a more perfect union."

The day after the verdict was a Sunday. I got up and I went to my church, Antioch Missionary Baptist of Miami Gardens.

I just thought it was important, especially on this Sunday. I wanted to clear my head and try to figure out my next steps and where I would go from this point forward. I was, of course, more than disappointed. I kept thinking about how people still judge African Americans as if they are already guilty—even, in Trayvon's case, in death. I kept thinking that there are so many times when no one knows who committed a crime. But in our case, we knew everything. Still, the killer walked free.

I tried not to bring those thoughts into church. But I knew God would give me unyielding spiritual strength.

I have a regular seat in our church: midway pew, in the middle, surrounded by friends and family. But on this Sunday, I sat alone in the back.

As the choir began singing, I silently gave my thanks to God; even the verdict was a kind of conclusion. That part I was glad about. I was sick of the trial, sick of going back and forth to Sanford. Tired of the endless process in the slow grind to justice. The verdict at least offered an end to all of that—the end of the trial—even if it wasn't the outcome we had fought so hard to bring about.

I sat through the service, praying, grieving, giving thanks to God and trusting that He would, as always, guide my path.

Then I went home, back to my purple bedroom. That numb feeling had returned. Once again, it was an out-of-body experience, a feeling that the jury's verdict, like Trayvon's death, wasn't real and I would wake up from this nightmare in the morning and things would be back to normal.

But the next morning only brought more of the same. The phone began ringing: Crump, as always, asking me to come forward with statements, interviews, media appearances.

"The media is trying to get in touch with you, and they want you to make a statement," he said, listing the television shows that were eager to speak with Tracy and me and pushing us to make a comment about the verdict.

I wasn't ready. I didn't think we should jump right out there again. Not yet. Not when we were so emotional, not when we were so bitter.

"We need time, Crump," I said. "I think we should have some time. So we don't say anything that we'll regret later."

I'm not the kind of person to just give voice to every violent or angry thought that passes through my mind. That's not who I am, but that's how I felt at that moment. My emotions were high. My feelings were ugly. I wasn't thinking about what to say publicly. I was thinking about what to do. My son was dead and his killer was free. Those were the facts. No turning back the clock.

How could I turn my anger into action?

How could we honor Trayvon in death and create a legacy where there was once a life?

I thought the best way was through the Trayvon Martin Foundation. We created it in the agonizing months after Trayvon's death. Donations would come in through the Miami Foundation, which handled the financial management. Our activities were limited to an Annual Remembrance Dinner and a Peace Walk and Peace Talk. But we needed other programs to continue Trayvon's legacy and, hopefully, bring about change. We created a mission statement: The Trayvon Martin Foundation is dedicated to embracing social and civic changes for justice through awareness of senseless gun violence. We began meeting—at Starbucks, IHOP, the Miami-Dade Public Library—and asking ourselves: how can we create programs to support families of gun violence, bring awareness of the effects of gun violence and, ultimately, end gun violence, before another child is killed?

Then, slowly, deliberately, Tracy and I reemerged. We had more to say.

July 26, a Friday, I attended the National Urban League in the Pennsylvania Convention Center, where I was scheduled to give my first major speech after the verdict. It had been thirteen days since the acquittal of the man who killed my son, and the National Urban League, America's oldest civil rights organization, created in 1910 "to enable African Americans to secure economic self-reliance, parity, power, and civil rights," seemed the ideal place to speak.

Six thousand people were in the audience that day in Philadelphia, including many of the leaders of the civil rights movement: Reverend Al Sharpton, Reverend Jesse Jackson, and National Urban League CEO Marc H. Morial. I was introduced, and a powerful, surprising wave of applause washed over me. I placed my hand over my heart, and all I could say was "Wow."

I was emotional, but I was determined that the audience wouldn't see the broken Sybrina. I was determined to show them the woman that had once been broken but who had somehow been able to get back up. The Sybrina who couldn't get out of her bedroom had been reborn. I was no longer walking alone; I was now the voice for Trayvon.

"Let me start off—because I have to put God first," I began. "I need to tell you my favorite Bible verse. It's Proverbs three, verses five and six, and it says, 'Trust in the Lord with all your heart and lean not unto your own understanding. In all your ways acknowledge Him, and He shall direct your path.'"

I paused. "Let me just say that I stand here before you today, only through the grace of God, only because of the spirit that lives within me," I continued. "Because, as a mother, Sybrina couldn't do it. Sybrina could not lose her baby. Sybrina could not lose one of her children. It's only through God that I stand before you today.

And as I said before, Trayvon was my son. But Trayvon is also your son."

That massive audience applauded again.

"I just ask you, as a mother, to wrap your mind around what has happened. Because I speak to you as Trayvon's mother. I speak to you as a parent. And the absolutely worst telephone call you can receive as a parent is to know that your son—your son!—you will never kiss again. I'm just asking you to wrap your mind around that.

"Wrap your mind around no prom for Trayvon," I said. "No high school graduation for Trayvon. No college for Trayvon. No grand-kids coming from Trayvon. All because of a law. A law that has pre-vented the person who shot and killed my son to be held accountable and to pay for this awful crime.

"What is my message to you?" I asked. "My message to you is: Please use my story. Please use my tragedy. Please use my broken heart to say to yourself, 'We cannot let this happen to anybody else's child.'"

Now the applause grew louder.

"And I hope I've delivered that message," I continued. "Because on the way here, I gave the driver one of my business cards, and it has a picture of Trayvon on there."

I held up one of the cards with Trayvon's picture on the front.

"And what he said was, 'That's my son, too!' So my message is coming across. And it's coming across the right way. It's coming across because I know that regardless of the color of someone's skin, that somebody is listening. That somebody wants to act and some-body wants to react. The only thing I say to you is: Nobody is hurting worse than me as a parent. Me as a mom. Because you know, as a mom, we are a little sensitive when it comes to our children, and we have every right to be.

"When they hurt, we hurt. When they're happy, we're happy.

"At times I feel like I'm a broken vessel. At times, I don't know if I'm going or coming. But I know beyond a shadow of a doubt that God is using me and God is using my family, to make a change, to make a difference.

"So lastly, I just want to tell you about the foundation that we have created in Trayvon's name. Because the verdict is not going to define who Trayvon Martin was.

"We will define his legacy.

"We will define who he is and what he was all about.

"I can't do it alone. I can't do it with just my family. So not only am I asking the Urban League family, I'm asking your individual families to take a look at our website. To get involved and stand up for something, please. Because we need your help, your support, and, more importantly, your voice. So that there are no more Trayvon Martins again."

I thanked the National Urban League, the audience, our attorneys and supporters. And that audience of six thousand people rose up once again to applaud and embrace me, and that embrace continued all the way back from Philadelphia to Miami, where God continued embracing me by leading me into the next phase of my life.

I kept having this dream, in which I saw myself in an endless field of purple.

And I saw ladies crying in agony and sorrow. They were lost and alone, even while they were somehow together. Then, suddenly, I saw them smiling and hugging one another in support. I somehow knew that these ladies were mothers. And I knew that, just like me, they were mothers who had lost their children to senseless gun violence. And while they once felt alone, they now had one another.

I saw these mothers sitting together in a circle in an enormous room. Then I saw them sitting together before tables filled with flowers, and everything was so pretty and so purple. There were different speakers coming up to speak to them. I had no clue what all of this meant. But I knew that it was a vision that God had given to me. When I awoke, I grabbed a pen and paper I kept near my bed, and I began writing down what I had seen in my dream. And when I was done writing about that purple dream in my purple bedroom, I had pages and pages of notes, all about that dream about mothers who found healing in one another.

The next morning, I knew my purpose, my mission. I knew the way that I was going to channel the not-guilty verdict into something positive. I had to do something to help other mothers, women who, like me, had lost their children to violence. Mothers who, in shockingly increasing numbers, would soon form a sorority of sorts. I would find a way to unite this sorority, once joined only by sorrow, in support. I would find a way to help the mothers work toward a common goal: to show that our grief doesn't define us; it propels us to do something to bring change. So that one day what happened to Trayvon, and has happened to other sons and daughters across America and the world, might someday soon never happen to another mother's child.

We would come together as a circle, because a circle is a symbol of unity and struggle—a circle never ends. I knew that the key to my healing was to help other mothers.

The event we launched would be called the Circle of Mothers. The participants were fifty mothers whose names you would never have known except for the children they lost—fifty mothers whose children had been cut down, fifty mothers now on a mission in the hope of ensuring that the violence doesn't touch other mothers, other fathers, other families.

The day after my dream I met with the Trayvon Martin Foundation team, and we began calling the mothers. They weren't hard to find. Their names had been in headlines from coast to coast. Others I met through people I knew, through pastors who, upon hearing about our losing Trayvon, told us, "The same thing happened to one of the members of our church."

Soon I had a long list of mothers to invite to our event. They included a Colorado state representative, whose only son was shot and killed while sitting in his car at a traffic light in Aurora, Colorado, in 2005; Cleopatra Pendleton, whose fifteen-year-old honor student daughter, Hadiya, a drum majorette who had performed during President Obama's second inauguration, was shot and killed while standing in a Chicago park after a gang mistook her and her friends for rivals; and the keynote speaker, the activist Afeni Shakur, whose son, the rapper Tupac Shakur, was killed in Las Vegas.

Sadly, there were so many others. But happily, almost everyone we contacted immediately said that they would attend.

We couldn't just have a room filled with broken moms; we also needed a team of support mothers to help lift us up, hug us, and most important, pray for strength for us. For help with that, I called on Lisa Nichols, a dynamic entrepreneur, life coach, and public speaker who has delivered her passionate message of empowerment to thirty million people around the world. I met Lisa in Philadelphia when I delivered that Urban League speech. After I spoke that day, Lisa came onstage with me, holding my hand and telling the audience to "Give the world notice!"

"Give the world notice, and the Lord will draw something up in you that you didn't even know you had!" she said, and I felt like she could have been speaking about me.

If Lisa Nichols could inspire thirty million people worldwide, just think what she could do for fifty mothers who had lost children to senseless gun violence.

"Whatever you want me to do, I'm here," she immediately said when I called her.

"I want to help other mothers," I told her. "I want to do something to help empower and heal the other mothers. I had a great group of family and friends around me, people who loved me and prayed for me and supported me, but I don't know if the other mothers had or have that same type of support."

Lisa Nichols arrived in Miami that next May 2014 when those fifty mothers gathered for the first of what would become an annual Circle of Mothers weekend.

Although I pray that not one more mother is added to our group, the weekends have been the most inspiring events of my life. We share our stories and our grief. We cry, we remember, and we support one another. We honor our children's lives by not just dwelling on their deaths. At that first event, we were inspired by the words of our keynote speaker, the now-late Afeni Shakur, and were led by Lisa Nichols, who would later say that she "guided the healing" by celebrating the mothers' lives "versus only focusing on their loss."

After it was over, we bonded as both mothers and sisters, emerging closer and stronger, and determined to bring about change.

Soon after that, Tracy led a similar event for fathers, called the Circle of Fathers.

Today, the Trayvon Martin Foundation lives on in my son's name, through various scholarship programs and mentoring initiatives, ranging from teaching kids Trayvon's age what to do and how to act if confronted by the police or other figures of authority, to holding our annual Circle of Mothers and Circle of Fathers weekends, which we have held now for three years strong.

And from these beginnings radiated a chance for real change.

Tracy and I, along with our attorneys, began fighting Stand Your Ground laws throughout our nation, addressing Congress on the issues of Stand Your Ground and racial profiling in our judicial system, and testifying before the United Nations about racial discrimination when the U.N. reviewed the killing of our son and the not-guilty verdict. President Obama would invite Tracy and me to the White House just before he announced his My Brother's Keeper initiative, a mentorship program for black and brown boys, and we could feel the power of that historic house and the winds of change building around us. Celebrities and athletes used their power and influence to continue advocating for our son even after the not-guilty verdict. *Ebony* magazine dedicated its September 2013 issue to Trayvon, with four different covers, three featuring a famous personality with their sons—the director Spike Lee, the basketball star Dwyane Wade, and the actor Boris Kodjoe—and a fourth cover with Tracy, Jahvaris, and me, and each cover had the headline "We Are Trayvon: Join the Movement to Change America." Oscar-winning actor Jamie Foxx hosted a fundraiser at his house for the Trayvon Martin Foundation, and he continued supporting us and our cause, calling upon his influential friends to join him in deploying their power to create positive change in our nation and greater equality for our children.

We have a long way to go. But it's a start.

Even as the killings continue and the number of parents who have lost children continues to rise, we, as mothers and fathers, continue to support one another as members of a community that share a parent's worst nightmare: the inconceivable tragedy of losing a child.

All I wanted was to be a mother, to work at my job and raise my kids and live a normal life. Then my son was killed and that world went with him, and God led me to another place, another world, and another life. I became a mother on a mission. A mission to bring awareness and change. So that the killing of Trayvon Martin would stand for something, so that the killing will someday stop and the healing will begin.

So that our children, and all children, can live in peace.

Rest in power, my son.

ACKNOWLEDGMENTS

We would like to thank all those who have been so supportive of our fight for justice over the past years, and those who continue to stand with us in our quest for change.

ACKNOWLEDGMENTS